ESSENTIALS OF EVANGELICAL THEOLOGY

Other Books by Donald G. Bloesch

Centers of Christian Renewal

The Christian Life and Salvation

The Crisis of Piety

The Christian Witness in a Secular Age

Christian Spirituality East and West (coauthor)

The Reform of the Church

The Ground of Certainty

Servants of Christ (editor)

The Evangelical Renaissance

Wellsprings of Renewal

Light a Fire

The Invaded Church

Jesus Is Victor!: Karl Barth's Doctrine of Salvation

ESSENTIALS
OF EVANGELICAL
THEOLOGY

Volume One:
God, Authority, and Salvation

DONALD G. BLOESCH

HarperSanFrancisco
A Division of HarperCollins*Publishers*

Dedicated to my wife
Brenda

6/92

First HarperCollins paperback edition published 1982.

Library of Congress Cataloging in Publication Date
Bloesch, Donald G., 1928–
  ESSENTIALS OF EVANGELICAL THEOLOGY.

  Includes index.
  CONTENTS: v. 1. God, authority, and salvation.
  1. Evangelicalism—Collected works.
2. Theology, Doctrinal—Collected Works.
I. Title.
BR1640.A25B57   230   77–15872
ISBN 0-06-060802-1

---

91 92 93 94 HAD 14 13 12 11 10 9

ACKNOWLEDGMENTS

Special thanks go to my wife who has been a genuine helpmate to me in my writing career. I am particularly grateful for her careful reading of this manuscript; her many suggestions have proved to be most helpful. Again, I wish to thank my colleagues at the Aquinas Institute in Dubuque for directing me to books and original sources that have helped clarify the Roman Catholic understanding of the faith. I am especially indebted to Benedict Viviano and Benedict Ashley. Finally, Miss Lillian Staiger of the library staff of Dubuque Theological Seminary should be given due recognition for her many services rendered in the procuring of needed books.

ABBREVIATIONS

Scripture references are from the Revised Standard Version, unless otherwise indicated by the following abbreviations:

New International Version	NIV
King James Version	KJ
New English Bible	NEB
Living Bible	LB
Jerusalem Bible	JB

CONTENTS

PREFACE

This book has been written in order to enunciate the salient tenets of evangelical faith. It is commonly said that evangelicalism connotes a particular kind of experience rather than a distinctive doctrinal stance. My contention is that to be evangelical means to hold to a definite doctrine as well as to participate in a special kind of experience. The experience of the forgiveness of sins through the atoning sacrifice of Christ and the assurance of salvation through the gift of the Spirit will always be paramount in evangelical religion. But doctrine is no less essential, since experience, even genuine experience, that is not rightly understood can promote heresy rather than orthodoxy.

I believe that the time has come to spell out evangelical essentials, the fundamental tenets of the faith once delivered to the saints. I make no claim that this is the only way to articulate the historic faith of the church, but it is one that stands in continuity with the Protestant Reformation and the evangelical awakenings.

My systematic theology will necessarily have a polemical ring, since in affirming certain truths I must also oppose competing interpretations. This book is an apologetics of a type, since it aims to defend the true faith against current misunderstandings, though always within the circle of faith. It is also a dogmatics, since I seek to interpret the faith to the church.

In enumerating the hallmarks of the historic faith from an evangelical perspective, one must acknowledge that all of these must be interpreted. None can be affirmed in an unqualified manner because all are capable of wide distortion. The total depravity of man, for example, can be expounded in such a way that it signifies no good whatsoever in man. Rightly understood it means that while man is a mixture of good and evil, evil is ascendant and intrudes into every area of his life. Again, the doctrine of justification by faith alone can be so taught that the impression is created that grace is cheap as well as free. The sovereignty of God can be taken to mean a God of arbitrary power who predestines some to damnation even apart from their personal response. Yet there is enough truth in all of these mottoes to warrant their continued use.

My theology is hopefully radical as well as conservative, since I seek to return to the roots of the faith and to the infallible standard of faith, Holy Scripture. While seeking to maintain continuity with the evangelicalism of the past, I believe it is proper to criticize any of the luminaries of our heritage in the light of the biblical norm, and this includes Calvin, Luther, Augustine, and Wesley.

At the same time I try to be irenic wherever possible: where bridges can be built that will contribute to Christian unity it is incumbent upon us to do so. It is time, for example, to resolve past conflicts between Calvinism and Arminianism and also between Calvinism and Lutheranism, since many of these conflicts have their roots in attempts to maintain logical consistency in doctrinal position at the expense of the mystery and paradox in faith. The same can be said for some, but not all, of the barriers dividing Reformation Protestantism and Roman Catholicism.

The crucial division in the church today is not sociological or political but theological. There is a growing need for evangelical unity as the cleavage in the church widens. Pluralism is a promising pathway in penultimate matters, but in ultimate matters it is confusing. It is rightly said today that we should love the oppressed and downtrodden, but we must love the truth most of all, and imbued with the truth we can then love our neighbor in the right way.

While holding to the fundamentals of the faith, I have diverged from contemporary fundamentalism and evangelicalism wherever I have detected misunderstandings of the faith. The bane of much conservative evangelicalism is a rationalism that denies mystery in faith and a sectarianism that breaks continuity with the catholic tradition. At the same time I see as the main enemy not an obscurantist orthodoxy but an attenuated liberalism which dissolves the faith in the spirit of the times (Zeitgeist). Liberals often use the vocabulary of evangelicals but not our dictionary, and this is why we must be doubly vigilant in the conflict that is looming.

The time is indeed appropriate to stress evangelical essentials. A secular humanism is penetrating the bastions of both mainstream Protestantism and Catholicism. The old liberalism is facing bankruptcy, but Evangelicalism too is in confusion. Among many Evangelicals there is a stress on marginal doctrines instead of those that are truly fundamental, and this tends to weaken evangelical initiative and credibility especially in the academic world today. It is sad but true that most Protestants, even conservative Protestants, are unfamiliar with the basic teachings of the historic faith. Thus we need again to make an effort at theological precision though always making a place for honest differences but within the theological circle.

Some persons indeed would not acknowledge me as evangelical in the traditional sense. One reason is that I accept the historical criticism of Scriptures (though in a qualified sense) and refuse to posit an absolute equation between the letter of the Bible and divine revelation. At the same time I affirm the unity of the biblical words with the self-revelation of Jesus Christ to whom these words are directed by the inspiration of the Spirit. These words are to be seen as a mode or channel by which we hear and know the living Word. I also wish to learn from modern philosophy and theology, even liberal theology which has often arisen as a valid protest against gross distortions of the faith in orthodoxy. I also believe that one should be free to criticize confessions and theologians of the past as well as the present in the light of Scripture. Moreover, I seek to forge ties with Roman Catholics and Eastern Orthodox of similar minds, since only a united church can bear a credible witness to a disunited world.

I do not presume to be speaking for all evangelicals. My own tradition is the Evangelical and Reformed church, now part of the United Church of Christ. I speak as one who is particularly indebted to the mainline Protestant Reformers, Luther and Calvin. I also speak as a chastened evangelical who seeks to come to terms with the theological and biblical scholarship of our time. The ghetto mentality that characterizes much current evangelicalism spells death to any creative endeavors in the area of systematic theology.

Finally I speak as a socially concerned evangelical, one who sees that the Gospel is a stick of dynamite in the social structure. We need to proclaim the whole Gospel to the whole man, and this includes relating Christian faith to the economic and political areas of life as well as the so-called religious area. At the same time we must beware of combining the Gospel with any social ideology whether it be feminism, socialism, free enterprise, pacifism, and so on, since this prevents social movements from coming under the scrutiny of a transcendent criterion.

It will be noticed that the format of this book is somewhat innovative, since it does not follow the traditional outline in general works of systematic theology. The chapter headings focus on controversial themes that have proven barriers to Christian unity in the past. Problems of methodology are for the most part subsumed

under the definition of "Evangelical" in Chapter II and the authority of Scripture in Chapter IV. I deal more extensively with theological methodology in a previous book of mine *The Ground of Certainty* (Eerdmans, 1971), where I lay the groundwork for a theology
of revelation.

Donald G. Bloesch

My friends, I was fully engaged in writing to you about our salvation—which is yours no less than ours—when it became urgently necessary to write at once and appeal to you to join the struggle in defence of the faith, the faith which God entrusted to his people once and for all.

JUDE 3 NEB

Evangelicals . . . regard as the only possible road to the reunion of the churches the road of biblical reformation. In their view the only solid hope for churches which desire to unite is a common willingness to sit down together under the authority of God's Word, in order to be judged and reformed by it.

JOHN R. W. STOTT

The great dividing issue for the soul is neither . . . the Bible nor the social question. For the Church at least . . . it is the question of a redeeming atonement. It is here that the evangelical issue lies.

P. T. FORSYTH

The doctrine of salvation by grace through faith is both the basic and the distinctive article of Christianity, by which it is distinguished from all man-made religions as the only true and divine religion.

JOHN T. MUELLER

I.

INTRODUCTION

The need for evangelicalism to rediscover its identity and to present a united witness to the church and the world is particularly acute in this time when a new modernism threatens to engulf mainline Christianity. The loss of the uniqueness of the Christ revelation is manifest in the rise of a syncretistic mysticism and a latitudinarianism which see saving grace present in all faiths, even in the circles of atheism and agnosticism. Natural theology is reappearing in a new guise with the emphasis now not on proofs of the existence of God, but on the discovery of the divine ground of authentic humanity. Many of the theologies of experience today assume that femininity, blackness, liberation, secularity, hope, and so on, are in themselves revelatory, and, therefore, the biblical revelation is rendered superfluous. Frederick Herzog, whose own theology has a marked immanentalist orientation (one that denies the transcendence of God over the world), nonetheless perceives the danger in the widespread departure from biblical norms: "A lot is being sold under the label Christianity that is actually the *desertion* of the Christian faith, nothing less than apostasy. Insofar as it still appears under the label Christian, it has to be understood as *counterfeit Christianity.*"[1]

That an evangelical renaissance is occurring today, partly in reaction to the secularization of faith and life in the modern world, can no longer be doubted.[2] Yet it is well to ask whether the same secularistic influences are present in evangelicalism, whether true Christianity is diluted even in that branch of the faith which ostensibly holds to the fundamentals. It is incumbent upon us to determine what is or is not authentic in the resurgence of conservative religion today, and this means to be cognizant of the dangers as well as the opportunities in the current evangelical revival.

One danger in modern evangelicalism is neo-Pietism, characterized by an emphasis on religious experience over doctrine.[3] Too many evangelicals today seek a continuous mountain-top experience and avoid controversial theological issues. Practical piety and mystical aware-

1

ness figure more highly than biblical or dogmatic theology. One interpreter candidly observes that modern "evangelicalism, with its roots in the open-air eighteenth century English preaching and the nineteenth century American frontier, centers not on Scripture, church, doctrine or sacraments, but on personal experience. Having the right kind of conversion, second-blessing, 'peace,' etc., becomes all-important, and without it all else may be suspect."[4] The experience of salvation must not be discounted, but it must be tested in the light of an objective criterion, the Holy Scriptures.

It is well to bear in mind that faith is deeper and wider than a spiritual experience: it is an acknowledgment of the claims of Jesus Christ and an obedience to his commands. It consists primarily in personal devotion to a living Savior, but it also entails a confidence in the apostolic testimony concerning who he is and what he has done. Our faith is directed not simply to the mystical presence of Christ or to the unconditional, but to Jesus Christ crucified and risen according to the Scriptures. The act of believing *(fides qua creditur)*, though supremely important, must never prevail over the content of faith *(fides quae creditur)*.

There is presently a resurgence of interest in spirituality in evangelical circles, but a spirituality that is not theologically and biblically based may be worse than none. P. T. Forsyth gives this timely word of warning: "A warm spirituality without the apostolic and evangelical substance may seem attractive to many—what is called undogmatic, or even unconscious, Christianity. It will specially appeal to the lay mind, in the pulpit and out. But it is death to a Church."[5]

There is a need for sound doctrine as well as the experience of the Spirit and the new life in Christ. John Wesley, whose contribution to evangelical renewal is beyond dispute, nonetheless sometimes minimized the importance of doctrinal fidelity in his emphasis on heart experience.[6] This tendency to downplay doctrine in favor of experience is, of course, much more evident in his later followers than in Wesley himself. We must constantly subject our doctrine as well as our life and experience to the criterion of the Scriptures, but we must at the same time strive for a true understanding of our faith (and Wesley would agree). We can never claim to possess the truth, but we should strive to keep and maintain the truth (cf. Luke 8:15; John 17:6–19; 1 Cor. 15:2; 2 Tim. 1:12–14).

One reason why Evangelicalism fell into partial eclipse in the early twentieth century—and why it still is not considered a live option by many earnest Christians—is that it lacked doctrinal sophistication and a basic biblical fidelity, and thereby created false stumbling blocks to the faith. Among the doctrinal distortions that the older Evangelicalism promoted, in one form or another, were: the separation of God's love from his wrath; that God loves only some and hates others; the portrayal of hell as a place of torture created by an angry, vindictive God; the idea that God's wrath can only be appeased by the sacrifice of an innocent victim; the view that unbaptized infants are destined for hell or are eternally condemned; the misunderstanding that God has three separate personalities; the insistence that everything recorded in the Bible is literal historical fact; and, the depiction of capitalism as the economic theory of biblical faith. People were confronted with an unattractive, legalistic, and obscurantist evangelicalism that offered no hope of triumphing over the then rising liberalism, which appealed to the latest findings and insights of modern science and philosophy.

Still another pitfall in modern evangelicalism has been its pronounced individualism and its lack of prophetic insight regarding social sin. It is to the credit of liberals such as Walter Rauschenbusch that they were profoundly aware of the corporate nature of evil and of the social imperatives of the faith. Carl Henry has sought to remind those in the tradition of fundamentalism that Christianity has far-reaching social implications, that its message pertains to the public as well as the private sphere of life.[7] The Gospel is in reality a world-changing message, but it has been reduced to a world-resisting message by an overemphasis on individual salvation to the neglect of community responsibility.[8] This stands in sharp contrast to the in-depth social involvement of many of the earlier evangelicals who were often in the vanguard of social reform movements.[9]

In our concern for social as well as personal holiness, however, we must beware of converting the Gospel into a political manifesto. The Gospel is a spiritual message which stands above all social ideologies (though it furnishes a theological rationale for the right kind of social action). The evangelical left is to be congratulated for its well-meaning attempt to relate the Gospel to the social arena, but at times it tends to lose sight of the transcendent dimensions of the Gospel message and too easily allies the Christian faith with the social expectations of political radicalism.[10] While the Gospel gives direction to the political enterprise, it must not be reduced to a political theology.

In the delineation of evangelical essentials I have sought to deepen the meaning of *evangelical*. *Evangelical* is not to be equated with a particular position on biblical inerrancy, since some who hold to this concept virtually deny every other evangelical doctrine (e.g., the Jehovah's Witnesses). The divine authority of Scripture will always be fundamental in evangelical theology, but the formal norm of faith (Scripture) must continually be subordinated to and interpreted by the material norm, the Gospel of reconciliation and redemption. This Gospel is the very heart and soul of evangelical theology.

I also seek to stand in the Reformed tradition, but Reformed is to be understood more broadly than Calvinistic, since I look to Luther as well as Calvin, to evangelical Pietism as well as Reformed orthodoxy, to the neo-Reformation theology of Barth and Brunner as well as the neo-Calvinism of Hodge and Warfield. Indeed, I gratefully acknowledge evangelical and Reformed motifs in some of the leading Catholic thinkers as well including Irenaeus, Augustine, Anselm, Thomas Aquinas, and Pascal. The genius of Reformed theology is to be always reformed in the light not only of Scripture, but also of the historical commentary on Scripture in the church tradition.

As can be inferred, I wish to be Catholic in the best sense of the word. We need a renewed appreciation of the priceless heritage of the church as well as of the Scripture that forms a part of this heritage. It is a common evangelical heresy to affirm that if we believe in the Word of God then we have no need for creeds or doctrines. Or it is said that if we only worship God in our hearts then we can do without rituals or symbols or even the discipline of public worship. It is well to bear in mind that Calvin reaffirmed the dictum of Cyprian that outside of the church there is no salvation.

My ancestral tree from a theological perspective includes Isaiah, Jeremiah, St. Paul, Augustine, Calvin, Luther, Kierkegaard, Forsyth, and Karl Barth. It also includes, in varying degrees, Pascal, Philip Spener, Richard Sibbes, Jonathan Edwards, Zinzendorf, and Abraham Kuyper. It excludes rationalists such as Justin Martyr, Clement of Alexandria, Abelard, Socinus, Erasmus, Lord Herbert of Cherbury, John Locke, and Christian Wolff. Mystics who verge towards a monistic or panentheistic orientation are also excluded: among these are Dionysius the pseudo-Areopagite, Evagrius, John Scotus Erigena, Meister Eckhart, Angelus Silesius, Schleiermacher, Alan Watts and Gerald Heard. On the other hand, I do not reject mysticism altogether, since some in this tradition have maintained a firm adherence to Jesus Christ as the only Savior from sin: Augustine, Bernard of Clairvaux, Pascal, and Gerhard Tersteegen. While aligning myself with the Reformed tradition with its emphasis on the sovereignty of grace and the total inability of man to come to salvation, I have sought to learn from those in the Arminian tradition (e.g., John Wesley) who rightly seek to do justice to human responsibility and activity in the salvific event.

I see evangelical theology at odds with modern existentialism, which is a child of the Renaissance with its emphasis on personal freedom and human autonomy. Those luminaries within the wider existentialist movement, however, whose thinking was still controlled by Scripture are to be regarded more as allies than enemies of the true faith. Here I would include Kierkegaard, Emil Brunner, Karl Barth, and to a lesser extent, Reinhold Niebuhr.

In modern Evangelicalism there exists a tension between Reformation theology and Pietism. Both these movements are important for an understanding of Evangelicalism, and both have very much to offer. In addition to the firm commitment of Calvin and Luther to *sola gratia* (salvation by grace alone) and *sola fide* (faith alone), we need to pay heed to the concerns of Spener and Wesley for the holy life. Protestant orthodoxy, especially in its later phases, became arrayed against Pietism and tended to devalue or even deny the mystical and existential elements in the faith. Modern neo-Pietism with its emphasis on religious experience and interpersonal relations underplays the doctrinal and intellectual dimensions of the faith. Evangelicalism must give due appreciation to both religious experience and doctrinal integrity, and certainly also to the call to ethical obedience, if it is to become a viable option for the church of the future.

NOTES

1. Frederick Herzog, "The Liberation of White Theology," *The Christian Century* 91:11 (March 20, 1974), [pp. 316–319], p. 318.

2. See Donald G. Bloesch, *The Evangelical Renaissance* (Grand Rapids: Eerdmans, 1973), and David F. Wells and John D. Woodbridge, eds., *The Evangelicals* (Nashville: Abingdon Press, 1975).

3. We here include the charismatic renewal, Camps Farthest Out, the Lay Witness missions, the Disciplined Order of Christ, the higher life movement, and the Faith at Work movement. The feminist movement within the churches could also be cited, since one of its tenets appears to be that theology must be primarily rooted in human experience, and for many this means women's experiences. See Nancy Hardesty, "Toward A Total Human Theology," *Sojourners* 5:5 (May/June 1976), pp. 35–37. The objective basis of faith is much more in evidence in Young Life and Campus Crusade for Christ, but even here an extrabiblical experientialism is intruding. We do not dispute the moving of the Spirit in all these movements nor the fact that in them evangelical motifs certainly persist in varying degrees.

4. John Warwick Montgomery, *Principalities and Powers* (Minneapolis: Bethany Fellowship, 1973), p. 169. Montgomery's statement is generally accurate, but it does not take into consideration that at their best the earlier revival movements held in balance the objective and subjective dimensions of salvation. Nor must it be forgotten that one of the prime fruits of the revivals was a real love for the Scriptures on the part of laymen resulting in the formation of Bible schools and Christian colleges.

5. P. T. Forsyth, *The Church and the Sacraments,* 2d ed. (London: Independent Press, 1947), p. 4.

6. Wesley says that true religion consists neither "in orthodoxy, or right opinions; which although they are not properly outward things, are not in the heart, but in the understanding." *The Works of John Wesley,* vol. 5 (Grand Rapids: Zondervan, 1958), p. 78. At the same time he agrees that there are some "fundamental truths" that are an essential part of true religion, but faith does not consist primarily in their affirmation.

7. See Carl Henry, *The Uneasy Conscience of Modern Fundamentalism* (Grand Rapids: Eerdmans, 1947) and his *Plea for Evangelical Demonstration* (Grand Rapids: Baker Book House, 1971).

8. See Carl Henry in *World Vision* 18:5 (May, 1974), p. 13.

9. Donald W. Dayton ably shows how social welfare in this country sprang directly from the ranks of evangelical Christianity. See his *Discovering An Evangelical Heritage* (New York: Harper & Row, 1976). On the crucial role of eighteenth century evangelicals (mainly Calvinists) in the social ferment that led to the American revolution see Alan Heimert, *Religion and the American Mind* (Cambridge, Mass.: Harvard University Press, 1966). For the social involvement of Pietism see Donald Bloesch, *The Evangelical Renaissance,* pp. 122–129.

10. I have in mind, for example, Virginia Mollenkott's asseveration that "the Bible supports the central tenets of feminism." In *Sojourners* (February 1976), p. 21. I do not doubt the reality of a biblical feminism with its emphasis on freedom for service, but this must be sharply distinguished from feminism as a secular ideology, which upholds the autonomy and essential independence of woman and makes self-fulfillment the primary goal in life. Many of the contributors to *Sojourners* would here be in agreement with me. I regard both *Sojourners* and *The Other Side* as beacon lights in the evangelical world, although my own orientation is closer to the Reformed than to the Anabaptist tradition, which has considerable influence in the evangelical left.

II.
THE MEANING OF
EVANGELICAL

For I am not ashamed of the gospel: it is the power of God for salvation to every one who has faith, to the Jew first and also to the Greek.

Romans 1:16

Christianity is not the sacrifice we make, but the sacrifice we trust; not the victory we win, but the victory we inherit. That is the evangelical principle.

P. T. Forsyth

Evangelical means informed by the gospel of Jesus Christ, as heard afresh in the 16th century Reformation by a direct return to Holy Scripture.

Karl Barth

Evangelical Christianity is theological in its character, biblical in its substance . . . and fundamental in its emphasis.[1]

John R. W. Stott

Of the various meanings associated with the term *evangelical,* the theological meaning is primary. *Evangelical* is derived from the Greek word *evangelion,* meaning message of salvation through the atoning sacrifice of Christ. It contains a missionary thrust because it is centered in the proclamation to the world of the good news of salvation. It also entails an appeal to conversion and decision on the basis of the free grace of God.

In its historical meaning *evangelical* has come to refer to the kind of religion espoused by the Protestant Reformation. It is also associated with the spiritual movements of purification subsequent to the Reformation—Pietism and Puritanism. The revival movements within Protestantism in the eighteenth and nineteenth centuries have also been appropriately termed *evangelical.*

When the term is used in its strict theological sense, it crosses all sectarian lines. The Second Council of Orange (529) can be deemed basically evangelical in view of its vigorous defense of the doctrine of free grace (God's favor toward the undeserving) and its condemnation of semi-Pelagianism (the claim that man can initiate the process of salvation). G. C. Berkouwer maintains that this judgment must be qualified, since it was also affirmed that man can cooperate with grace in the attaining of his salvation.[2] Among the fathers and theologians of the Roman Catholic church in whom evangelical themes and emphases can be detected are Ambrose, Augustine, Bernard of Clairvaux, Thomas Aquinas, and Pascal. Even some who are more often associated with an other-worldly mystical spirituality can be mentioned in this connection. Thérèse of Lisieux preferred to speak of a lift rather than a ladder to heaven, the lift of free grace.[3] "Faith is the only means," said John of the Cross, "whereby God manifests himself to the soul in his divine light, which surpasses all understanding."[4]

Evangelical theologians, especially of the neo-orthodox persuasion, have protested against the biblical–classical synthesis in which the dynamic categories of biblical faith were subsumed under the static categories of Hellenistic philosophy. Yet voices were also raised in the medieval church against the growing accommodation to Hellenistic philosophy. Peter Damian was among those who railed against any compromise with the world of speculative thought. Three hundred years before the Reformation Bonaventure warned the church against a dependence on Aristotle and other pagan philosophers that would "turn the thinking of men toward themselves."[5]

An evangelical witness can also be discerned in contemporary Catholicism, though this witness has been muted by the rise of a neo-Catholicism with a markedly anthropocentric orientation. Father Jerome Hamer, a Belgium Roman Catholic priest, criticized the delegates at the 1973 World Council of Churches' Conference on World Mission in Bangkok for discussing salvation for many days without once mentioning "justification by faith" or "God's righteous wrath against sin." Louis Bouyer in his noted *Spirit and Forms of Protestantism* has maintained that the salient principles of the Reformation are authentically Catholic.[6] Opening himself to criticism from both the right and left, Hans Küng appeals to the message of Scripture over the consciousness of the church and accepts the Reformation principle of justification by faith alone.[7] The lay theologian Ralph Martin contends that it is not sufficient to hold up Jesus as model: He must above all be acknowledged as Savior of the world, "the one who by his life, death, and resurrection crushes the power of Satan, takes away our sins" and "restores us to union with God."[8]

Eastern Orthodoxy with its concept of *theosis,* the divinization of man through faith and love, reflects a spirituality that is more remote from the concerns of evangelical faith. Yet in this branch of Christendom, too, an evangelical note has been sounded even though its impact has been minimal. Greek Orthodox Patriarch Cyril Lucaris (sixteenth and seventeenth centuries) is perhaps the best known example of those who sought to incorporate evangelical motifs in the theology of their church. He drew up a confession which explicitly affirmed justification by faith, the authority of Scripture over the authority of the church, and the doctrine of predestination. Yet his views were resisted from the beginning and finally condemned in several church councils.[9]

It can be shown that authentic evangelicalism is rooted in the catholic heritage of the church as well as in Scripture. Yet there is a cultural inheritance in the church tradition that is not part of the spiritual inheritance of the faith once delivered to the saints. There is a need to discriminate between truth and error in the church tradition in the light of Scripture.

EVANGELICALISM AND CATHOLICISM

Evangelicalism and Catholicism are the two themes in the Christian symphony, and Christianity, biblical Christianity, is not complete without either of them.[10] Each of these types of theological orientation has its own peculiar emphasis, which accounts for areas of tension between them. Ideally they are complementary, but this is not always apparent.

While Evangelicalism is oriented about the primitive message of the New Testament, Catholicism is just as concerned about the institution and rites of the church. Whereas Evangelicalism upholds the particularity of the historical revelation as attested in Scripture, Catholicism gives more weight to the universality of grace and the universality of the community of faith. While Evangelicalism's concern is with outreach and mission, the concern of Catholicism is continuity with the tradition. The vicarious atonement of Christ figures much more highly than the incarnation in Evangelical theology and piety; Catholicism on the other hand puts much more emphasis on the incarnation of Christ and the body of Christ, which is the Church. If Evangelical theology appeals to the events of sacred history, Catholic thought is preoccupied with the channels of salvation, the means of grace. Evangelicalism is noted for its protest against idolatry, while Catholicism puts a high premium on symbols and aids to salvation. This iconoclastic strain in Evangelicalism is especially pronounced in Puritanism which condemned all visible representation of God in the worship of the Church.

It can be said that Evangelicals stress the why more than the how, the cross more than the incarnation.[11] The deity of Christ is seen in light of his saving work. Christology and soteriology are viewed as an integral whole. It is not Christ in himself but Christ for us that is particularly valued."To know Christ is to know His benefits"(Melanchthon). It should be noted that the two natures of Christ and the doctrine of the Trinity are not an integral part of the New Testament evangel. Yet they are still of fundamental importance because they are implicit in the scriptural witness and are crucial in the explication of this witness. The deity of Christ has especially been stressed by Evangelicalism against Liberalism.

At the time of the Reformation there was a pressing need to emphasize certain biblical themes that had been obscured or diluted in the development of Roman Catholicism. Among these were the primacy of Scripture, salvation by grace, justification by faith alone, and the cruciality of preaching. Luther and Calvin were both cognizant of the perils of the semi-Pelagianism that was reasserting itself in the Roman church. Many Roman Catholic scholars today acknowledge the validity of the Reformation fear of a religion of works-righteousness, though they maintain that such a religion did not represent authentic Catholicism.[12]

Karl Barth has made the astute observation that Catholicism is characterized by a "both-and" philosophy, whereas Evangelical Protestants stress "either-or." Catholicism affirms both grace *and* free will, faith *and* works, Scripture *and* the church, Christ *and* Mary. Protestants of the Reformation tradition have reacted against this by stressing grace alone *(sola gratia)*, faith alone *(sola fide)*, Scripture alone, *(sola scriptura)* and Christ alone *(solus Christus)*. It must be acknowledged, however, that in much popular Protestantism synergism (salvation through both grace and free will) is even more evident than in Catholicism, and human reason and experience figure more prominently than Scripture in determining the norms for faith. It should also be recognized that some in academic Catholicism insist vigorously upon *sola gratia, solus Christus,* and even the primal authority of Scripture. For all its validity Barth's allegation must to some degree be qualified.

In his provocative book *Christ's Church: Evangelical, Catholic and Reformed* Bela Vassady indicts the Roman church for not being sufficiently catholic.[13] He argues with some cogency that this church by its

Romanizing and Latinizing tendencies represents a narrowing and confinement of the catholic vision. It is only fair to add, however, that Vassady wrote his book before the Second Vatican Council, which signified a valiant effort in the direction of a more ecumenical stance.

A true Evangelicalism will be Reformed in the theological as well as the historical sense in that it will include many emphases associated with Reformed Christendom. Among these are the sovereignty of grace, glory to God alone, and unconditional election. An authentically Evangelical church will also affirm *ecclesia semper reformanda*—the church always being reformed, the church ever in the process of reformation.

Besides its Reformation moorings, Evangelicalism is also indissolubly linked with the tradition of evangelical revivalism, which includes the Anabaptists, the Pietists, and the Puritans. Evangelicalism numbers among its forefathers not only Luther, Calvin, Zwingli, and Knox but also Menno Simons, Philip Spener, Richard Baxter, John Owen, John Wesley, Count Zinzendorf, and Jonathan Edwards. Pietism sought a fulfillment of the Reformation in a reformation of life as well as doctrine. In addition to the Word and sacraments as the marks of the true church, Pietism stressed the importance of fellowship and mission. Puritanism was noted for its concern for a reformation or purification in worship as well as in life. All these movements stressed the necessity for the new birth, the experience of the heart, and the reality of regeneration which served as a complement to the Reformation emphasis on justification. In recovering the experiential side of the faith, evangelical revivalism reestablished continuity with the tradition of Catholic mysticism;[14] at the same time its pronounced ethical thrust, which extended even into the nineteenth century, sharply distinguished it from that strand in mysticism which was more philosophical than biblical.

Protestant Orthodoxy too must figure in any assessment of Evangelicalism. This movement, which was especially vigorous in the seventeenth and eighteenth centuries, was known for its concern for precision and clarity in the formulation of doctrine. It includes such noted spokesmen as Martin Chemnitz, Johann Gerhard, Francis Turretin, J. H. Heidegger, Abraham Kuyper, Ernest W. Hengstenberg, Charles Hodge, A. A. Hodge, Herman Bavinck, and Benjamin Warfield. True Evangelicals will be concerned for right doctrine as well as the right way of living. And yet Evangelicalism, because it values a personal faith in Jesus Christ over loyalty to creeds and dogma, cannot simply be equated with or subsumed under Protestant Orthodoxy. Protestant

Orthodoxy tended in the direction of a Christian rationalism and thereby obscured the mystical dimensions of the faith.

Finally we must give attention to neo-Orthodoxy (the movement associated with Karl Barth and Emil Brunner) as still another manifestation of Evangelicalism. By its emphasis on the uniqueness of the Christ revelation and its strictures on philosophical theology it was able, for a time, to recover a vital, living biblical faith. Nevertheless, by underplaying and in some cases denying the inspiration of the Scriptures and the urgency of evangelism it did not succeed in spearheading a genuine revival of Evangelical theology and piety.[15] In its often lackadaisical and sometimes negative attitude toward the church and sacraments neo-Orthodoxy was also not sufficiently catholic.[16]

It is my contention that Evangelicalism to be complete and effective must be Catholic as well. Catholicism to be authentic must be Evangelical as well. Paul Tillich referred to the Protestant principle and Catholic substance, which are equally important for the faith.[17] My preference is to speak of the evangelical message and the catholic heritage, both of which are necessary for a biblical, ecumenical church.

The term *Evangelical* is wider and narrower than *Protestant*. It is wider since it includes godly men and women of biblical piety in the Catholic churches and in some of the sects. It is narrower since there are two kinds of Protestantism—the evangelical and the liberal, and as J. Gresham Machen has rightly said, these cannot be harmonized.[18]

As has been indicated, the term *Evangelical* is also narrower than *Catholic,* since it excludes any confidence in one's own merit and any trust in the Church that is not subordinated to Scripture. Yet Evangelicals in their concern for freedom in Christ do not intend to minimize the crucial role of the Church in our salvation. Barth claims that "the meaning of Protestantism (both Lutheran and Reformed) was in the beginning not a lessening but a heightening of the force of all the claims which Catholicism makes for the Church."[19]

That a true Evangelicalism is at one with a true Catholicism is attested by such spokesmen for the Evangelical faith as P. T. Forsyth, John Nevin, Nathan Söderblom, Wilhelm Löhe, and Count Nicolaus Ludwig von Zinzendorf—all of whom were noted for the breadth of their ecumenical vision. Calvin and Luther too should be included, for they sought to stand in the historic tradition of the Roman church and appealed to many of the church fathers as well as Scripture. Yet the polemical climate of their time prevented them from giving due appreciation to certain emphases in the Catholic heritage whose biblical support is more implicit than explicit (e.g., the doctrine of the saints).

Though acknowledging the need for continuity with the Catholic tradition, I insist that Evangelicalism is characterized by certain features that were given prominence at the time of the Reformation and should be given attention again today. Yet these need to be united with catholic themes and concerns if we are to witness the full recovery of biblical Christianity in our time.

EVANGELICALISM AND LIBERALISM

While Evangelicalism is at odds with historic Roman Catholicism and Eastern Orthodoxy on some important points, it wages a different kind of battle with Liberalism. In traditional Catholicism the simple Gospel message tends to be obscured by church dogma and the intricacies of ritual. In Liberalism the Gospel appears to be either reduced to ethics or translated into ontology or dissolved into mysticism. The focus of attention is placed either on moral and spiritual values or on an experience of inner enlightenment which requires philosophical conceptualization.

Liberal theology is associated with some of the leading scholars in the history of the church. Within Protestantism it includes such luminaries as Friedrich Schleiermacher, Albrecht Ritschl, Ernst Troeltsch, Adolf Harnack, Wilhelm Herrmann, and Emanuel Hirsch; on the American scene are Horace Bushnell, Harry Emerson Fosdick, Edward Scribner Ames, Shailer Mathews, D. C. Macintosh, and Henry Nelson Wieman. In more recent times we can mention Rudolf Bultmann, Paul Tillich, Fritz Buri, Harvey Cox, J. A. T. Robinson, Langdon Gilkey, Daniel Day Williams, John Macquarrie, John Cobb, Jürgen Moltmann, and Dorothee Soelle. Among Catholic liberals today are Gregory Baum, Rosemary Ruether, Michael Novak, David Tracy, Donald Goergen, Louis Evely, and Piet Schoonenberg. Not all of the persons mentioned above fit neatly into the ideal type of liberal theology, but they nevertheless approximate it in various degrees.

Liberal theology places a high premium on personal autonomy and freedom. It is characterized by an appeal to interior norms, such as conscience and religious experience. It is disposed to view Jesus as a moral ideal or symbol of divine love instead of a sin-bearer and mediator. It sees the value of religion mainly in its ethical and social fruits; this is generally true even of liberals who stress the importance of mystical experience, though it is not always so apparent with them. The Bible tends to be treated as a text book on religious and moral evolution. There is a general inclination to regard man as innately good and capable of realizing his spiritual potential with the aid of divine grace. An attempt is invariably made to bring the Christian faith into dialogue with the modern world and to make its abiding insights creditable to its cultured despisers.

The orientation of liberal theology is not so much theological as psychological-anthropological. It takes for its point of departure not the divine incursion into history nor the self-attesting Scriptures but the exploratory outreach of man's reason. While evangelical theology appeals to the Protestant Reformation and the heritage of Pietism and Puritanism, liberal theology has an acknowledged affinity to the Renaissance and Enlightenment, though it also finds kindred spirits among some of the rationalists and radical mystics in the patristic and medieval periods.

Evangelical theology has been impelled to uphold and defend certain tenets of the historic faith that palpably conflict with modern life and world views and that ipso facto disturb the proponents of an "enlightened" Christianity. Among these are the absolute sovereignty and transcendence of God; the divine authority and inspiration of Scripture; the radical sinfulness of man; the deity of Jesus Christ; His vicarious, substitutionary atonement; the eschatological and superhistorical character of the kingdom of God; a final judgment at the end of history; the realities of heaven and hell; and evangelization as the primary dimension of the Christian mission.

Karl Barth has gone so far as to indicate a preference for historical Catholicism over neo-Protestantism: "If I today became convinced that the interpretation of the Reformation on the line taken by Schleiermacher-Ritschl-Troeltsch . . . was correct . . . I could not indeed become a Catholic tomorrow, but I should have to withdraw from the Evangelical Church. And if I were forced to make a choice between the two evils, I should, in fact, prefer the Catholic."[20]

In contradistinction to liberal theology, whether in its neo-Protestant or neo-Catholic guise, evangelical theology stresses the moral regeneration of the will over rational and spiritual insight; crisis over process; God's gracious initiative over man's religious quest; the service of God's glory over the fulfillment of the self; scriptural norms over cultural mores; biblical proclamation over rational apologetics; the cross as substitution over the cross as moral ideal; and, the historical particularity of the revelation of Jesus Christ over the general wisdom and experience of the religious community.

Evangelicals resist the tendency to reduce piety to practice, since this prepares the way for moralism. The privatization of piety is likewise opposed because this fosters ghettoism. Piety, in the biblical perspective, is the fear of the Lord combined with an adoring love for him born out of gratefulness for his mercy. True piety is inseparable from Christian practice, but it is also its precondition. The vertical relationship to God is the basis for the horizontal relationship to one's neighbor.

Against the new modernism a catholic evangelicalism draws sharp lines of distinction between faith and unbelief, theology and culture, the sacred and the profane. It sees any attempt to identify the sacred and profane as a form of pantheism that contradicts the biblical affirmation that only the living God is holy and all human culture and religion stand under his judgment.

For authentic evangelicalism the test of a sound theology is not whether it is successfully correlated with general wisdom but whether it is in conformity with its object, the revealed Word of God. Theology may utilize the language and insights of secular thought, but it must beware of synthesizing the content of faith with philosophical meanings (the temptation in Liberalism), since faith is thereby diluted in the process. In evangelical theology we do not try to bring together the answer of faith and the creative questions of the culture (as in Tillich); instead our aim is to challenge the culture to begin asking the right questions.

Despite all that has been said the Evangelical response to Liberalism is not an unqualified no. Karl Barth on at least one occasion pointed to the portrait of Schleiermacher in his home and remarked, "He too is a Christian." There are some things in the Liberal tradition that can be appreciated and even belong to an ecumenical evangelical vision. Among these are the self-critical spirit, a sensitivity to social injustice, an earnest desire to communicate to the world outside the church, an openness to truth wherever it appears, and a readiness to learn from other religious persuasions. It is a sad but irrefutable fact that many of those who call themselves Liberals have a very illiberal spirit and refuse even to carry on a dialogue with Evangelicals. But this does not controvert the valid insights that are to be found in Liberal theology. The Puritan father John Robinson manifested a truly liberal spirit when he declared: "The Lord has more truth and light yet to break forth out of his holy Word." It is important to remember, however, that Evangelical theology upholds an openness under the Word; it does not seek a higher truth or experience beyond the Word.

A catholic evangelicalism, in contrast to fundamentalism, will not isolate itself from the world of critical scholarship. It will not accommodate the faith to the modern world view but will earnestly try to understand it and learn from it wherever possible. Evangelical theology will give a qualified approval to the historical-critical method, but it will reject the naturalistic philosophy of many of the higher critics. It will display a readiness to take into account scientific discoveries and new scientific evidence, even if this calls into question certain reputed historical facts or opinions of the world and man found in the Bible. The theory of evolution is not a scientific fact, however, and therefore Evangelical theology has been basically right in its continued opposition to Darwinism and especially social Darwinism. Evangelicals will value the scientific method (though not as a pathway to knowledge of God), but they will always be on the alert against scientism, the naturalist philosophy that makes use of science for its own ends.

Against radical-liberal theology a catholic evangelicalism will not seek to downgrade the church in favor of a churchless Christianity or a purely ethical or mystical religion. Forsyth spoke for many when he said that what is needed is "not the dechurching of Christianity, but the Christianizing of the Church."[21] Religion needs to be incarnate in community, but true community must be anchored in the transcendent.

Authentic Evangelicalism distrusts appeals to religious experience that are not corroborated by Scripture. There are tensions and even opposition between Evangelicalism and mystical and spiritualistic movements. While the first rests its case on the historical revelation mediated in the Scriptures, mysticism is based on the experience of immediacy. Benjamin Warfield went too far when he averred that one could not be both a mystic and a Christian,[22] but his warning contains an element of truth. Evangelical theology views with considerable reserve the spiritualists of the radical Reformation as well as mystics who were heavily influenced by neo-Platonic philosophy such as Dionysius the pseudo-Areopagite, John Scotus Erigena, and Meister Eckhart.[23] It is even more averse to modern immanentalist mysticism as represented by Alan Watts, Teilhard de Chardin, Kazantzakis, Thomas Altizer, Bernard Meland, and J. A. T. Robinson.[24]

Paul Tillich, despite the fact that he has one foot in the spirituality of the Lutheran Reformation, belongs more properly to the classical mystical tradition. His spiritual kinship to neo-Platonic mysticism rather than to biblical personalism is revealed in his conception of a God beyond the divine-human encounter, which he describes as the abysmal ground of all being. In Tillich we see a synthesis of the liberalism of the Enlightenment and the mysticism of Plato and Plotinus, which has constantly reasserted itself in the Christian mystical tradition.[25]

We must indeed be on guard against the Platonizing and spiritualizing of the Christian faith, but we must not embrace a fanatically antimystical posture that excludes the genuine contributions of the great mystics of the church.[26] In the dialogue with Roman Catholicism and Eastern Orthodoxy on the one hand and neo-Protestantism on the other,[27] it is well to keep in mind that there are various types of mysticism, some of which have more affinity with biblical faith than others. Many of the Catholic mystics were avowed theists despite the neo-Platonic bent of their thought, and quite a few were well versed in the Scriptures. Luther himself was positively influenced by such mystics as Johann Tauler and the author of the *Theologica Germanica*. Though he broke out of the conceptual framework of mysticism (neo-Platonism), he nonetheless perceived that faith itself includes an overpowering sense of the majestic presence of God. In this experience the humanly rational is transcended, and the soul is enveloped in awe and rapture.[28]

Bengt Hoffman has challenged the antimystical bias in recent Lutheran and Reformed scholarship and maintains that Luther can best be understood against the background of Germanic mysticism.[29] It can, with some justification, be argued that Hoffman overlooks the synergism that is almost endemic to mysticism and too easily reconciles the evangelical faith of the Reformation with pre-Reformation mystics.[30] At the same time his work is a welcome antidote to the antipathy toward mysticism that has pervaded Protestant scholarship since Ritschl. It also contains a potent reminder that the great missionary thrust within Protestantism, as well as the flowering of charitable enterprises, is to be traced to the Pietistic movements, which have their basis in the mystical side of the Reformation.

A SYSTEMATIC EVANGELICAL THEOLOGY?

Evangelical theology in its completed form is a systematic whole, though our human systems are but broken reflections of the absolute system, the plan of salvation in the mind of God. Our theology, since it is a human enterprise, needs to be constantly revised and reformed. Yet since the message of faith is rational, it can be understood. The revelation in the Bible throws light not only upon the purposes of God but also upon the human situation. It is incumbent upon us to present to the world a reasonably coherent, intelligible gospel, and theological reflection is geared to this end. Our theological method is reason in the service of revelation to the greater glory of God.

At the same time the truth of faith cannot be translated into a finalized, coherent system which denies the mystery and paradox in faith. This is because this truth is suprarational as well as rational. Our human system must always be one that is open to revision in the light of new insights into the Word of God and the human situation. It can never be a closed, airtight, logically consistent, perfected system of truth.

All the doctrines of the Christian faith presuppose one another and include one another. The doctrines of the Virgin Birth and the bodily resurrection of Christ are included in the deity of Christ. These particular doctrines had to be emphasized in the early twentieth century, but now the very divinity of Christ is called into question, and the battle must be waged on this front.

It may be that in the future, to safeguard the message of faith, some doctrines will have to be emphasized that are not here mentioned as evangelical essentials. We have in mind such themes as the Trinity, the apostolicity of the church, the communion of saints, angelology, and the sacraments, though some of these are included in this book under different headings.

Evangelical theology aims not only to be faithful to Scripture, but also to expose the unfaithfulness of the Christian community to Scripture. It must warn the church of threats to the faith from both within and without. It should say yes to the Evangel but no to modern heresies. Therefore theology has both a positive and a negative side, a dogmatic and an apologetic task. Yet the latter must always be subordinated to the former and in fact included within it. Apologetics (the defense of the faith against unbelief) is not a preparation for dogmatics (the systematic explication of the faith to the church); instead dogmatics is the foundation for apologetics.

Among the current heresies that Evangelical theology must combat is universalism, the doctrine that all mankind either is saved or will be saved. Both Karl Barth and Karl Rahner have given impetus to this heresy, though neither is technically a universalist. Barth's quasi Christomonism, in which all people are included in the body and kingdom of Christ, and Rahner's idea that all people are "surrounded" by the grace of God have created a new mood which tends to disregard or deny the wrath of God against sin and the reality of being spiritually lost. Both Barth and Rahner, however, make a place for each of these ideas, though the latter idea is considerably qualified.

Other heresies that currently pose a threat to the church are a creeping unitarianism, which calls into question the deity of Christ; situationalism, which denies absolute moral principles; religious naturalism, which discards the idea of a transcendent, theistic God; syncretistic mysticism, which disclaims the historical uniqueness of Jesus Christ; and, a secular, political theology which identifies salvation with liberation from economic and political oppression.

Against the current mood of social activism in the churches, Evangelical theology will stress the spiritual mission of the church, but not in such a way as to give any support to individualistic, privatistic religion. It will not disavow the social dimension of the faith but instead try to see this dimension in its proper context. It will protest against the misconceptions that social reform is the mission of the church and that the heart of the Christian message is the Sermon on the Mount rather than the atoning sacrifice of Christ on the cross. While standing against the new Social Gospel, it will at the same time seek to discover the social implications of the biblical Gospel.

Evangelical theology does not pretend to have the *whole* truth, but it does profess to know the *real* truth. It is not agnostic concerning the reality of God and the plan of salvation, but it is also not gnostic in the sense of claiming access to a secret knowledge into the mysteries of God beyond the ken of ordinary Christians. It bases its claim only on the knowledge of faith anchored in the testimony of Scripture, which is available to all Christians.

Evangelical theology is a *theologia viatorum* (a theology of wayfarers), not a *theologia comprehensorum* (a theology of those who have arrived conceptually). It sees itself on a pilgrimage to a heavenly city where faith will be supplanted by direct vision, but at present it is content simply to walk by faith.

Evangelical theology, however systematic, is not to be confused with a Christian philosophy or with philosophy of religion. Its basic concern is not an overall view of the world but the faithful explication of the Word of God and the heralding of this Word to the world. Its appeal is not to the natural knowledge of God, which is inevitably inadequate and misleading, but to the revelation of Jesus Christ given in Holy Scripture, a revelation that is absolutely unique and once for all times. In this perspective reason is not a stepping stone to faith but a useful instrument in the hands of faith.

THE BANE OF MODERN EVANGELICALISM

Evangelicalism, particularly in America, has had difficulty in presenting a credible witness to the world today because of its concentration on peripheral and nonessential matters. By focusing its attention on such matters it has become isolated not only from the contemporary theological debate but also from its own heritage. Eschatology (the doctrine of the last things: death, resurrection, etc.) is not peripheral, but the chronology of events in the last days certainly is, and this is what preoccupies many of those of an evangelical or fundamentalist persuasion. What many conservatives tend to overlook is that the premillennial reign of Christ on earth, the seven dispensations, and the pretribulation rapture are not to be found in the thinking of the Protestant Reformers, and such ideas were also generally alien to the early Puritans and Pietists. It is certainly permissible to hold to such views as pious opinions but to elevate them into dogmas of the church is to flirt with heresy on the right. A catholic evangelical theology will insist that the blessed hope is not the rapture of the church but the second coming of Christ. Edward J. Carnell has aptly pointed out that eschatology has never been made a test of orthodoxy or true faith in the mainstream of Evangelicalism, and it surely should not be today.[31]

Another bane of latter day Evangelicalism is that too often it has sought to equate the logical conclusions of dogma with dogma itself. It has thereby placed itself in the position of viewing as cardinal tenets of the faith such ideas as biblical inerrancy, double predestination, the second blessing, and the millennial reign of Christ on earth. We do not deny the element of biblical truth in all these doctrines, but in and of themselves they cannot be considered evangelical essentials. There is an important sense in which the Bible does not err and there are blessings of the Spirit after conversion, but these doctrines also lend themselves to profound misunderstandings if not seen in their proper context. We need to remember that both the Jehovah's Witnesses and Christadelphians affirm the total inerrancy of Scripture, and yet neither of these cults can be considered Christian, let alone evangelical. Both prove to be systems of works-righteousness and thereby contravene the very core of evangelical faith. Some Pentecostal groups, despite their marked biblicism and fundamentalist fervor, actually hold to a Unitarianism of the second person and consequently can only be regarded as heretical.[32] Several sects have elevated Sabbatarianism (strict observance of the Sabbath) into a fundamental of the faith and are therefore also outside the pale of authentic evangelicalism.

As has been indicated there are fundamentals of the faith that are not included as major headings in this book, but if they are truly fundamental they are given proper treatment under one or more of these headings. The Trinity, for example, is discussed in its relation to both the sovereignty of God and the deity of Christ. Though not part of the primitive message of the faith, it is a cardinal doctrine of the faith, a Catholic truth as well as an Evangelical essential, though perhaps not one that needs to be stressed as much today as some others.

There is a need for a catholic evangelicalism that will maintain continuity not only with the heritage of the Reformation but also with the whole catholic heritage. It will assess the tradition of the church and its own particular tradition not uncritically but in light of the Word of God in Scripture. A catholic evangelicalism will seek to go through the Reformation and beyond it, not merely behind or around it, as many Anglo-Catholics do. It will place Scripture over the ecclesiastical tradition bearing in mind that the Word that God speaks to the church cannot be simply equated with the word of the church itself. At the same time it will value the history of theology as an important albeit imperfect commentary on Scripture. It will view the church as a herald of grace rather than a dispenser of grace. It will see the clergy as servants of grace more than mediators of grace.

Yet in its emphasis on free grace the Evangelical church should take care not to minimize the means of grace—the visible aids whereby the Holy Spirit comes to us. And surely the church is the chief of these instruments or means through which we come to know the saving truth of Jesus Christ. May we not indeed refer to the church as our Mother just as we refer to God as our Father and Jesus Christ as our Savior?[33] Both Luther and Calvin employed this terminology, and we must bear in mind that the Reformers themselves sought a theology that would be at the same time Evangelical and Catholic.

NOTES

1. Note that quotations from John R. W. Stott in the introductory sections in this book are taken from his *Christ the Controversialist* (London: Tyndale Press, 1970).

2. G. C. Berkouwer, *The Conflict with Rome,* trans. David H. Freeman (Philadelphia: Presbyterian & Reformed Publishing Co., 1958), p. 78.

3. For the evangelical motifs in Thérèse of Lisieux, see Ida Friederike Görres, *The Hidden Face,* trans. Richard and Clara Winston (New York: Pantheon Books, 1959).

4. John of the Cross, *Ascent of Mount Carmel II,* ch. 8:1.

5. In Max Lackmann, *The Augsburg Confession and Catholic Unity* (New York: Herder & Herder, 1963), p. 141.

6. Louis Bouyer, *The Spirit and Forms of Protestantism,* trans. A. V. Littledale (Westminster: Newman Press, 1961).

7. See especially Hans Küng, *Justification,* trans. Thomas Collins, Edmund E. Tolk, and David Granskou (New York: Thomas Nelson & Sons, 1964), p. 252. In his more recent writing one can discern in Küng a movement away from biblical authority to the authority of experiential verification. While the Gospel remains the primary criterion, there is also an appeal to universally lived human experience. See Hans Küng, *On Being a Christian,* trans. Edward Quinn (Garden City, N.Y.: Doubleday, 1976), pp. 65 ff, 84 ff.

8. Ralph Martin, *Unless the Lord build the house . . .* (Notre Dame: Ava Maria Press, 1975), p. 21.

9. See C. Samuel Calian, "Cyril Lucaris: The Patriarch Who Failed" in *Journal of Ecumenical Studies,* 10:2 (Spring 1973), pp. 319–336.

10. We are including other Catholic traditions besides the Roman in the category of Catholicism.

11. As John Wenham puts it, in Reformed or evangelical thinking the weight is placed on "the moral marvel of substitution," not the "metaphysical marvel of incarnation." John W. Wenham, *The Goodness of God* (Downers Grove, Ill.: InterVarsity Press, 1974), p. 193.

12. See Harry J. McSorley, *Luther: Right or Wrong?* (Minneapolis: Augsburg Publishing House, 1969).

13. Bela Vassady, *Christ's Church: Evangelical, Catholic and Reformed* (Grand Rapids: Eerdmans, 1965), pp. 19ff.

14. A certain rapport with mysticism can be perceived in the early Luther, but it is much less evident in the later Luther and Melanchthon as well as in Protestant Orthodoxy. While the mystical dimension of the faith is certainly present in Calvin, it is patently less visible in later Calvinism.

15. See Donald G. Bloesch, "Whatever Became of Neo-Orthodoxy?" in *Christianity Today,* 19:5 (December 6, 1974), pp. 7–12.

16. See, for example, Emil Brunner, *The Misunderstanding of the Church,* trans. Harold Knight (Philadelphia: Westminster Press, 1953).

17. Paul Tillich, *Systematic Theology,* vol. 3 (Chicago: University of Chicago Press, 1963), p. 245.

18. J. Gresham Machen, *Christianity and Liberalism* (Grand Rapids: Eerdmans, 1923).

19. Karl Barth, *Theology and Church,* trans. Louise Pettibone Smith (New York: Harper & Row, 1962), p. 313.

20. *Ibid.,* p. 314.

21. P. T. Forsyth, *Positive Preaching and the Modern Mind* (London: Independent Press Ltd., 1953, fourth imp.), p. 193.

22. Benjamin Warfield, *Studies in Theology* (New York: Oxford University Press, 1932), p. 666.

23. This is not to overlook the evangelical themes that characterize such a noted mystic as Meister Eckhart, including an emphasis on grace over works, but we maintain that the neo-Platonic cast of his theology obscured and blunted the force of these themes. See infra p. 49. Johann Tauler sought to

avoid the excesses of metaphysical speculation, which in Eckhart's case tended in the direction of pantheism, and thereby gave Germanic mysticism a more biblical thrust.

24. See especially J. A. T. Robinson, *Exploration into God* (Stanford, Cal.: Stanford University Press, 1967) where he states the case for what he terms "secular mysticism" with the accent not on withdrawal from the world but on "a deeper immersion in existence."

25. Neo-Platonism is also very much in evidence in the thought of the German existentialist Karl Jaspers who speaks of man's liberation in terms of his "ascent from God to the Godhead." Karl Jaspers, *Philosophical Faith and Revelation,* trans. E. B. Ashton (New York: Harper & Row, 1962), p. 284.

26. Emil Brunner's *Die Mystik und Das Wort* (Tübingen, W. Germany: J. C. B. Mohr, 1928), a polemic against the mysticism of Schleiermacher, is even in Barth's view an unfair assessment of that great figure in liberal theology. Schleiermacher cannot be wholly identified with mysticism, since he also reflects concerns of the Enlightenment as well as of the Protestant Reformation.

27. One side of neo-Protestantism is rationalistic, but the other side has its roots in romanticism and mysticism. Mysticism can appear in both an idealistic and naturalistic garb.

28. Rudolf Otto documents these mystical notes in Luther in his *The Idea of the Holy,* trans. John W. Harvey (New York: Oxford University Press, 1958), pp. 94–108, 204–207.

29. Bengt R. Hoffman, *Luther and the Mystics* (Minneapolis: Augsburg Publishing House, 1976). Hoffman acknowledges that Luther's position cannot be harmonized with the neo-Platonic mysticism of the pseudo-Dionysius, but he maintains that Luther was favorably disposed toward the more evangelical mysticism of Bernard of Clairvaux, Johann Tauler, and the *Theologica Germanica.*

30. Hoffman's work needs to be read in conjunction with Steven Ozment, *Homo Spiritualis* (Leiden: E. J. Brill, 1969), which underlines the contrast between Luther's spirituality and mysticism. Ozment perhaps unduly minimizes the influence of the mystics on Luther, but he does show that Luther's theology and piety have a distinctiveness of their own. Friedrich Heiler, in our opinion, does justice to the mystical strand in Luther without compromising his essential biblical and evangelical stance. See his *Prayer,* trans. and ed. Samuel McComb (New York: Oxford University Press, 1958).

31. Edward John Carnell, *The Case for Orthodox Theology* (Philadelphia: Westminster Press, 1959), p. 118.

32. See David Reed, "Aspects of the Origins of Oneness Pentecostalism," in Vinson Synan, ed., *Aspects of Pentecostal-Charismatic Origins* (Plainfield, N.J.: Logos International, 1975), pp. 143–168.

33. For relevant Scripture texts see Psalm 87:5 and Galatians 4:26, 27.

III.

THE SOVEREIGNTY OF GOD

For dominion belongs to the Lord, and he rules over the nations.

Psalm 22:28

I know that thou canst do all things, and that no purpose of thine can be thwarted.

Job 42:2

Thine, O Lord, is the greatness, the power, the glory, the splendour, and the majesty; for everything in heaven and on earth is thine; thine, O Lord, is the sovereignty, and thou art exalted over all as head.

1 Chronicles 29:11 NEB

God has contrived to exclude our glorying; that we should be wholly and every way dependent on God, for the moral and natural good that belongs to salvation; and that we have all from the hand of God, by his power and grace.

Jonathan Edwards

God's participation in man's affairs is much more than that of a fellow sufferer on a divine scale, whose love can rise to a painless sympathy with pain. He not only perfectly understands our case and our problem, but He has morally, actively, finally solved it.

P. T. Forsyth

In a time of religious transition when old traditions are being challenged, the question is often raised as to whether it is still desirable or even possible to hold on to the idea of the sovereignty of God. Particularly in the shadows of Dachau, Auschwitz, and Hiroshima can one continue to affirm a God who is both omnipotent and compassionate at the same time? We contend that if we are to remain true to the biblical heritage of our faith, as well as to the consensus of the catholic tradition, we must maintain the idea of a God of sovereign power. On the other hand, the biblical idea of sovereignty must be sharply distinguished from philosophical notions which have made this general concept untenable particularly for those of a sensitive conscience who rightly perceive that arbitrary power excludes vicarious identification or suffering love.

CREATOR AND LORD

The God of the Bible is depicted as the Creator of the universe and the Lord of history. He is not the Unmoved Mover or the Undifferentiated unity but the Almighty One who calls the worlds into being and whose "kingdom rules over all" (Ps. 103:19). He is not the "Idea of the Good" (as in Plato) nor the "superessential One" who is beyond the good (Plotinus),[1] but the righteous Sovereign who wills the good. He is not an ideal of pure reason (as in Kant), but a Supreme Intelligence who plans and shapes man's destiny. Nor is he a necessary postulate of reason, as Kant also asserts; instead he is the One who remains hidden until he gives himself to be known in revelation. He is not a self-contained Absolute, who is unaffected by the world, but the living Lord of history, an Active Agent more than a Passive Subject.

Biblical religion portrays God as the power above all other powers (cf. 1 Chron. 29:11; Isa. 40:22, 23; Ps. 22:28; 47:7, 8). Daniel declares: "The Most High God rules the kingdom of men, and sets over it whom he will" (Dan. 5:21). It is he "who executes judgment, putting down one and lifting up another" (Ps. 75:7). Wealth and honor come from his hand, and might and power are of his disposing (1 Chron. 29:12). No force can oppose him (Ps. 76:7; Job 42:2). In the words of Jeremiah: "The fierce anger of the Lord will not turn back until he has executed and accomplished the intents of his mind" (Jer. 30:24). He uses the evil powers in the world as tools for his purposes. Luther could describe the Turk (at that time the ravager of Europe) as both "God's rod" and "the devil's servant."

A helpful distinction has sometimes been made (by Luther and others) between the kingdoms of nature, grace, and glory. God rules over the kingdom of nature in his role as Creator and Providential Protector. He rules over the kingdom of grace, the community of faith, in his role as Redeemer and thereby through his Son, Jesus Christ. The kingdom of glory signifies the reign of God over the new heaven and earth, the transformed and redeemed world, which is still in the future.

On the basis of the scriptural testimony the church through the ages has affirmed the doctrine of creation *ex nihilo* (out of nothing). This means that the world was created by divine fiat; God did not have to mold the world out of a material that was preexistent or coeternal. This is not immediately evident in Genesis 1, but the doctrine is certainly anchored in the scriptural witness as a whole. Isaiah proclaims that God created the darkness as well as the light (Isa. 45:7).[2] In Revelation 4:11 we read: "For thou didst create all things, and by thy will they existed and were created" (cf. Prov. 8:22–30; Isa. 37:16; 2 Macc. 7:28; Acts 17:24; Heb. 11:3).

God is related to the world not as Eternity is to time but as Creative Act is related to the creation (Torrance). He is not simply the ground or depth of being but the Lord of being and the Lord over being. As the omnipotent God he is the source of all created life and its preservation.

In patristic and medieval thought the idea was often present that God was compelled to create because of a superabundance that had to find an outlet. The world was explained as a necessary overflow of the divine being. We shall say more of this in the last section of this chapter. In the biblical view God created the world out of love, not metaphysical necessity. The world does not simply proceed from the Logos, but it is an act of the freedom of God.

The freedom of God, indeed, is another way to express his sovereignty. God's freedom means that he is grounded in his own being, is determined and moved by himself. This is to say, God exists in and of himself and cannot be explained by any prior cause. The medieval school men intended this idea when they spoke of the aseity of God (his state of being self-originated).

This One who creates in freedom and rules in love must not be confused with man's own idea of perfection, with a philosophical first principle. The true God lies beyond the confines of man's perception and conception. He is to be sharply distinguished from the idols of man's vain imagination. Karl Barth has put this very succinctly:

Just because He is this free and loving God, He is not interchangeable with any creature in heaven or on earth, or with the likeness of any product of human imagination. He is sovereign, and His name is holy above every other name, and not to be named with any other in the same breath.[3]

To affirm God as Creator and Lord also means to affirm the essential goodness of creation and the meaningfulness of history. In Gnosticism it was commonly thought that God is so remote and transcendent that he is not related in any positive way to the material world, which was formed by a lesser deity or demiurge. In order to find God man must rise above the realm of the material (where evil resides) and ascend to the realm of pure spirit. Salvation lies outside of time, history, and corporeality. Christianity asserts on the other hand that the one and only God not only created the material world but redeemed and sanctified it through the incarnation of his Son.

OMNIPOTENT WILL

The true God is active and dynamic will, not simply the depth or ground of reason. His will is supreme and unique, not arbitrary and overwhelming. Here a distinction must be made between the speculative idea of absolute power *(potestas absoluta)*, which swallows up all creaturely independence, and the biblical idea of sovereign freedom.[4] We must not think of God as having an unrestricted or arbitrary power, for this would be the sovereignty of whim or chance or caprice. His power is not irresistibly efficacious, it is not a naked freedom and sovereignty; rather it is in the service of his love. God's power does not violate his love or holiness (Job 37:23). He should not be thought of as the God who can do anything, but as the God who can do everything to express and fulfill his loving purpose. His sovereignty is not caprice but the liberty to interpose in judgment and mercy as he pleases (H. R. Mackintosh). God's power should be distinguished from power itself, for he is in control of his power.

At the same time we must not fall into the mistaken notion that God's will must be in accord with an abstract idea of love or justice. There is no necessity or justice to which God must conform. He is his own necessity, and he wills justice because it is his nature to do so. He declares what is right (Isa. 45:19). "What he desires, that he does" (Job 23:13). God's will is conditioned and limited only by itself.

God's sovereignty means that he is immutable. He does not change in his innermost being and in his ultimate vision and purpose for the world. "The grass withers," Isaiah says, "the flower fades; but the word of our God will stand forever" (Isa. 40:8; cf. Ps. 102:25–27; James. 1:17). God remains faithful to his promises; he will not swerve from the plan that he has for the nations and his people (cf. Job 23:13; Mic. 7:19, 20; Mal. 3:6).

Yet God is not the unchangeable, as philosophers understand this. For the Greeks, God's immutability means that he is immobile, in which case we no longer have a truly sovereign God. We concur with Barth: "As this omnipotent God, He is also distinct from the unchangeable, whose unchangeableness inevitably means utter powerlessness, complete incapacity, a lack of every possibility, and therefore death."[5] It is interesting to note that the phrase "God repented" frequently appears in the Old Testament (cf. Exod. 32; 14; 2 Sam. 24:16; 1 Chron. 21:15; Jer. 26:19; Jon. 3:10). Some theologians maintain that this can be taken only metaphorically, but I believe that it points to the truth that God has the freedom to change his mind or the ways in which he deals with his people, though he remains inflexible in his ultimate purpose for them. God is not immobile, but he is immutable at least in several basic senses: he is unchanging in his basic purposes; his being is indestructible; and his promises are inviolable.

In order to avoid the pitfall of Hellenistic abstractionism, Karl Barth, in his discussion of the perfections of God, replaces the classical term *immutability* with *constancy (Beständigkeit)*. This means that God is true to himself or self-consistent; he remains faithful even when men are faithless (2 Tim. 2:13). He does not lie but keeps his Word (Ps. 89:34, 35), and this is the ground for Christian ethics. According to Barth the true God is the living one and as such contains within himself both rest and motion, but he nonetheless maintains his constancy as the loving one in freedom.

Whereas the living God of the Bible is not to be confounded with the immobile God of Hellenistic philosophy, he must also be sharply distinguished from the modern idea of a God who is ever changing. Emil Brunner rightly censures this notion: "A God who is constantly changing is not a God whom we can worship, He is a mythological Being for whom we can only feel sorry."[6] In process theology and philosophy God is essentially dependent on the world and is enriched by the maturation of his creation. Process philosopher Charles Hartshorne has redefined the absolute as "the totally relative."[7] A definition more in keeping with biblical faith would be: He who may or may not relate himself to everything or anything.

Another related error is to equate God's omnipotence with the notion of omnicausality. In this way God becomes bound to the reality which is distinct from himself. God's omnipotence does not mean that he is the direct or sole cause of all that happens; rather he is Lord over all that happens. It means that God is omnicompetent, capable of dealing with all circumstances, that nothing can ultimately defeat or thwart his plan for his people. I agree with Barth: "Because God's power is the power of His personality, the power of His knowing and willing, we can say that it also belongs to God's will not to will many things."[8] God's omnipotence cannot be resolved into his omnicausality because this would make God a "prisoner of His own power."[9] God is both self-determined and self-limited, in the sense that he refuses to will some things.

Any discussion of God's omnipotence will invariably include the doctrine of predestination. A sovereign God has a sovereign plan and purpose which he chooses to realize in the world. But predestination is a theological concept and must not be confused with the philosophical concept of fate or destiny. It means that God's election of men to salvation in Jesus Christ (which is how the Bible understands election) does not override the freedom of man but is realized in and through this freedom, though it is the new freedom given in Christ and not natural free will. Predestination is not a *decretum absolutum* that tends to deny the free movement of history but a working out of the purposes of God in history. It does not mean that God wills whatever comes to pass but that God's will and purpose are to be fulfilled despite the perpetual defiance of his will in human history. When predestination is conceived as the eternal determination of whatever comes to pass, the dimension of the historical is lost. With Thomas Aquinas, who affirmed that God wills some things contingently and not necessarily, we reject the determinist view that all things happen by "an absolute necessity."[10]

In opposition to some of the older Calvinists we contend that God's decrees are not an eternal aspect of his nature but spring out of his sovereign freedom.[11] The sovereignty of God means that God's will is free not only to carry out the decree of election but also to determine it.

It is appropriate now to consider the doctrine of the omniscience of God, for not only God's will but his knowledge is said to be omnipotent. The Psalmist declares: "Our Lord is great, all-powerful, of infinite understanding" (Ps. 147:5 JB). "The Lord's wisdom founded the earth," Proverbs says, "his understanding established all the universe and space. The deep fountains of the earth were broken open by his knowledge, and the skies poured down rain" (Prov. 3:19, 20 LB; cf. 15:11 LB). And again from the Psalms: "Even before a word is on my tongue, lo, O Lord, thou knowest it altogether. . . . Thy eyes beheld my unformed substance; in thy book were written, every one of them, the days that were formed for me, when as yet there was none of them" (Ps. 139:4, 16). We read in 2 Chronicles: "For the eyes of the Lord run to and fro throughout the whole earth, to show his might in behalf of those whose heart is blameless toward him" (16:9).

The meaning of God's omniscience is that there is no concealment from God. "God's knowledge," says Barth "does not consist only in His knowing all things before they are and have been", but "in His actually knowing them when they are still future."[12] Yet we must utter here a word of caution: although God knows the future before it happens, he does not literally know the concrete event until it happens. We cannot affirm a preestablished harmony between the eternal plan of God and the events of history, for this would mean a closed or static universe in which real history and freedom become illusions. It would also tend to deny the reality of human sin and discord in history. We affirm the reality of God's foreknowledge and also his sovereignty over all events in time and space, but we do not hold to a rigid foreordination that excludes the free movement of history. Nothing happens, to be sure, apart from God's sanction, but this is not to say that God expressly wills everything that happens. There are some things that happen that God does not will and that have their reality precisely in God's negation instead of his affirmation (Barth). To believe in the omniscience of God means to affirm an overarching providence that sustains the world in its sin and misery but which is not the direct cause of its sin and misery.

Equally crucial in the discussion of the perfections of God is his omnipresence or ubiquity. This must be construed not as spacelessness but as God's freedom to be in space. Again Barth is right in affirming a spaciality in God just as there is time in God. True eternity includes the potentiality of space and time. God's omnipresence means that he is present *to* all creatures, but there is no identity between God and the creature. It does not mean that his being literally permeates all matter but that everything is included in his overall vision (Prov. 15:3; 2 Chron. 16:9). God's ubiquity should be understood in terms not of inactive extension in the universe but of sovereign dominion over all space.

Omnipresence means that God is both transcendent and immanent. Everything is immediately accessible to him, but he is not confined or contained in any space or place. He is free to enter every place because every place is within his grasp and power. He is eminent, towering above the world of the creature, but he is also imminent, exceedingly close to every creature. Augustine said that God is "nearer than hands and feet." And as Luther put it: "God is closer to everything than anything is to itself."

God's eternity is his exaltation over time, just as his omnipresence is his exaltation over space (Emil Brunner). His eternity is not to be viewed as a negation of time as in Platonic and neo-Platonic philosophy, for then time becomes an illusion. Eternity is not timelessness nor the endless duration of time; it is rather the "fulfillment of time." Karl Barth speaks of a "divine timefulness" thereby making it not incongruous for God to create time and to dwell in time. The eternity of God signifies his sovereign rule over time.

In discussing God's sovereignty we must also say something of his infinity. *Infinity* in the Christian sense means the freedom of God from all creaturely limitations. Everything that belongs to his being is without measure or quantity. Infinity does not mean that God is formless or characterless. It signifies that he is not dependent on anything else for his existence. God's infinity is his unlimited power but never separated from and always informed by his illimitable love.

Likewise we must affirm God's spirituality, meaning that he is not flesh and blood as man is and thereby not subject to corruption. He is not the superlative of human nature and possibilities (as in Mormonism) but one who infinitely transcends such possibilities. At the same time he does not exist in opposition to matter. Matter is not an aspect of his nature, but it is a channel of his power.

Again we must speak of a personal God, or to borrow Francis Schaeffer's terminology a Personal-Infinite God. This means that God is a Personal Spirit who can and does relate himself to the world of the creature. He is not an infinite silence or nameless depth but a divine Thou who addresses man. He is not simply "the power of the future" (as in Moltmann and Pannenberg) nor a Primal Mover in the past (as in deism); rather he is an existent being who lives and moves among his children here and now. A personal God cannot be a totally impassible God. As Barth says, "The personal God has a heart. He can feel, and be affected. . . . He cannot be moved from outside by an extraneous power. But this does not mean that He is not capable of moving Himself."[13] We agree with Joseph Ratzinger that to confess God as a person "necessarily includes the acknowledgement of God as relatedness, as communicability, as fruitfulness. The unrelated, unrelatable, absolutely one could not be person."[14]

A personal God, who loves and cares, can be solicited in prayer. Prayer can work miracles because God makes himself dependent on the requests of his children. This does not detract from his sovereignty but instead attests it in a striking way. This is the God who chooses to work out his purposes in cooperation with his children. As Forsyth has aptly said, his will is inflexible, but his ways are flexible.

In speaking of the sovereignty of God we must also affirm the sovereignty of Jesus Christ. Christ is not only Prophet and Priest, but also King. He shares in the sovereignty of the Father. All things were created in him and through him and for him, and all things hold together in him (Col. 1:15f). All things have been put under his feet, and he has been made head over all things (Eph. 2:21, 22; cf. 1 Cor. 15:27; Rev. 17:14). This does not mean that he is King of the world in the same way as he is King of the church. He is King in the church by his deity and humanity, but in the world by his deity only (Luther). The resurrection of Jesus Christ signifies the supreme act of the sovereignty of

God, and his heavenly ascension connotes his elevation over the whole world.

We should add that it is only in Jesus Christ that we know the living God and his sovereignty over the world. We experience the wrath and judgment of God outside of Christ, but we do not really know the breadth of his love and power until we have faith in Christ.

Moreover, it is necessary to uphold the sovereignty of God the Holy Spirit who implants within man the principle of the new life. The Holy Spirit is not only the originator of the new life but also the one who develops it, preserves it, and perfects it on the day of resurrection. Besides his work of regeneration and sanctification, the Holy Spirit empowers the people of God to witness boldly before the world concerning the truth of the Gospel. Though man through sin is radically disabled, he can be sovereignly empowered to testify to others and thereby be instrumental in their salvation. The life of the church rests not on evangelistic strategies or promotional techniques but on God the Holy Spirit who speaks and acts where he wills.

The work of the Holy Spirit also testifies to the sovereignty of God in the realm of the knowledge of God. Man cannot know God apart from the special illumination of the Holy Spirit given in the context of the hearing of God's Word. Man cannot on his own grasp or comprehend the truth of revelation but must be seized by this truth if he is to know it.

H. Richard Niebuhr has made the astute observation that evangelical Protestantism is characterized by its stress on the sovereignty of God instead of the vision of God (as in Roman Catholicism).[15] The accent is thereby placed on spiritual and ethical obedience, the attempt to bring our wills into conformity with his will. In this perspective, a passion to change the world takes precedence over the desire to transcend the world.

HOLY LOVE

God in his essence is both love and holiness, and therefore it is of a holy love that we must speak when referring to divinity. God is love, but his love exists in tension with his holiness, indeed it is informed by his holiness. There is both a kindness and a severity in God (Rom. 11:22), and neither must be emphasized to the detriment of the other. God's steadfast love endures forever (Pss. 136:1; 138:8), but it endures as a consuming fire. We see a basic distinction between the love and holiness of God but at the same time an interpenetration and indivisibility.

Holiness connotes separation from all that is unclean (from the Hebrew *qādōsh*), and this applies to God par excellence. Rudolf Otto has trenchantly observed that the concept of the holiness of God leads to the assertion that God is "Wholly Other," since man is both a creature and a sinner.[16] Indeed, man is separated from God not only by ontological fate but also by historical guilt. Our iniquities have made a separation between God and ourselves (Isa. 59:1, 2), and therefore God can only be approached via a Mediator whose righteousness is acceptable to divine holiness, namely, Jesus Christ.

Kierkegaard referred to the "infinite qualitative difference" between God and man,[17] and this is because God is holy as well as sovereign. His holiness is his otherness, his majesty, his separateness. A holy God must be intolerant of sin and can only demand purity of heart on the part of his subjects. This is why the true God must be approached in "fear and trembling," in deep-felt awe and reverence. The encounter with the Holy gives rise to a sense of one's own unworthiness as well as to a sense of the majesty of God (cf. Isa. 6:1–5).

The love of God is generous, sacrificial, self-giving. It is the love that issues in forgiveness, but it is a costly forgiveness resulting in the death of God's own Son. It is also costly for the Christian, since it calls him to a life of discipleship under the cross. The love that comes from God accepts the sinner as he is, in his sins, but because it is also a holy love, it demands that the sinner change his ways.

Holy love is not weakness or permissiveness but contains a severity that is totally foreign to the popular understanding of love. Its method is to uproot and attack all that is not of God. It is a judging as well as a redeeming love. It entails the disciplining and chastising of the children of God (Prov. 3:11, 12; Heb. 12:6). Love can be so merciful that it sometimes appears devoid of mercy. Meister Eckhart rightly observed, with reference to the Song of Solomon: "Love is as strong as death and harder than hell" (Song of Sol. 8:6).[18] The holy love of a sovereign God evokes adoration, not admiration. It elicits awe, not pity, as might be the case if his love were indulgent or permissive.

Holy love does not cancel the demands of the law but seeks the fulfillment of these demands. This is why the holy love of God made inevitable the vicarious atonement of Christ on the cross. A sinful mankind could be reconciled to a holy God only by one who paid the penalty for sin by dying on the cross. And this one was the Son of God himself who alone could represent mankind because of his incarnation, and who alone could render a perfect sacrifice because of his deity.

The holy love of God is inseparably related to his wrath. The concept of the wrath of God fell into disfavor with the rise of liberal theology which tended to see it as divine petulance and, therefore, not worthy of the God of Christian faith. But the erosion of this concept is also to be laid at the feet of orthodox theology which, in effect, separated God's wrath from his love and thereby proclaimed a God who was divided against himself. The wrath of God must properly be understood as the necessary reaction of his holiness to sin. It is one form of his holy love. The wrath of God is an objective reality emanating from the nature of God himself. Wrath is not what God is in himself, but it signifies what he can be in relation to the world of the creature. Wrath is not the basic disposition of God toward his people, since God is "slow to anger," but nonetheless it connotes the searing reaction of God to continued violations of his law. It is his righteous indignation against wrongdoing. Some liberal theologians have interpreted the wrath of God as referring only to the subjective experience of the sinner as he encounters God's love. But this is to lose sight of the character of God's love as holy love, a love that can become angry because of human sin.

For Martin Luther wrath is the strange work of God, and love in Christ is his real or proper work. Wrath proceeds from the nature of God himself, but it is not identical with his true nature, which is revealed in Christ. The danger in this dichotomy is that God's love tends to be divorced from his wrath and holiness. Yet it contains the element of truth that God's love is made known only in Christ and that outside of Christ God must necessarily appear as wrathful. At the same time was not God's wrath against sin also manifested in Christ, and does not Jesus Christ himself personify and reveal both the love and the holiness of God? Can God's holiness and wrath really be known apart from his love in Jesus Christ?

In the philosophy of Heraclitus and much of the monistic mysticism of the Orient, it is said that God includes all opposites within himself —good and evil, light and darkness, being and nonbeing.[19] In biblical faith, on the contrary, God signifies a purity of love that excludes and judges evil. The true God is neither beyond good and evil nor does he encompass good and evil, but he is the perfect good that negates evil and sets it off as an antithesis to his holy will. His wrath proceeds from his goodness and love, not from any darkness or shadow within himself, since he is altogether light (1 John. 1:5).

THE HOLY TRINITY

God is sovereign but not solitary. God is not simply a unity but a triunity. He is differentiated within himself. He not only exists but also coexists as Father, Son, and Holy Spirit (cf. Matt. 3:16, 17; 28:19; John 14:16, 17; 2 Cor. 13:14; Eph. 4:4–6). Because he has love and fellowship within himself his sovereignty can be one of love.

The doctrine of the Trinity is not clearly enunciated in the Scriptures, but it is definitely suggested.[20] It is not so much a revealed truth as an immediate implication of the fact, form, and content of revelation. It is a truth consonant with revelation and implicit in revelation. It is directly related to the doctrines of the preexistent Word and the deity of Christ.

This doctrine, which was defined and sharpened in the early councils of the church beginning with Nicaea, asserts that there is one divine being in three persons. There is a trinity of persons and a unity in essence. It should be recognized that *persons* in the early church did not mean personalities in the modern sense (which indicates autonomy) but objective modes of being.[21] Barth is correct when he affirms that God exists in three modes of being, but these are distinctions, as he acknowledges, that pertain to the inner life of God himself and not merely to dimensions of his activity (as in the heresy of Modalism). This is why orthodox theology speaks of the ontological or essential trinity and not just of the economic trinity, which refers to the way in which God relates himself to the world. The Trinity must be thought of neither as one God in three manifestations nor as a symmetrical triad of persons with separable functions; instead the Trinity signifies one God in three modes of existence—Father, Son, and Spirit, and each of these participates in the activity of the other.[22]

The first impetus toward the formulation of the doctrine of the Trinity emerged in the conflict with Arianism which held that Christ, being a creature, was unlike the Father. The semi-Arians asserted that Christ was of a similar substance to the Father *(homoiousios)*. Against these trinitarian heresies the Nicene Creed affirmed that Christ was of one substance with the Father *(homoousios)*. The significance of this credo is that the Logos who was incarnate in Jesus of Nazareth is none other than God himself. It is not sufficient to hold that Christ was *like* God: instead we must boldly affirm that God was *in* Christ, reconciling the world to himself (2 Cor. 5:19).

A trinitarian monotheism is a concrete monotheism which depicts a living God who reaches out in love, who becomes incarnate in human flesh. In a mystical monotheism everything concrete disappears in the infinite abyss. God becomes the impersonal Absolute, an undifferentiated substratum, beyond plurality and diversity. Trinitarian faith asserts on the contrary that "the highest unity is not the unity of inflexible monotony. The model of unity or oneness towards which one should strive is . . . not the indivisibility of the atom, the smallest unity. . . . The authentic acme of unity is the unity created by love."[23]

The God of absolute, arbitrary power, which has its roots in metaphysical speculation, is not a trinitarian God, since it depicts a God apart from Jesus Christ. The true God revealed himself decisively and fully in Jesus Christ. In Jesus we see a God who gives himself in love and who desires man as a covenant partner in the working out of his purposes in the world.

God is monarchial but not exclusively so. He is trinitarian. He is not only a monarch but also a friend and savior. Monarchianism, one expression of the subordinationist heresy, made God remote and distant from his creation. It has its source in the philosophical climate of the ancient world that depicted the Absolute as static and impassible. The trinitarian God is not lifeless but living. He is not static and immobile but dynamic and mobile though ever constant in his inmost being and purpose.

Against the subordinationists the early church insisted that though the members of the Trinity have different functions they are equal and coeternal. While there is a distribution of functions of the Trinity in the activities of creation and redemption, there is no subordination of one over the other in the essential life within the Godhead.[24] For the subordinationists everything depended on preserving the unity and monarchy of God. A distinction was made between God in his self-manifestation and God in his abysmal nature. The Godhead of Christ was seen as inferior to the Godhead of the Father.[25] Origen, for example, refused to call Christ *autotheos* (possessing in himself the divine nature). The two dangers in subordinationism are polytheism, in which we have several gods, and agnosticism, in which God in himself becomes unknowable. Arianism was one form of subordinationism, since it saw Christ as a heavenly mediator between the infinite God and man but not as God himself. Neo-Platonic mysticism—which reappeared in the thought of John Scotus Erigena, pseudo-Dionysius, Meister Eckhart, and Ruysbroeck—is another form of subordinationism, since it posits an undifferentiated Godhead beyond the God manifested as a trinity. Such a God is none other than a solitary being, unrevealed and virtually unknown.[26]

To bypass the Trinity is to end either in deism or pantheism. In the first God becomes remote and distant, and in the second God becomes indistinguishable from the depth or core of the world. The true God is neither totally outside the world nor is he incorporate in the world. He is a transcendent living Lord who has incarnated himself in the world but who remains essentially independent from the world.

The doctrine of the Trinity is not an explanation but a definition of the being of God and life of God. The Trinity itself remains a mystery even to faith. It reflects the truth that God is intelligible but incomprehensible (Aquinas). It bears witness to the affirmation that God is known truly, but not exhaustively, in his self-revelation in Jesus Christ.

Cyril Richardson considers the three terms of reference to the Trinity an arbitrary way of conceiving the richness and complexity of a dynamic God.[27] He acknowledges that such a God demands at least two terms, or better, an indefinite number. John Macquarrie has given this retort with which we fully concur:

The unbroken unity of a monolithic God from whom had gone forth neither Word nor Spirit would be something less than a God who could be worshipped. If we move from stark unity to twoness or duality, then we are in very grave danger of introducing a split that cannot be bridged, and of ending up in some kind of Gnostic or Manichaean dualism in which both the world and its creative agent have been so far removed from the hidden God that a fundamental opposition is set up. We have to move on to threeness, to the completion of the circle, when the Spirit who has proceeded from the Godhead to work in the creation lifts that whole creation to God and, above all, builds the community of the Spirit among the finite spirits.[28]

We would add that threeness is not only appropriate in the context of the worship and fellowship of the church but that it is also necessary to do justice to the biblical revelation concerning the being and activity of the true God. This is definitely implied in Macquarrie's statement, since his aim is to be both a biblical and catholic theologian, though he sometimes leans too heavily on secular philosophy in his explication of the biblical faith.[29]

SOLI DEO GLORIA

Among the perfections of God not yet mentioned is his glory. The glory of God signifies his splendor, majesty, and radiance particularly as these make an impression upon the world of the creature. Emil

Brunner contends that the divine glory is that which God possesses in relation to the world. God's glory is the reflection of the being of God from the creation back to him. Barth speaks of the divine glory as the overflowing perfection of God and particularly as "His overflowing self-communicating joy."[30]

God wills his own glory for the sake of his creation. In himself he has full satisfaction and stands in need of nothing. Yet his children lack virtually everything. Since he is the highest good, he owes it to his children to make them aware of his perfections so that their spiritual quest and hunger will be fulfilled.[31] Barth declares that God "satisfies Himself by showing and manifesting and communicating Himself as the One who He is."[32] He glorifies himself by revealing himself. God's glory is the shining of his light in the darkness of this world.

God wills to glorify himself in his creation but even more in his Son (John 13:31, 32; 14:13). In Barth's words: "God's glory really consists in His self-giving, and this has its centre and meaning in God's Son, Jesus Christ. . . ."[33] Jesus Christ is the radiance and effulgence of the glory of God (Heb. 1:3). In Christ we see the splendor and marvel of the very being of God himself (John 17:5).

God seeks his own glory for the sake of the salvation of his people (Ps. 108:5, 6; Isa. 30:18). He seeks to draw them to himself and to share his glory with them (cf. Isa. 60:1–3; John 17:22). By opening the eyes of his children to his glory he demonstrates his love for them, for his glory is their salvation. In this light we can understand the Psalmist: "Not to us, O Lord, not to us, but to thy name give glory, for the sake of thy steadfast love and thy faithfulness" (115:1).

John Calvin in particular saw that man's deepest need is to lose himself in the glory of God, and this is why he emphasized *Soli Deo gloria* (glory to God alone). For him, as for the Psalmist, the one who longs for the saving help of God must ever cry, " 'All glory to the Lord!' " (Ps. 40:16 NEB). He saw that man is fulfilled only by living solely for Him who is the ground and mainstay of man's life. In Calvin's mind glory must not be given to anything less than God, whether this be the church, the state, or the pope, for this is idolatry. Only one who is at the same time the Infinite Creator and the Sovereign Redeemer can command our unconditional adoration.

Calvin perceived the close relation between *Soli Deo gloria* and the Christian life. The glory of God is the foundation for active service and obedience. When man seeks his own welfare and power rather than God's glory, then his good works are turned into evil works. "Surely the first foundation of righteousness is the worship of God. When this is overthrown, all the remaining parts of righteousness, like the pieces of a shattered and fallen building are mangled and scattered."[34] Calvin saw that worship comes before bread, God's glory before human livelihood, even though God is truly glorified when we help others to secure their livelihood. This theological motif is reflected in the *Shorter Westminster Catechism:* "Man's chief end is to glorify God, and to enjoy Him forever" (question 1).

Of course Calvin and his followers were not the only Christians to uphold *Soli Deo gloria.* Luther and Ignatius Loyola were also known for this emphasis.[35] So was Jonathan Edwards who stands in the tradition of Calvinism but who was deeply original as well as profoundly biblical.[36] God, he maintained, has sought to exclude all human glory so that we should be wholly dependent on Him for our salvation. We should recognize that everything we have is "from the hand of God, by his power and grace."[37] All of these men placed the glory of God and the advancement of his kingdom over every temporal and material concern. In their eyes God's glory is to be valued even more than human happiness.

Yet in the tradition of Christian mysticism, especially where the neo-Platonic influence was most felt, the glory of God was definitely subordinated to the fulfillment and blessedness of the self. The mystics were more concerned with the discovery of God in the depths of the soul and the perfection of the self in God than with giving glory to God by upholding Jesus Christ before the world. Meister Eckhart contended that a man ought not to work or live for anything outside him, nor for God nor for his glory among men; instead man should live "only for that which is his being, his very life within him."[38] And hear these words of Schleiermacher: "A religious man must be reflective, his sense must be occupied in the contemplation of himself. Being occupied with the profoundest depths, he abandons meanwhile all external things, intellectual as well as physical. . . ."[39] In the radical mysticism of Angelus Silesius the realization of the self is considered so crucial that even the life of God is dependent on it: "I know that without me God cannot live for an instant; if I come to nothing, then He must give up the ghost."[40]

While audacity of this kind must obviously be rejected by earnest evangelicals, it should be recognized that *Soli Deo gloria* does not mean the annihilation of man. When man dedicates himself to the glory of God he finds himself in God's kingdom, he discovers himself as a child of God. The glory of God does not reduce man to nothing but instead gives him hope and confidence. Irenaeus put it very aptly: "The glory of God is man fully alive."

The question can now be posed: how does man give glory to God?

Whereas God glorifies himself by revealing his glory, we glorify God by acknowledging and upholding the glory that is in his Son, Jesus Christ (2 Cor. 9:13; 1 Pet. 1:7; Rev. 5:12). God's light radiates in the darkness, and it is incumbent upon us to bear witness to this light in our words and deeds. At no time is God more glorified than when we bow down before him in praise and adoration out of gratefulness for what he has done for us in Jesus Christ. God is given glory, too, when we bring before him our supplications asking for his aid, for this demonstrates our absolute dependence upon his mercy. Glory and honor are also given to God when we seek the total welfare of our neighbor, his physical and material welfare as well as his eternal salvation.

It is obvious that God's glory takes precedence over one's own salvation. Moses prayed that God might blot his name out of the book of life for the sake of the sins of Israel (Exod. 32:32), and Paul was willing to be cut off from Christ for the sake of his erring brethren (Rom. 9:3). The early Calvinist ordinands in New England were asked by their superiors if they would be willing to be damned for the glory of God. This, of course, obscures the complementary truth that God is indubitably glorified when people are deeply concerned about their own salvation, for this means being in communion with God's Son, Jesus Christ. Yet it points to the truth that God's glory takes precedence over the good of the self, though paradoxically the self only finds its highest good by giving up its own claims and prerogatives for the sake of the kingdom of God (Matt. 6:33; 10:39; 16:25; Luke 9:24).

It should be recognized that God is glorified in the condemnation of man as well as in his salvation (Ezek. 28:22). God even makes the wrath of men to praise him (Ps. 76:10; Rom. 3:7). God's glory is no less evident in hell than in heaven because his purposes are being fulfilled in, through, and despite man's error and rebellion. No man can defeat the grace of God, though man can damn himself by not acknowledging God's grace and glory.

The essence of biblical piety is the desire to give glory to God in everything we say or do. And we glorify God when we love him as our Creator and Redeemer and fear him as our King and Judge. We glorify God when we surrender any claim to righteousness on our part and trust his righteousness alone, as revealed in his Son Jesus Christ. We glorify God when we dedicate ourselves to the great commission—the proclamation of the good news of salvation to a lost and despairing world. We glorify God when we feed the hungry, clothe the naked, and visit the sick in prison, since Christ has identified himself with the poor and ailing in our midst (Matt. 25:31ff.).

EROSION OF THE BIBLICAL VIEW OF GOD

The concept of an Almighty God who relates himself to his creation in self-giving love was subverted first by the apologists of the early church who tried to make the faith palatable to its cultured despisers and then by the medieval school men who sought a biblical–classical synthesis in which they borrowed heavily from Graeco–Roman philosophy. God became identified with the self-contained, static Absolute of Platonic, neo-Platonic, or Aristotelian speculation. To be sure, pagan ideas were checked, and both the Trinity and the creation of the world by divine fiat were stoutly affirmed by the mainstream of Catholic theology. At the same time these particular doctrinal emphases were not always so apparent in the mystical tradition of the church. The neo-Platonic concept of emanation figured more prominently in the thinking of Dionysius the pseudo-Areopagite and John Scotus Erigena than the biblical idea of creation. For John Scotus Erigena God in himself is the ideal of motionless unity, and the creation is a process of the unfolding of the Divine Nature. Though the Trinity was outwardly affirmed, God was often defined in terms of the undifferentiated Absolute that is neither light nor darkness, love nor wrath. This Nameless Being or Primal Unity is not easily reconciled with the Heavenly Father of biblical faith.

Some of the Christian mystics in the tradition of neo-Platonism spoke of God as simple essence without activity. We maintain that essence does not preclude action, since God's action cannot be severed from what he is in himself. God is not pure essence unmoved and unmoving, but his own inner history is a history of action (Barth).

Especially significant is how the philosophical concept of the impassibility of God made its way into the Christian faith and became virtually accepted as the orthodox position on the being of God. This is the view that God is not affected by the world, that he is not touched by human suffering. Plato declared that divinity is beyond "either joy or sorrow."[41] In Aristotle the metaphysical and ethical perfection of God is described as *apatheia,* meaning imperturbability and dispassionateness. Such ideas infiltrated the Christian church, though they were always resisted to a degree. It was generally asserted in the early and medieval church as well as in the Reformation and Protestant orthodoxy that Jesus Christ suffered in his human nature but not in his divine nature. Needless to say, this way of thinking about God and Christ contravenes the biblical picture of a God who is not an Eternal Rest or an Unmoved Mover but One who is restless "until he establishes Jerusalem" (Isa. 62:1, 7). This is a God who agonizes over his children and who becomes "enraged" at the sin of the nations (Is. 34:2). The truth in the concept of divine impassibility is that God is incapable of corruption and that his innermost being and ultimate purpose are unchanging. Barth draws a helpful distinction between God in "the impassible glory and blessedness of His own inner life" and God in his self-determination in Jesus Christ whereby he makes himself vulnerable to the pain of his creation,[42] and I think that this can be substantiated by Scripture.

Anders Nygren has documented the thesis that the Platonic concept of love as Eros came to predominate over the biblical Agape.[43] Irenaeus was one of the few among the church fathers who retained the idea of Agape, while Dionysius combatted this idea in favor of Eros. Nygren maintains that the medieval *Caritas,* as we find it in both Augustine and Thomas Aquinas, signified a synthesis of Agape and Eros, with Eros being dominant. While Agape is outgoing, self-giving love, Eros is aspiring, self-regarding love. It is not the love that goes out to the sinner but the love that seeks its own realization and perfection in God. The goal of the Christian, consequently, came to be interpreted as union with God rather than the glorifying of God in the service of one's neighbor. God was seen as man's highest good *(summum bonum)* who alone can satisfy man's deepest need. Despite the significant role given to God, the anthropocentric character of such religion is unmistakable.

The Platonic and neo-Platonic principle of plenitude also intruded into Christian speculation and served to subvert the doctrine of divine sovereignty. In this idea existence is the consequence of a system of "eternal" and "necessary" truths inherent in the very logic of being. Being-itself is said to have a fullness or plenitude which necessarily overflows thereby causing a temporal, material, and variegated universe. In Plato the created universe is an exhaustive replica of the world of ideas. In the system of Dionysius the principle of plenitude results in a cosmological chain of being with infinite variety. Absolute Being is not only the logical ground but also the dynamic source of a diverse universe. Deity becomes self-expansive and creative energy, and this idea existed in tension with that of a Self-Sufficing Perfection. God's love came to be seen as creative and generative more than redemptive.

Many of those theologians who affirmed the creation of the world by God nevertheless tended to maintain that God was moved by a metaphysical necessity, since being must invariably give rise to the real existence of all possible things. Abelard concluded that it was intrinsically impossible for God to make or leave unmade anything other than the things that he actually made.[44] In the thought of Nicholas of Cusa the divine perfection is the infinite actualization of all that is simply and absolutely possible. In this general tradition, the conceptual possibility in the mind of God must necessarily result in its full realization in actuality. The essence of God was therefore seen as his power to create or produce, whereas in the biblical view God's power is subordinated to his love.

For Thomas Aquinas "the Absolute, if good or rational, must generate variety in a measure proportional to his power—which could only mean, infinitely, though within the restrictions imposed by the logical impossibility of some things."[45] Yet Thomas in an effort to safeguard the divine freedom contended that though the will of God always chooses the good it chooses it "as becoming to its own goodness, not as necessary to its goodness."[46] While he was decidedly influenced by neo-Platonism Thomas nonetheless sought to maintain the biblical view that God creates through a personal free act and not deterministically. Lovejoy says that Thomas was able to hold to this biblical position only at the cost of inner consistency and that he never really succeeded in breaking free from the principle of plenitude.[47]

Despite their rejection of the neo-Platonic idea of emanation, medieval scholastics blurred the distinction between the Creator and the creature by retaining the neo-Platonic notion of a graded hierarchy of being from the highest to the lowest and viewing creaturely existence as directly grounded in the eternality of God. Thomas Torrance comments: "What it implied was an eternal positing or even co-existence of creaturely being with God's eternal Being which made it difficult to deny the *aeternitas mundi,* even if it could not be affirmed, or at least not to be convinced of the ultimate changelessness of nature, i.e., of all that is not God."[48]

The sovereignty of God was again compromised by the growing sacramentalism in the church which tied his grace to the rites and rituals of the church. But the sovereign God of the Bible cannot be put in a box. Though he remains ultimately true to his promises, he sometimes withholds his grace from his unrepentant children and sometimes reaches out to those outside the circle of faith. He is characterized by a "sovereign unpredictability" (David Du Plessis). Although God is not bound to the means of grace, we are so bound, and the outpouring of his grace must not be misconstrued as necessarily or even primarily occurring apart from human instrumentality.

Luther, Calvin and other Reformers protested against the biblical-

classical synthesis and for a time succeeded in recovering the biblical
doctrine of an Almighty God who acts in love. With their Christocentric
emphasis they interpreted the perfections of God in terms of his revelation in Jesus Christ, they rediscovered the reality of God as Sovereign
Creator and Merciful Redeemer, and the reality of his love as Agape.
Yet in their distinction between the revealed and secret will of God,
they returned to the philosophical idea of God as naked power. Calvin's
concept of double predestination tended to divorce the justice of God
from his love. In Luther's *Bondage of the Will* we again meet with the
speculative idea of unlimited power *(potestas absoluta),* though the
biblical idea asserts itself in many of his other writings. When God is
portrayed as the sole actor, when it is said that God does all *(Allwirk-
samkeit),* this excludes any kind of creaturely causality. Zwingli was
highly influenced by neo-Platonism in his *De Providentia* where he
begins with the speculative idea of Absolute Being rather than the
biblical idea of a living Lord and Redeemer. In Zwingli's thought all
evil as well as all good is due to the causality of God.

In much modern philosophy and theology the biblical view of God
has been supplanted by an all-embracing Absolute Spirit (as in monistic idealism and mysticism) or a Life-force or Creative Process in the
world (as in naturalism). For Hegel the Absolute is both the ground and
the culmination of the infinite forward surge that is world history.
"Without the world," he says frankly, "God were not God." In Schleiermacher the Divine is the ground of all finite meaning and comes to
self-consciousness in human nature. For him the Father refers to the
unity of the Divine Essence and not to one of the supposed distinctions
in it. God's omnipotence is defined in terms of his omnicausality. Both
Schleiermacher and Ritschl disclaimed the idea of the wrath of God[49]
and thereby lost sight of the biblical vision of a holy God who judges
and condemns as well as creates and saves. Paul Tillich, who leans
heavily on both Schleiermacher and Hegel, as well as on the neo-
Platonic tradition in Christian mysticism, posits a "God above God,"
that is, one that transcends the God of theism. This deity, which is
described as the infinite depth and ground of all being, incorporates the
personal element but is himself not a Person.[50]

The dialectic theology of Karl Barth and Emil Brunner represents
a remarkable reversal in theological thought, since the living God of
biblical revelation is again confessed against the God-concepts of philosophical theology. In some of his writings Barth admittedly verges
toward a theopanism and Christomonism in which the grace of God is
said to permeate everything, but he sharply distinguishes his position

from any kind of pantheism or panentheism when he maintains that God in His freedom is not bound or confined to any creaturely space or place. Barth and Brunner also clearly differentiate the ideas of divine predestination and providence from any kind of philosophical determinism. Regrettably the dialectical or neo-orthodox theology did not make a permanent impression upon the academic theological establishment and is now in partial eclipse.

Process philosophy, presently in vogue especially in America, posits a God who is bound to the world, at least in his concrete nature (as in Whitehead and Hartshorne). Teilhard de Chardin is also a major influence in this school of thought.[51] A common axiom is that God is the soul of the world just as the world is the body of God. God is fulfilled or completed in the pleroma of the universe (Teilhard de Chardin). For Whitehead it is as true to say that the world creates God as that God creates the world.[52] God does not call the world into being (as in the biblical view), but he saves it by presenting it with persuasive ideals. In process thought both God and the world are in the grip of creativity. Hartshorne remarks: "What is not to be decided, even by God, is that progress . . . there shall be."[53] What we are left with is a God who, though infinite in some of his aspects, is essentially finite and at the mercy of the creature.

In opposition to process philosophy and theology I contend that the true God is essentially independent of the world though he makes himself dependent in his relationship to his children. God needs man only in relation to the realization of his plan for the world, not because there is any deficiency in himself.

Especially noticeable is the wide gulf between the God of biblical faith and the God of modern culture-religion (in both its conservative and liberal modes). The God of folk religion is a God of sentimental love, not holy love. He is the One who forgives no matter what we do. He is the "Man Upstairs" who is approached as an indulgent father, not as a Sovereign King. This is the God who is a means to man's own happiness, who enables man to attain self-fulfillment.

Modern evangelicalism opposes this kind of God, but it too is sometimes inclined to place a limit on the sovereignty of God. It is said that God only offers man salvation but does not effect salvation. Salvation is made dependent on man's own free will rather than divine election. In popular evangelicalism God is portrayed as powerful, but not invincible. His loving mercy is exalted but not his universal Lordship. God, it is thought, desires our worship, but little recognition is given to his kingship over all areas of life including politics and economics.

In some strands of evangelicalism, especially in fundamentalism, God's revelation is depicted as a static deposit of truth that is directly accessible to man's reason. But this subverts the idea that God is sovereign even in his revelation, that God remains hidden until he gives himself to be known. The knowledge and grace of God are not simply available to man even in the Bible, and this means that God remains the Master and man the servant even in the area of the knowledge of God.

An authentically evangelical theology will uphold the supremely personal God of biblical religion over the suprapersonal God of speculative philosophy on the one hand and the crudely personal God of culture-religion on the other. It will side with the transcendent God of the prophets over the immanent God of the mystics. It will proclaim the infinite God of the historic catholic faith over the finite God of modernistic theology. It will appeal to the concrete Absolute, as seen in Jesus Christ, over the metaphysical principle of pure abstraction. The God of the Scriptures is a supremely moral deity who demands our obedience, not an infinite abyss beyond good and evil wholly detached from the creature; nor is he the tolerant, benign deity of the folk tradition who merely desires our friendship. This God is jealous of his rights and solicitous for the welfare of his children (cf. Exod. 20:5, 6; Deut. 6:-14–19). He is neither an unfeeling Primal Source nor "the fellow-sufferer who understands" (Whitehead), the one who needs us just as we need him. He is not to be equated with "the personality-producing forces of the cosmos" (Shailer Mathews), but he is the sovereign king who rules the cosmos. The true God is the holy, majestic Lord who gives himself in love but who demands our faith and love in return. He creates not because the Good must necessarily be productive or creative (as in Plato and Plotinus), but because he chooses to do so in his sovereign freedom.

Against the classical philosophical tradition evangelical theology maintains that the perfections of God are not compromised in the humiliation and incarnation of Christ but instead nowhere more fully and dramatically revealed. Here in the condescension of Christ we see that omnipotence, as the Bible understands it, can be manifested in self-limitation, self-denial, and self-emptying. This indeed stands in contrast to the historical philosophical tendency to conceive of absolute power in terms of self-expansion. At the same time we must affirm that Christ, even in the form of a servant, remains King and Lord of the universe. His absolute power, however, is now decisively attested as being in the service of his omnipotent love.

NOTES

1. This idea is also present in philosophic Hinduism, which depicts the Supreme Being as beyond all ethical distinctions. It should be noted that Plotinus sometimes infers that the Good is included in the One.

2. This text is sometimes seen as directed against Persian dualism, in which there is a perpetual conflict between the god of light and the god of darkness. Whatever be the case, the theme that Isaiah is enunciating is not exceptional in Old Testament thought, though this must not be taken to mean that God is the direct cause of evil. In Gen. 1:3–5 darkness is the result of a work of division, not of creation. It is, in Barth's words, what God does not will, and yet it is thereby given a provisional reality by the fact that it is set apart from light. The point is that nothing, not even evil and darkness, can be removed from the dominion of God. One interpreter comments that the darkness here described is "not the mythological darkness of the primeval abyss" but is "like the sea which Yahweh has bound within its limits." John L. McKenzie, *Second Isaiah* (The Anchor Bible) (Garden City, N.Y.: Doubleday, 1968), p. 77.

3. Karl Barth, *Church Dogmatics* II, 2, ed. G. W. Bromiley and T. F. Torrance (Edinburgh: T. & T. Clark, 1957), p. 685.

4. The speculative idea of the *potestas absoluta* as found in later medieval theology is derived partly from the Stoic idea of an inexorable Fate or Destiny and partly from the neo-Platonic view that the essence of God is his power to create or produce. It also stems from a misunderstanding of the biblical idea of sovereignty as arbitrary self-assertiveness. There is, however, a genuinely biblical concept of absolute power, but in this perspective God's power is always subordinated to his love. Creation is interpreted not as an irresistible overflowing of being but as a free act of sovereign love.

For Emil Brunner's discussion of the *potestas absoluta* see his *The Christian Doctrine of God,* trans. Olive Wyon (Philadelphia: Westminster Press, 1950), pp. 266 ff., 325.

5. Karl Barth, *Church Dogmatics* II, 1, eds. G. W. Bromiley and T. F. Torrance (Edinburgh: T. & T. Clark, 1957), p. 523.

6. Emil Brunner, *The Christian Doctrine of God,* p. 269.

7. See especially Charles Hartshorne, *The Divine Relativity* (New Haven: Yale University Press, 1948). The fuller position of Hartshorne is that God is both absolute and relative in that his eternal ideas are unchangeable, but his concrete being is ever changeable. He speaks of his God as "finite-infinite" to which we would oppose the "personal-infinite" God of the historic Christian faith.

8. Karl Barth, *Church Dogmatics* II, 1, p. 544.

9. *Ibid.,* p. 587.

10. For a perceptive discussion of Aquinas' view, see Harry J. McSorley, *Luther: Right or Wrong?* (Minneapolis: Augsburg Publishing House, 1969), pp. 138–182. In this respect we likewise concur with the Puritan theologian William Ames, who had a marked influence on Jonathan Edwards, that the "will of God does not imply a necessity in all future things, but only a certainty in regard to the event. Thus the event was certain that Christ's bones should not be broken. . . . But there was no necessity imposed upon the soldiers. . . ."

William Ames, *The Marrow of Theology,* ed. John D. Eusden (Boston: Pilgrim Press, 1968), p. 99. Ames like Edwards distinguished between natural necessity and the foreordination and providence of God.

11. For a brilliant critique of the determinism of the Calvinist decretal theologians see James Daane, *The Freedom of God* (Grand Rapids: Eerdmans, 1973).

12. Karl Barth, *Church Dogmatics* II, 1, p. 558.

13. *Ibid.,* p. 370.

14. Joseph Ratzinger, *Introduction to Christianity,* trans. J. R. Foster (New York: Herder & Herder, 1970), p. 128.

15. H. Richard Niebuhr, *The Kingdom of God in America* (New York: Willett, Clark, 1937), p. 20 f.

16. See Rudolf Otto, *The Idea of the Holy,* pp. 25–30, 50–59. Otto's emphasis was on mystical awe more than the conviction of sin in the encounter with God.

17. Søren Kierkegaard, *The Sickness Unto Death,* trans. Walter Lowrie (Princeton, N.J.: Princeton University Press, 1941), p. 207.

18. Raymond Bernard Blakney, ed. and trans., *Meister Eckhart: A Modern Translation* (New York: Harper & Row, 1941), p. 124.

19. See R. C. Zaehner, *Our Savage God* (New York: Sheed & Ward, 1974), p. 74 f. Also cf. Alan Watts who conceived of God as "the total energy-field of the universe, including both its positive and negative aspects, and in which every discernible part or process is a sort of microcosm or hologram." In his *Behold the Spirit* (New York: Vintage Books, 1971), p. xviii. Also cf. Hegel who viewed all opposites as moments or constituents in a living process of thought.

20. While the New Testament can definitely be said to affirm the triunity of God though not the creedal trinitarian formula, this is only hinted at in the Old Testament. The most frequent appelation for God in the Old Testament, the Hebrew word *Elohim,* connotes a divine plurality in unity. The noun is plural, but it is generally, though not always, used with singular verbs. See B. W. Anderson, "Names of God" in George A. Buttrick, ed., *The Interpreter's Dictionary of the Bible* (New York: Abingdon Press, 1962), pp. 407–417.

21. Barth rightly recognizes that the modern concept of personality includes the attribute of self-consciousness and this, therefore, creates problems for the doctrine of the Trinity. To hold that there are three distinct centers of consciousness, three self-conscious personal beings, comes close to tritheism.

22. Orthodox theology, nonetheless, associates particular activities with each member of the Godhead: the Father is Creator, the Son reconciler, and the Spirit revealer and indweller. Yet all members participate in each of these activities. The New Testament can speak of God the Father dwelling in Christ, the Holy Spirit being given to Christ, and of God the Father dwelling in us and we in him (cf. John 1:32; 14:10, 11; 1 John 2:24; 4:15).

23. Joseph Ratzinger, *op. cit.,* p. 128.

24. Orthodox theology (in the West) asserts a relationship of dependence of the Son on the Father and of the Holy Spirit on the Father and Son, but this refers to their modes of operation, not to their essential being.

25. Against this view John Chrysostom declares: "The Son is in reality neither less than, nor inferior to, the Essence of the Father." *Saint John Chrysostom: Commentary on Saint John the Apostle and Evangelist,* trans.

Sister Thomas Aquinas Coggin (New York: Fathers of the Church Inc., 1957), p. 63.

26. It is a matter of debate among Eckhart scholars whether he remains within the orthodox scholastic tradition or whether he basically thinks within the framework of neo-Platonism. John D. Caputo, Thomas Molnar, and others forcefully remind us that for Eckhart the Godhead is prior to the trinitarian distinctions, and therefore he is properly a neo-Platonist in this regard. Rudolf Otto on the other hand contends that Eckhart's God is not the same as that of neo-Platonism, since He is not static but ever creative: the modeless, void Godhead is at the same time Father, Son, and Holy Spirit. (Rudolf Otto, *Mysticism East and West* [New York: Meridian Books, 1960]). Similarly the Eastern Orthodox scholar Vladimir Lossky holds that Eckhart affirms not a descent from pure unity into multiplicity (as in Plotinus) but a movement of plenitude which proceeds from the Father to the Son and returns to the perfect unity of deity through the Spirit. (Vladimir Lossky, *Théologie négative et connaissance de Dieu chez Maître Eckhart, Etudes de Philosophie Médiévale,* vol. 48 [Paris: J. Vrin, 1960], pp. 32–39).

We believe that Eckhart tries to hold together two disparate conceptions of God, the neo-Platonic and traditional Catholic, and ever again neo-Platonic motifs tend to overshadow the biblical ones in his thinking. He sometimes asserts that the Godhead is the simple unity of pure thought (not-being rather than being) and is prior even to the Father. Similar themes are found in Ruysbroeck, who speaks of a God above God who is of "simple essence without activity." This same tradition reasserts itself in Fichte and Schleiermacher in the nineteenth century and in Paul Tillich in the twentieth.

27. Cyril Richardson, *The Doctrine of the Trinity* (Nashville: Abingdon Press, 1958), p. 113.

28. John Macquarrie, *Thinking About God* (New York: Harper & Row, 1975), pp. 127, 128.

29. Macquarrie tends towards panentheism in his view that God does not exist without the world and that the ontological priority of God is not incompatible with the eternality of the world. See his *Thinking About God,* pp. 118, 151. He calls his position an "organic theism" as over against monarchial theism.

30. Karl Barth, *Church Dogmatics* II, 1, p. 653.

31. We here have in mind the necessity of love to redeem, not the metaphysical necessity of goodness to create or produce. Once God had created the human race, his own love impelled him to care for us even in our sin.

32. Karl Barth, *Church Dogmatics* II, 1, pp. 666, 667.

33. *Ibid.,* p. 670.

34. John Calvin, *Institutes of the Christian Religion,* ed. John T. McNeill, trans. Ford Lewis Battles. II, 8, 11, p. 377.

35. Cf. Luther: "The glory of God is to be sought before all and above all and in all things, and all our life eternally is to redound to God's glory alone, not to our advantage, not even to our blessedness or any good thing, whether temporal or eternal." See *D. Martin Luthers Werke* (Weimarer Ausgabe, 1883 ff.) [henceforth known as W. A.] II, 94. Quoted in Philip Watson, *Let God be God* (Philadelphia: Fortress Press, 1948), pp. 44, 45.

36. This does not mean that Edwards is exclusively biblical. Like Augustine

and Calvin he gave due appreciation to the holiness and sovereignty of God, but he failed to perceive the radicality and universality of divine love, since he restricted its redemptive outreach to a select number of the elect.

37. Jonathan Edwards, "Miscellaneous Remarks" in *The Works of Jonathan Edwards,* vol. II, ed. Edward Hickman (London, 1879), p. 560.

38. *Meister Eckhart's Sermons,* trans. Claud Field (London, 1932), p. 32.

39. Friedrich Schleiermacher, *On Religion,* trans. John Oman (New York: Harper & Row, 1958), p. 132.

40. Quoted in Thomas Molnar, *God and the Knowledge of Reality* (New York: Basic Books, 1973), p. 42. Cf. "Without me God cannot live nor without Him can I" in Angelus Silesius, *The Book of Angelus Silesius,* trans. Frederick Franck (New York: Vintage Books, 1976), p. 137.

41. Plato, *Philebus,* 33. In *The Dialogues of Plato* Trans. B. Jowett, vol. 2 (N.Y.: Random House, 1937), p. 366.

42. Karl Barth, *Church Dogmatics* II, 2 (Edinburgh: T. & T. Clark, 1957), p. 166.

43. Anders Nygren, *Agape and Eros,* trans. Philip S. Watson (Philadelphia: Westminster Press, 1953).

44. For Abelard's position see Arthur Lovejoy, *The Great Chain of Being* (Cambridge, Mass.: Harvard University Press, 1953), pp. 70–73.

45. *Ibid.,* p. 75.

46. *Ibid.,* p. 74.

47. Ibid., p. 78 f.

48. Thomas Torrance, *Theological Science* (London: Oxford University Press, 1969), p. 60.

49. Ritschl held that this idea, which implies a negation of the love of God, was already vanishing in the Old Testament, and in the New Testament it could only be maintained eschatologically as a description of God's attitude toward the unrighteous.

50. Paul Tillich, *The Courage to Be* (New Haven: Yale University Press, 1958), p. 186.

51. For a sympathetic introduction to Teilhard's thought see Donald P. Gray, "The Phenomenon of Teilhard" in *Theological Studies* (March 1975) 36:1, pp. 19–51. A devastating critique of Teilhard is given by the conservative Catholic scholar Thomas Molnar in his *Utopia the Perennial Heresy* (New York: Sheed & Ward, 1967). For a cogent criticism of Teilhard from an evangelical perspective, see D. Gareth Jones, *Teilhard de Chardin: An Analysis and Assessment* (Downers Grove, Ill.: InterVarsity Press, 1969). A somewhat more positive appraisal of Teilhard but still with reservations is to be found in Doran McCarty, *Teilhard de Chardin* (Waco, Texas: Word Books, 1976).

52. Alfred North Whitehead, *Process and Reality,* reprinted. (New York: Macmillan, 1941), p. 528.

53. Charles Hartshorne, "Whitehead's Idea of God" in *The Philosophy of Alfred North Whitehead,* ed. P. Schilpp (Chicago: Library of Living Philosophers, 1941), [pp. 515–559], p. 554.

Compare Teilhard de Chardin who referred to "a progressive 'humanization' of mankind." In Pierre Teilhard de Chardin, *Christianity and Evolution,* trans. René Hague (New York: Harcourt Brace Jovanovich, 1969), p. 140.

IV.
THE PRIMACY OF SCRIPTURE

Every word of God proves true. . . . Do not add to his words, lest he rebuke you, and you be found a liar.

Proverbs 30:5, 6

Did not our hearts burn within us while he talked to us on the road, while he opened to us the scriptures?

Luke 24:32

All scripture is given by inspiration of God, and is profitable for doctrine, for reproof, for correction, for instruction in righteousness. . . .

2 Timothy 3:16 KJ

Who does not know that the Holy canonical Scripture is contained within definite limits and that it has precedence over all letters of subsequent bishops, so that it is altogether impossible to doubt or question the truth or adequacy of what is written in it?

Augustine

It is impossible for me to recant unless I am proved to be wrong by the testimony of Scripture. My conscience is bound to the Word of God.

Martin Luther

The whole counsel of God, concerning all things necessary for his own glory, man's salvation, faith and life, is either expressly set down in Scripture, or by good and necessary consequence may be deduced from Scripture: unto which nothing at any time is to be added, whether by new revelations of the Spirit, or traditions of men.

Westminster Confession I, 6

ITS DIVINE AUTHORITY

Evangelical theology appeals to the authority of Scripture because it sees Scripture as the written Word of God. The precise relationship between divine revelation and the human writings which comprise the canonical Scripture has been and still is a subject of debate in both evangelical Protestant and Roman Catholic circles, but there is no gainsaying the fact that Scripture is given a crucial role in the determining of doctrine because of its divine authority.

Scripture cannot be rightly understood unless we take into consideration that it has a dual authorship. It is not only a human witness to divine revelation, but it is at the same time God's witness to himself. The Bible is not partly the Word of God and partly the word of man: it is in its entirety the very Word of God and the very word of man. If we contend as do many liberals that the Bible is fundamentally a human account of a particular people's experiences of God or the product of a heightened religious consciousness, that it only leads us to divine truth, then we have an ebionitic view of Scripture.[1] On the other hand if we affirm, as do many within the camp of orthodoxy and fundamentalism, that the Bible is predominantly a divine book and that the human element is only a mask or outward aspect of the divine, then we have a docetic view of Scripture. Some would even say that the Bible is an exact reproduction of the thoughts of God, but this denies its real humanity as well as its historicity.

While it is important to underscore the inseparability of the biblical text and divine revelation, one must not make the mistake of equating them. In Bavinck's view: "Scripture is . . . not the revelation itself, but the description, the record, from which the revelation can be known."[2] "It should . . . be remembered," Barth declares, that the biblical writings as such are "not the Revelation" but instead "the witness to the Revelation, and this is expressed in human terms. . . ."[3] Berkouwer replies to those evangelicals who object to describing Scripture as a human witness:

Calling Scripture a human witness . . . does not at all mean a separation of Scripture and revelation, but rather an honoring of integral Scripture. The witness is indeed directed to that which is witnessed to. It is not a relativizing of Scripture, but the acknowledgment of its meaning, intention, and function when it witnesses *of* Christ and therefore as God's Word is distinguished *from* him.[4]

Yet we must go on to affirm that Scripture is more than a human witness to revelation: it is revelation itself mediated through human words. It is not in and of itself divine revelation, but when illumined by the Spirit it becomes revelation to the believer. At the same time it could not become revelation unless it already embodied revelation, unless it were included within the event of revelation. Scripture is not simply a "pointer to revelation" (as Brunner has asserted), but by the action of the Spirit it is a veritable bearer of revelation, a vehicle or "conduit of divine truth" (C. Henry).

While in his earlier writings Barth sometimes gives the impression of calling into question the revelational status of Scripture, he becomes more consciously orthodox in his *Church Dogmatics* I. Continuing to maintain the distinctiveness of the scriptural witness from revelation, he is also insistent on its unity with revelation "in so far as revelation is the basis, object and content of this word."[5]

> As the Word of God in the sign of this prophetic-apostolic word of man Holy Scripture is like the unity of God and man in Jesus Christ. It is neither divine only nor human only. Nor is it a mixture of the two nor a *tertium quid* between them. But in its own way and degree it is very God and very man, i.e., a witness of revelation which itself belongs to revelation, and historically a very human literary document.[6]

While we must resist the temptation to posit a direct identity between Scripture and revelation (since this could lead to bibliolatry), we do affirm an indirect identity in that by the work of the Holy Spirit the very human words of the prophets and apostles are conjoined with the Word spoken by God to them. God's Word is consequently not the Bible in and by itself but the correlation of Scripture and Spirit (Barth). The revelation comes to us in the veiled form of the language of Zion, but at the same time it is not known except in and through this language. It can be seen that the most appropriate symbol of the Word of God is not the Bible as a closed book but the cross of Christ shining through the pages of the open Bible.

While Barth was unable to maintain his understanding of the three-fold unity of the Word of God as revealed, written, and proclaimed (because of his stress on the transcendence of the Word over the words), in his emphasis on the revealing work of the Spirit he is closer to the intention of the Reformers than is modern fundamentalism in this regard.[7] The Reformers too spoke of the necessity for the unity of the Holy Spirit and the biblical word, and only this unity is the divine criterion for faith. Luther declared: "Thus Scripture is a book, to which there belongeth not only reading but also the right Expositor and Revealer, to wit, the Holy Spirit. Where He openeth not Scripture, it is not understood."[8] Just as the Bible only makes sense when illuminated by the Spirit, so the Spirit only gives sense in and through the biblical witness. "Do not seek the Spirit through solitude or through prayer," Luther said, "but read Scripture. When a man feels that what he is reading is pleasing to him, let him give thanks; for these are the first fruits of the Spirit."[9] In Calvin's view the truth of Scripture cannot be discerned as the Word of God apart from "the sealing of the Spirit" which imparts to the conscience of believers "such certainty as to remove all doubts."[10] As he saw it, the work of the Spirit is not to supplement or supersede the heavenly doctrine in Scripture but to authenticate it and to bring it home to our hearts.

The mainstream of historic evangelicalism has also perceived the indispensable role of the Holy Spirit in bringing us the veritable Word of God, though a rationalistic strand in modern evangelicalism has obscured this truth. Jonathan Edwards' position is described as follows: "God's Word is really *God's* Word when it is accompanied by the Spirit dwelling in the human heart; when unaccompanied by the Spirit it is simply another natural, human word."[11] Packer rightly observes that "the Holy Spirit is . . . the one who, in a mystery for which the Incarnation provides the only analogy, caused the verbal witness of man to God and of God to himself to coincide."[12] Carl Henry, seeking to do justice to the written word, underlines the unity of Spirit and Scripture: "The rule of the Spirit does not remove man from the will of God objectively revealed in the Bible, and emancipate him to moral self-sufficiency. The Spirit rules in and through the written word, which he has inspired."[13]

It should be recognized that God's Word is not only revealed in the Scripture by the Spirit but also concealed by human finitude and sin. With the Reformers and the neo-Reformation theology of Barth and Brunner, and against the Christian rationalism of the Enlightenment and its modern representatives including Pannenberg and Langdon Gilkey, we hold that the revelation in Scripture is not open to general reasonableness but is disclosed only to the ears and eyes of faith. It is as if light shone through biblical characters on a stained glass window in a cathedral. The light is objectively shining but because of our blinded eyes we cannot make out the images on the window. It is only when the Spirit opens our eyes from within that we can perceive the message on the window and receive it into our hearts. The truth of revelation is objectively given in biblical history, but revelation also encompasses the interior work of the Holy Spirit by which this truth is gratefully acknowledged and received (cf. Eph. 1:17, 18; Gal. 1:12).[14]

We affirm that Scripture is not only a human witness and medium of divine revelation but also a divinely inspired witness and medium. In 2 Tim. 3:16 we read: "All scripture is inspired by God and profitable for teaching, for reproof, for correction, and for training in righteousness. . . ." (cf. 1 Cor. 2:13; 2 Pet. 1:21). With Warfield we hold this to mean that all Scripture is breathed out by God, is a product of the creative activity of the Spirit of God. It must not be taken to mean (as in Protestant liberalism) that the writers were simply assisted and illumined by the Spirit: they were so guided by the Spirit that what was actually written had the very sanction of God himself.

While revelation refers to the action by which God discloses himself and the truth of his Gospel to his church, inspiration refers to the divine election and guidance of the biblical prophets for the express purpose of ensuring the trustworthiness and efficacy of their witness through the ages (cf. Isa. 30:8; Hab. 2:2). God's Spirit was operative upon both the writers and their writings, and he continues to be present in their testimony throughout the history of the church, preserving it from corruption. By the gift of inspiration the biblical writings are made the repository of divine truth as well as the unique channel of divine revelation.

Inspiration, which pertains basically to the verbal witness of the prophets and apostles and which is completed, is to be distinguished from illumination, which denotes the ongoing action of the Spirit in awakening men and women in every age to the truth of what is given in Scripture. In our view inspiration is both conceptual and verbal, since it signifies that the Spirit was active both in shaping the thoughts and imagination of the biblical writers and also in guiding them in their actual writing. We read that the Spirit of the Lord came upon the prophet *and* his words (Isa. 59:21; cf. Exod. 31:18; II Sam. 23:2; Prov. 30:5, 6; Isa. 49:2; Jer. 1:9; 1 Cor. 2:13). Verbal inspiration must not be confused with perfect accuracy or mechanical dictation. Warfield explains inspiration as the *concursus* of divine and human activity.[15] The divine activity does not supersede the human but works confluently with the human so that the Scriptures are the joint product of both God and man. The writers are not to be thought of as simply the pens of the Holy Spirit (as a number of seventeenth century divines taught) but as partners with the Spirit so that the end product can be attributed to coauthorship.

We also affirm the plenary inspiration of Scripture, meaning that Scripture in its totality is inspired. The words of both prophets and apostles are deemed authoritative (2 Pet. 3:2), and the New Testament letters are called Scripture along with the Old Testament (2 Pet. 3:15, 16; I Tim. 5:18). This does not mean, however, that all Scripture has equal value. We oppose the so-called "flat view" of Scripture which does not consider levels of revelation and the fulfillment of revelation in Jesus Christ. All of Scripture is binding upon the church, all of Scripture is a product of the Holy Spirit, but not all Scripture attests equally to the incarnation and atoning work of Jesus Christ, to the Gospel of reconciliation and redemption, which is the formal norm of Scripture.[16] Luther relegated some books in the Bible to the level of Law, whereas other books give a forthright and potent testimony to the message of salvation, the center and apex of Scripture.

In contradistinction to both Barth and Forsyth, we hold that the doctrine of inspiration is preeminently concerned with the written product and not just with the writers and readers of Scripture. Yet we share with these men a dynamic view of both revelation and inspiration. The will and purpose of God have been fully and adequately revealed in Jesus Christ for all time and, therefore, revelation in this sense is final and complete. Since the original witness to this revelation is also complete, inspiration too is something that is finished.[17] In another sense, however, revelation continues in that people in every age must be awakened to the significance of the Christ-event for their lives. But continuing revelation does not signify a new revelation, simply the clarification and illumination of what has already been disclosed definitively and conclusively in the sacred Scripture.

Against a certain Marcionite tendency in modern liberalism and existentialist theology, we affirm that the revelation of Jesus Christ is present in the Old Testament as well as the New. The Old Testament was not simply a preparation for the New Testament, but the Gospel was already anticipated in the Old Testament though not in final or definitive form. This is why Calvin could preach a series of sermons on the Gospel according to Isaiah. Jesus Christ, in his preexistent state, was present to the patriarchs and prophets of Old Testament history, though his full identity was hidden from them. They looked forward to the fulfillment of time (kairos) when Jesus Christ would be incarnate in human form, but they were nevertheless in continuity with Christ. In this sense it can be said that the church had its beginnings in the ancient history of the Hebrews.

The divine authority of Scripture was seriously undermined by the rise of higher criticism, and while not discounting the solid gains that were made, we must not ignore the damage that was also caused by many of the critics who were heavily influenced by an evolutionary philosophy of history.[18] When the Old Testament is seen as the climax of a continuing cultural and religious development, or when revelation is believed to be contingent on the level of man's spiritual maturity, then the very meaning of revelation as supernatural intervention into earthly history is subverted. Historical criticism has enabled us to recapture the humanity of Scripture, but we must not lose sight of its divinity if we are to recover the Bible as an authoritative guide for the church of today.

SCRIPTURAL PRIMACY

A conflict that had already emerged in biblical times concerns the relation between the written Scriptures and the rabbinical and ecclesiastical traditions. Jesus himself made the Scriptures the ruling norm.[19] The Pharisees on the other hand added their traditions to the Scriptures while the Sadducees subtracted the supernatural from Scripture. Jesus accused the Pharisees of making the word of God void (Mark 7:13; Matt. 15:6) and reprimanded the Sadducees for being ignorant of it (Mark 12:18–27).

For the most part both the patristic fathers and the medieval theologians before the fourteenth century taught that the Bible is the unique and sole source of revelation.[20] To be sure, it was generally assumed that the Scriptures need to be supplemented and interpreted by the church tradition. In the Eastern church it was believed that the *Philokalia,* an anthology of patristic texts on prayer, clarifies and illumines what the Bible holds in secret and which cannot be easily grasped by our limited understanding. Yet the traditions of men cannot add anything new to what is already contained in the Scriptures, either explicitly or implicitly. The priority of Scripture over tradition was clearly enunciated by Thomas Aquinas: "Arguments from Scripture are used properly and carry necessity in matters of faith; arguments from other doctors of the Church are proper, but carry only probability; for our faith is based on the revelation given to the apostles and prophets who wrote the canonical books of the Scriptures and not on revelation that could have been made to other doctors."[21]

In the fourteenth and fifteenth centuries, with the rise of nominalism and the flowering of mysticism, an appeal was made not only to Scripture but also to mystical experience and the church tradition. Roman Catholic theologians came to speak of a parallel source of truth —the oral tradition which continues in the history of the church. According to Gabriel Biel, Scripture and tradition should be held in equal esteem. Heiko Oberman contends that this was also the view of the Council of Trent, though some contemporary Catholic theologians are of the mind that Trent made no decision on this matter.[22] In late medieval theology it was also assumed that the church authenticates Scripture and therefore has a certain primacy over Scripture. In the words of Duns Scotus: "The books of the holy canon are not to be believed except insofar as one must first believe the church which approves and authorizes those books and their content."[23]

Many Catholic scholars today (including Karl Rahner, Hans Küng,

Yves Congar, and George Tavard) speak of only one source of revelation, sacred Scripture. While contending, however, that all the truth of salvation is contained in Scripture, they affirm that the teaching office of the church gives the authoritative interpretation of Scripture. Yet although the church tradition interprets the truth of revelation, it does not create this truth. Congar goes so far as to declare, "Scripture has an absolute sovereignty."[24]

Against the prevailing view in their time that church tradition is on a par with Scripture, the Reformers resolutely maintained that there is only one source of revelation, Holy Scripture. Scripture, moreover, contains not only the revealed, divine truth but the *whole* revealed truth. For the Reformers the church is under the Word and simply attests and proclaims it but does not authorize it. "The church of God," said Luther, "has no power to establish any article of faith, and it neither has established nor ever will establish one."[25] Augustine had declared: "I should not believe the gospel except as moved by the authority of the Catholic Church."[26] Calvin explains that when this remark is seen in its proper context it is clearly understood that Augustine was not maintaining that Scripture is authenticated by the church but only that Scripture has its most potent appeal when reverence is given to the church as well.[27] Luther also seeks to interpret Augustine's statement in an evangelical sense, but in the "papist" sense, he says, it is "false and un-Christian. Everyone must believe only because it is the word of God, and because he is convinced in his heart that it is true."[28]

Luther gave poignant expression to the newly emerging consensus of the Reformation when he referred to the Word as the judge and creator of the church. At one place he pointed to Scripture as the light and the church tradition as the lantern. He spoke approvingly of Bernard of Clairvaux who said that he would rather drink from the spring itself (the Scriptures) than from the brook (the fathers of the church). For Luther and other Reformers, as well as for Bernard, the brook is helpful mainly in leading us back to the spring.

The Reformers intended not to denigrate the church, but to make clear that the church must be a servant of the Word, not its master. They were even willing to affirm that the true church, the church which subordinates itself to the Word, is infallible, though this infallibility is derivative and relative. Zwingli declared that the true church "depends and rests only upon the word and will of God. . . . That Church cannot err. . . . That is the right Church, the spotless bride of Jesus Christ governed and refreshed by the Spirit of God."[29] And as Luther put it: "The church cannot err for the Word of God which it teaches cannot err."[30]

Against their Catholic opponents the Reformers contended that Scripture authenticates itself and interprets itself. It gains its credence neither from the church nor from reason but from the One to whom it testifies and who is himself its living center, Jesus Christ.[31] By the power of his Spirit it is able to impress upon the minds of its readers and hearers the trustworthiness of its doctrine and the urgency of its message (cf. Luke 24:32; 2 Tim. 3:15, 16). It is not Scripture in and of itself but Scripture ruled and imbued by the Spirit of God that convicts people of their sins and convinces them of the truth.

The Reformers also staunchly affirmed the perspicuity of Scripture, its inherent clarity. They meant by this that its basic message is clear even to the unsophisticated layman, and therefore every person can go to the Bible directly to search and find the truth. The doctrinal mysteries need to be expounded by theologians so that one can perceive them rightly, but everything necessary for salvation is plainly attested in the Scriptures. The language in certain parts of Scripture will also prove difficult to the layman, but God's truth shines through even obscure terminology. Luther maintained that the clearness of Scripture is two-fold: the one kind is external, referring to the objective testimony in Scripture and the other internal, referring to the illumination of the Spirit.

If you speak of the *internal* clearness, no man understands a single iota in the Scriptures by the natural powers of his own mind, unless he have the Spirit of God; all have obscure hearts. The Holy Spirit is required for the understanding of the whole of Scripture and of all its parts. If you allude to the *external* clearness, there is nothing left obscure and ambiguous, but all things brought to light by the Word are perfectly clear.[32]

In neo-Protestantism the consciousness of the ecclesial community again came to take precedence over the Scriptures. For Schleiermacher the Holy Scripture as the witness to Christ is subject to the judgment of "the corporate spirit." It is the result of faith, not the basis of faith. Culture came to be seen as a source or norm of theology in addition to Scripture.

Modern neo-Catholicism reflects a similar orientation. Karl Rahner, for example, refers to the church's "awareness of faith" as "a theological supreme court."[33] Avery Dulles holds that the living magisterium is endowed with authority from Christ to interpret rightly the Word for the community.[34] In some neo-Catholic circles reference is made to the infallibility of the people of God, which takes precedence over the infallibility of the Word.

Against both Roman Catholicism and neo-Protestantism the dialectical theology vigorously asserted the primacy of Scripture over the church as well as over religious experience. Karl Barth declared: "Scripture is in the hands but not in the power of the Church."[35] It was his conviction that

the Church is most faithful to its tradition, and realises its unity with the Church of every age, when, linked but not tied by its past, it today searches the Scriptures and orientates its life by them as though this had to happen today for the first time. And, on the other hand, it sickens and dies when it is enslaved by its past instead of being disciplined by the new beginning which it must always make in the Scriptures.[36]

Dietrich Bonhoeffer, who shared with Barth a dynamic view of revelation, also subordinated the church to the criterion of the divine Word in Scripture:

The Word of God seeks a *Church* to take unto itself. It has its being *in* the Church. It enters the Church by its own self-initiated movement. It is wrong to suppose that there is so to speak a Word on the one hand and a Church on the other, and that it is the task of the preacher to take that Word into his hands and move it so as to bring it into the Church and apply it to the Church's needs. On the contrary, the Word moves of its own accord, and all the preacher has to do is to assist that movement and try to put no obstacles in its path.[37]

In identifying ourselves with the theology of crisis over neo-Protestantism and Roman Catholicism we do not mean to deprecate the role of the church or deny the movement of the Holy Spirit in the church. Yet while Scripture is inspired by the Spirit, the church is assisted by the Spirit (Max Thurian). The role of the Spirit is to awaken the church to the truth contained in the Scriptures and then to empower the church to proclaim this truth. With the Reformers and the dialectical theologians, we contend that Scripture when illumined by the Spirit authenticates itself. The church simply recognizes the truth that Scripture upholds and then applies this truth to the world.

Our position is that the Spirit both indwells the church and judges the church by the Word. The Word functions normatively over the church as the Sword of the Spirit. With Berkouwer we have definite reservations concerning the contention of Roman Catholic scholars that the Spirit is the church's immanent life principle, since this seems to deny the transcending, judging role of the Spirit. An American Benedictine Kilian McDonnell reflects Reformation motifs when he declares: "The Word always calls the church and constitutes it. And having constituted it, warns, judges, purifies, strengthens, nourishes, edifies it."[38]

Evangelical theology holds that Scripture has primacy not only over the church but also over religious experience. The Word, said Luther, must be believed "against all sight and feeling and understanding." The Word must indeed be experienced, but this is the experience of faith itself, which transcends the reach of man's perception as well as the power of man's conception. Moreover, the experience of faith is forever critical of itself as an experience and always points beyond itself to the Word. Luther averred that our theology is certain because "it snatches us away from ourselves and places us outside ourselves, so that we do not depend on our own strength, conscience, experience, person, or works. . . ."[39]

This brings us to the perennial misconception that Reformation theology elevates the individual conscience as the ultimate authority. In the words of Forsyth: "The Reformation . . . stood not for the supremacy of conscience, but for the rescue of the conscience by the supremacy of Christ in it."[40] Luther averred that his conscience was bound to the Word of God, and this is why he could not go against conscience. In evangelical theology the authority for faith is nothing in us but something within history (Forsyth). It is the voice of the living God speaking to us in the sacred history mirrored in the Scriptures. This voice to be sure also speaks to us in our conscience, but its basis and origin are beyond man's conscience and imagination. Conscience, like experience, can be a trustworthy guide only when it is anchored in the divine revelation given in Holy Scripture.

In addition we affirm the primacy of Scripture over dreams, signs, and wonders. Also to be included in this connection are proofs and evidences of the faith. In the book of Deuteronomy we read that a prophet or dreamer of dreams who gives a sign that comes to pass must not be listened to if what he says contradicts the word of God (13:1–5). Forsyth gives a timely warning on seeking after proofs and empirical evidences for faith:

They are tests of nature and not of faith, tests of feeling rather than insight, tests of empirical experience instead of soul experience, of success rather than of devotion. We withhold full committal till we have tested things in life. We make no inspired venture of faith, but we put Christ on His mettle to see if He is effective in thought or practice. We turn pragmatists and trust Christ because He works; which may come suspiciously near to trusting Him because it spiritually pays and enhances our spiritual egoism.[41]

Signs and wonders have a place in the life of faith, but they are to be seen not as the basis for faith but as illuminations of the truth of faith for those who already believe (cf. Rom. 15:19; II Cor. 12:11–13; Heb. 2:4). We are not to seek after signs or put God to the test, but we should be open to the signs which he is already working for his people. The most authentic signs are those that form part of the message of faith itself, such as the resurrection of Jesus Christ from the grave. In this light we can understand these words of our Lord: "This generation is an evil generation; it seeks a sign, but no sign shall be given to it except the sign of Jonah" (Luke 11:29).

Likewise we must resist any claim to a new revelation, one that completes or even supersedes Scripture and does not merely illumine or clarify Scripture. Various cults and sects have arisen in the modern age which in effect deny Scripture as the original and fundamental vehicle of divine revelation, the sole and unique source of saving truth. We can here mention Mormonism, Christian Science, Anglo-Israelism, the Unification Church of Sun Myung Moon, the Church of the Living Word, Bahaism, and to a lesser degree Seventh Day Adventism and the Community of True Inspiration.[42] Against these new religions we affirm with Luther: "No one is bound to believe more than what is based on Scripture."[43] We also concur with Watchman Nee's timely word of wisdom: "All the revelation today is but the light regained from the word of the past."[44]

Again, we must assert the primacy of Scripture over culture. Too often in the past theologians have drawn upon the creative thought of their culture as well as the Bible in constructing their theology. Although Albrecht Ritschl believed that theology should derive its content from the New Testament and from no other source, he in fact unwittingly accepted the guiding principles of the then current philosophy (Kantianism) including the conflict of man with nature and the need to gain mastery over nature. Schleiermacher, in his *Speeches on Religion,* upheld not the biblical Christ, the divine Savior from sin, but a cultural Christ, the principle of mediation between infinite and finite. Karl Barth on the contrary was strident in his criticisms of what he termed culture-Protestantism and contended that the basic content of our faith must be derived from Scripture alone *(sola Scriptura).* For him culture is not a norm or source for theology but the field in which theology functions and addresses itself.

In concluding this section on Scriptural primacy, we must bear in mind that the ultimate, final authority is not Scripture but the living God himself as we find him in Jesus Christ. Jesus Christ and the message about him constitute the material norm for our faith just as the Bible is the formal norm. The Bible is authoritative because it points beyond itself to the absolute authority, the living and transcendent Word of God. Against both fundamentalism and the old Catholicism we do not conceive of the authority of Christian faith in heteronomous terms. Our authority is not an external standard that impresses itself upon the soul, but a Word from God that enters into the depths of the soul and creates its own response. As Forsyth put it:

> The authority in theology is not external to the matter it works in. It is spiritual. It is inherent in the fontal fact, and connate to the soul. It belongs to the revelation as such, and not to any voucher which the revelation created, like a book or a church. It is an authority objective to us in its source, but subjective in its nature and appeal.[45]

We must go on to affirm, however, that the absolute authority of faith, the living Christ himself, has so bound himself to the historical attestation concerning his self-revelation, namely, the sacred Scripture, that the latter necessarily participates in the authority of its Lord. The Bible must be distinguished from its ground and goal, but it cannot be separated from them. This is why Forsyth could also say: *"The Bible is not merely a record of the revelation; it is part of the revelation.* It is not a quarry for the historian, but a fountain for the soul."[46]

Jesus Christ is the one who speaks, the message of the Bible is the word that he speaks within history, and the church is the mouth through which he speaks. Just as the church is subordinated to the Bible, so the Bible in turn is subordinated to Jesus Christ, who embodies the mind and counsel of God. To put it another way, the church is the phonograph by which we hear the voice of Christ on the record, the Scriptures.[47] To carry the illustration further, it is the Holy Spirit who sets the phonograph in motion. The authority of the Bible is operative within the context of the church by the action of the Spirit. Where these analogies fall down is that Christ is free to speak his Word in a slightly different way for every age and culture, though he remains faithful to the Word that he uttered once for all in the history of the biblical revelation.

Forsyth points to this higher criterion within the Bible, the canon within the canon, when he says: "The gospel of God's historic act of grace is the infallible power and authority over both church and Bible. It produced them both. They both exist for its sake, and must be construed in its service."[48] The ruling criterion of the Gospel, however, must not be construed as referring only to particular sections of Scripture, but it is either implicit or explicit in the whole of Scripture.

The authority and infallibility of the Bible as well as of the church are derivative, having their basis in Christ and his Gospel. We must listen to the dictates of the Bible and also to the counsel of the universal church because they have their ultimate sanction in God himself. When these authorities seem to disagree, this means that we have not really made contact with the real Word of Scripture or the true head of the church, who are one and the same. We must subject the discordant voices that we hear to Christ's self-witness within the Scriptures thereby bringing a transcendent norm to bear upon the point of contention. Yet this transcendent norm is not within our possession: to hear the voice of the living Christ is a miracle of grace which we can hope and pray for but cannot take for granted.[49]

INFALLIBILITY AND INERRANCY

Evangelical theology affirms both the infallibility and inerrancy of Scripture, but these terms must be qualified in the light not so much of modern historical research but of Scripture's own judgment concerning itself. The biblical authors did not claim to possess a synoptic or absolute perspective concerning the truth that they attested and proclaimed. The Psalmist declared: "Such knowledge is too wonderful for me; it is high, I cannot attain it" (Ps. 139:6). And again: "Teach me, Lord, the meaning of your laws" (Ps. 119:33 Today's English Version). Job testified: "Therefore I have uttered what I did not understand, things too wonderful for me, which I did not know" (Job 42:3; cf. Dan. 12:8). Peter describes the prophets as seeking and striving to understand what the Spirit of the Messiah was teaching them (1 Pet. 1:10, 11). Some prophecies, moreover, undergo revision in the Scriptures. Jesus, for example, assures us that John the Baptist is the object of the prophecy of Malachi (in Mal. 4:5) even though he referred explicitly to Elijah (Matt. 11:10).[50] Paul is careful not to equate his own opinions on marriage with the mind of God, though he claims to have the Spirit of Christ (1 Cor. 7:12, 25, 40).

We must also bear in mind that the prophets and apostles were men of their times though the message that they attested transcended their age and every age. The enlightened biblical Christian will not shrink from asserting that there are culturally conditioned ideas as well as historically conditioned language in the Bible. Both Luther and Calvin recognized that in the hermeneutical task a distinction must always be made between the inward content and the outward form of the Bible.

Calvin, in his attempt to reconcile historical and cultural elements in the Bible with its divine inspiration, referred to the accommodation of the Holy Spirit. As he saw it the Holy Spirit accommodated himself to the thought-forms and language of the people of that age in order to impress upon them the heavenly doctrine which speaks to every age. Calvin was here anticipated by Origen and Augustine, who also acknowledged the condescension of the Spirit to our human ways of communicating and understanding. The Puritan William Gouge perceived the possibility of error if we concern ourselves only with the words as such and not with the Word: "This Word is properly and truly the right sense and meaning of the Scriptures; for except that be found out, in many words there may seem to be matter of falsehood."[51]

The Lausanne Covenant gives this potent witness: "We affirm the divine inspiration, truthfulness and authority of both Old and New Testament Scriptures in their entirety as the only written word of God, without error in all that it affirms, and the only infallible rule of faith and practice."[52] We can heartily assent to this statement but with the proviso that the infallible truth of Scripture is not something self-evident. The doctrine or message of Scripture, which alone is infallible and inerrant, is hidden in the historical and cultural witness of the biblical writers. They did not err in what they proclaimed, but this does not mean that they were faultless in their recording of historical data or in their world view, which is now outdated. The Scriptures are entirely trustworthy in what they purport to give us, but this trustworthiness is a property not simply of the letter of the Bible but of the Spirit, the primary author of the Scripture. Apart from the work of the Spirit, the inherent, transcendent truth of the Scripture cannot be perceived. This is why our ultimate criterion is not the Scripture in and of itself but the Word and the Spirit, the Scripture illumined by the Spirit.

The Reformers were very emphatic that Scripture does not err, but we must ask in what sense. Luther declared: "But everyone, indeed, knows that at times they [the fathers] have erred, as men will; therefore, I am ready to trust them only when they give me evidence for their opinions from Scripture, which has never erred."[53] At the same time he can make a statement like this: "When one often reads [in the Bible] that great numbers of people were slain—for example, eighty thousand—I believe that hardly one thousand were actually killed. What is meant is the whole people."[54] He said of the book of Job that though he tended to regard it as real history, he did not believe that everything happened just as reported and that some ingenious, pious and learned man added to the story characters and circumstances.[55] As is well-known, he was exceedingly critical of the emphasis on works in the Epistle of James, though he was not willing to bar this book from the canon.[56] The various authors of both Testaments, he said, built not solely with "gold, silver, and precious stones" but also with "wood, hay, and stubble."[57] Moreover, he freely acknowledged that there was failure as well as success in prophetic prediction. There is little doubt that Luther's ultimate authority was the Word enlightened by the Spirit and not simply the *graphē* or writing of Scripture: "I care not if thou bring a thousand places of the Scripture for the righteousness of works against the righteousness of faith, and cry out never so much that the Scripture is against me. I have the Author and Lord of the Scripture with me, and on whose side I will rather stand than believe thee."[58] He steadfastly declared: "When our opponents interpret the scriptures against Christ, we are prepared to hold fast to Christ against scripture."[59]

Calvin, too, upheld biblical infallibility and inerrancy without falling into the delusion that this means that everything that the Bible says must be taken at face value. He felt remarkably free to exercise critical judgment when dealing with textual problems. He tells us, for example, that Jeremiah's name somehow crept into Matthew 27:9 "by mistake," and no reference is made to the autographs as a way out of this difficulty. Again, he was prone to doubt the Petrine authorship of 2 Peter despite its claim to be written by the apostle Peter; at the same time he firmly held to the inspiration and canonicity of this epistle. While referring to the Bible as "the certain and unerring rule," he clearly meant by this the rule for faith. He contended that the biblical writers when referring to matters of science might well be speaking "in mere accommodation to mistaken, though generally received opinion."[60] He warned that we must not expect to learn natural science (specifically astronomy) from Genesis 1, which is composed in popular phenomenal language. Calvin was committed to a high view of the Scriptures, even regarding them as the oracles of God, but this did not prevent him from examining the text critically.

Many latter day evangelical Christians have felt the need to extend the meaning of inerrancy to cover purely historical and scientific matters, even where the treatment of these in the Bible does not bear upon the message of faith.[61] It is no longer sufficient to declare that Scripture is the infallible standard for faith and practice: it is now regarded as *totally* inerrant.[62] A view of error is entertained that demands literal, exact, mathematical precision, something the Bible cannot provide.

The extrabiblical criterion of scientific exactitude is imposed on the Scriptures, and certainty is thereby made to rest on objective, external evidence rather than on the internal witness of the Holy Spirit (as with the Reformers). Such persons mistakenly believe that this approach insures the canons of orthodoxy whereas in reality it is a suicidal position that rests the case for Christianity on the shifting sands of scientific and historical research. The discovery of one discrepancy in Scripture can then discredit the entire Christian witness. The defenders of total or absolute inerrancy are quick to assert that they uphold only the inerrancy of the autographs, which are nonexistent, thus allowing for the possibility of copying errors in Scripture.

This position has been increasingly questioned in recent years in the light of the advances in textual and historical criticism as well as the new understanding of revelation.[63] In addition, the rise of pseudo-Christian cults that champion biblical inerrancy has been a source of embarrassment to those who contend that this doctrine is the foundation stone and practical guarantee of orthodoxy.[64] Because of the ambiguity related to the word "inerrancy," Clark Pinnock has proposed that "we ought to suspend it from the list of preferred terminology for stating the evangelical doctrine of Scripture, and let it appear only in the midst of the working out of details."[65]

We are not willing to abandon the doctrine of inerrancy, but we must take the Scripture's own understanding of this concept instead of imposing on Scripture a view of inerrancy drawn from modern empirical philosophy and science. Berkouwer perceptively reminds us that inerrancy in the biblical sense means unswerving fidelity to the truth, a trustworthy and enduring witness to the truth of divine revelation.[66] It connotes not impeccability, but indeceivability, which means being free from lying and fraud. He warns us that we must not identify the precision of journalistic reporting with the trustworthiness of the Gospel records. The man of faith must not be surprised by what Abraham Kuyper has termed "innocent inaccuracies" in Scripture.[67] The Scriptures do not lie in their witness to the heavenly truth which God revealed to the prophets and apostles, not only the truth of salvation but also the truth of creation; yet this does not mean that everything reported in the Scriptures is factually accurate in the modern historical sense.[68] Nor does such a judgment detract in the slightest from the full inspiration of the Scriptures. As we have seen, it is possible and necessary to affirm that the Spirit accommodated the truth of the Gospel to the mind-set and language of the writers. They were both children of their times and prophets to their times, since they were witnesses and bearers of a transcendent truth. As Paul averred, "we have this treasure in earthen vessels, to show that the transcendent power belongs to God and not to us" (2 Cor. 4:7).

We should also bear in mind that not only the historical and cultural perspective of the biblical writers was limited but also their theological and ethical ideas. It is only when their testimony is related to and refined by the self-revelation of Jesus Christ that it has the force of infallible authority. The Law of God is both fulfilled in and transcended by the Gospel, and this means that it is properly understood only in the light of the Gospel. Any text when taken out of its proper context and when divorced from the culminating revelation in the Bible becomes susceptible to error. In the light of its inspired meaning, however—the meaning which the Spirit gives it in its relationship to the incarnation and self-revelation of Jesus Christ—it is inerrant and infallible.

Both sides in the fundamentalist-modernist controversy were mistaken. The fundamentalists rigorously maintained that Scripture contains no discrepancy or flaw as modern science would understand this. The modernists, on the other hand, appealed to eternal religious and moral insights that are contained in Scripture but that are available to people of every age and culture. The truthfulness and reliability of Scripture can only be properly measured in the light of its own criterion, the Gospel of the cross, embodied in Jesus Christ, and attested to in both the Old and New Testaments.

We are not persuaded that the idea of infallibility or inerrancy should be replaced by indefectibility, as Hans Küng urges.[69] *Indefectibility* means abiding or remaining in the truth despite errors even in doctrinal matters. This seems to call into question the absolute normativeness of Scripture in the church's understanding of the truth of revelation. With the Reformation we wish to maintain that the heavenly doctrine of Scripture is infallible but that this doctrine can only be discerned by the eyes of faith. In the last analysis it is the consensus of faith and not historical science that can and must decide on the inerrancy and credibility of Scripture. We cannot affirm with some of our evangelical brethren that an unbiased investigation will disclose that the Bible does not err. Only an investigation made by faith and to faith will disclose that the Scriptures are indeed the infallible and inerrant Word of God. While faith alone can grasp the significance of Scripture, this very faith is dependent on Scripture for its reality and sustenance.

The Bible contains a fallible element in the sense that it reflects the cultural limitations of the writers. But it is not mistaken in what it purports to teach, namely, God's will and purpose for the world.[70] There are no errors or contradictions in its substance and heart. It bears the imprint of human frailty, but it also carries the truth and power of divine infallibility. It is entirely trustworthy in every area in which it claims to be trustworthy. We vigorously dissent from the position of Rosemary Ruether that Scripture is basically "an unreliable witness."[71] Nor can we go along with Hanson who seeks to substitute the uniqueness and sufficiency of Scripture for its inspiration and infallibility.[72] The Scriptures are infallible because their primary author is God himself, and their primary content is Jesus Christ and his salvation (cf. John 5:46, 47; 2 Tim. 3:15). Yet we have the infallible, perfect Word of the living God enclosed and veiled in the time-bound, imperfect words of sinful men. As Abraham Kuyper averred: "The 'shadows' remain humanly imperfect, far beneath their ideal content. The 'spoken words,' however much aglow with the Holy Ghost, remain bound to the limitations of our language, disturbed as it is by anomalies."[73] The divine content, of course, cannot be separated from its human form and is available to us only in its human form. It is only when people of faith are given spiritual discernment that they can perceive the priceless treasure of God's holy Word in the earthen vessel of the human word.

This must not be taken to mean (as in liberal theology) that the Scriptures are a mixture of truth and error and that it is human reason that therefore decides what can be believed. Because of the superintendence of the Holy Spirit we have in the Bible an accurate portrayal of the will and purpose of God. Yet we reverently acknowledge that the biblical writings are not uniform in their witness to Christ and that the kernel of the Gospel is always to a certain degree hidden in the husk of culturally conditioned concepts and imagery.[74] Only reflection done in faith can grasp what is of abiding significance and what is marginal and peripheral.

It is inadmissible to treat the Bible as though it were a source book of revealed truths that can be drawn out of Scripture by deductive or inductive logic. The truth of the Bible can only be known as the Spirit makes it known in the event of revelation, yet even here there is no direct perception of truth but only a submission and reception which are adequate for salvation but not for comprehension. The truth in the Bible is enveloped in mystery and therefore can only be dimly perceived (1 Cor. 13:9, 12). Indeed mystery and revelation often seem to go together (cf. Mark 13:11; 1 Cor. 2:7; Rom. 16:25). This does not mean that the Word of God is basically unknowable but that it cannot be known exhaustively and that it remains mysterious even to faithful reason (Rom. 11:33). Mystery does not connote obfuscation but an illumination that eludes rational assimilation. "Though transcending logic in the sense of going beyond it," Macquarrie observes, "mystery is neither absurd nor opaque. It has its own translucency."[75] God is truly revealed even as he comes to us in a form that signifies his veiling (Barth). With Pascal we can say that there is in the self-revelation of God as we find it in Scripture "sufficient clearness to enlighten the elect, and sufficient obscurity to humble them."[76]

While it is important to recognize the element of mystery in revelation, we must stay clear of the opposite error of denying the element of rationality. This is the temptation in mysticism and existentialism. What is revealed is not simply a spiritual presence but a rational message. Revelation is both a *dandum* (event) and a *datum* (objectively given truth), and the two cannot be separated. Yet this truth, because it can only be apprehended in part and because it disrupts and challenges the natural inclination of reason, can never be assimilated into a rational or logical system. The central tenet of Christianity—God becoming man in Jesus Christ—will always remain (at least in this life) a paradox to human reason and indeed can only be grasped by the inwardness of faith (Kierkegaard). At the same time faith also seeks understanding, as Augustine and Anselm forcefully remind us; and there can be at least a certain measure of understanding because the object of faith is not a mystical void or infinite abyss wholly beyond the rational, but the historical embodiment of true rationality, the very wisdom of God (1 Cor. 1:24).[77]

THE HERMENEUTICAL TASK

This brings us to the hermeneutical task, the problem of interpretation. If the infallibility of the Bible were self-evident, if the divine truth of Scripture were directly accessible, then the hermeneutical task would be quite easy, but for better or worse it is much more complicated.

We must first recognize that the Bible is not principally a source book of data on Israel's history (as Wellhausen alleges) but a witness to divine revelation, a witness that points beyond itself to a supernatural reality. This means that in order for us to come to a true understanding of the basic content of the Bible, our inward eyes must be opened to the divine message to which the texts attest. But this is no longer a matter of historical analysis and research but of spiritual discernment. The divine truth of the Bible can only be known by a miracle of divine grace.

Nonetheless, the believer who truly seeks for the spiritual meaning of the biblical texts can prepare himself for the divine-human encounter which comes to one through wrestling with the text. He can amass historical knowledge through a scientific examination of the text, knowledge which can help him to appreciate the context in which the revelation was given, though the encounter with this revelation is not necessarily contingent on such knowledge.

We see the hermeneutical task in a series of stages. First, one must come to the Bible with an open heart and a searching mind. This presupposes that the seeker is a believer, one who has already been grasped by the spiritual reality to which the Bible attests. We agree with Barth that one must approach sacred Scripture without any overt presuppositions or at least with a critical attitude towards one's presuppositions. We affirm this against Tillich who has declared that one must "read the Bible with eyes opened by existentialist analysis."[78] We also oppose Bultmann who contends that one must come to the Bible with a preunderstanding concerning the meaning of human existence. Going on to the second stage one must now examine the text critically, and this means using the tools of literary and historical criticism. He must seek to ascertain what the writer actually intended. He must try to discern the cultural matrix in which the text was written (Sitz im Leben).

Yet one must not be content with historical-grammatical exegesis, but must proceed to theological exegesis, which means seeing the text in the light of its theological context, relating the text to the central message of Holy Scripture. He must now subject his own preconceptions to the scrutiny of Scripture itself. He must listen to the voice of the living Christ within Scripture. Historical criticism must give way to spiritual discernment, which must ultimately be given to the critic by the divine author of Scripture (cf. Luke 24:45). The text is no longer the interpreted object but now the dynamic interpreter (Bengel).

Finally, the interpreter must relate the text, now understood in the light of Scripture itself, to the cultural situation of his time. He must translate the theological meaning of the text into the language and thought forms of modern man so that his hearers are presented with a coherent and intelligible message.

Yet though the theological exegete can make the message of faith intelligible, only the Holy Spirit can make it credible and knowable. The illumination of the Spirit is necessary not only for the interpreter but also for the hearer if a real translation of meaning is to take place.

Historical criticism is not to be disregarded, but it has a secondary or ancillary role. It can enable us to understand the cultural and historical background of the text, but it cannot uncover the spiritual significance of the text, the meaning that was in the mind of the Holy Spirit and that was at least in part grasped by the biblical authors. Karl Barth has these pertinent words on this subject:

Historical criticism has led to a better understanding of the Scriptures than was possible in the past, for those situations which show the historical and secular aspects of the Bible have also something to teach us. . . . However, in course of time, historical criticism has assumed exaggerated importance, so that there is a tendency to identify the real meaning of Scripture with its historical significance.[79]

There has been much resistance to historical criticism in conservative evangelical circles. According to E. J. Young: "A man may practice the principles of criticism or he may be a believer in evangelical Christianity. One thing, however, is clear: if he is consistent, he cannot possibly espouse both."[80] George Eldon Ladd, on the other hand, has shown that higher criticism, including form criticism, can be helpful in the exegesis and exposition of the biblical text.[81] What has made many evangelicals understandably suspicious of historical criticism is that it has too often been associated with a naturalistic philosophy or world view that denies a priori the very possibility of supernatural intervention into human history. Brevard Childs has warned against using the principles of criticism with liberal presuppositions.[82]

It is necessary to understand that historical criticism in the sense of historical-literary investigation can only take us so far, and then we must go on to what Forsyth calls "the highest criticism," seeing every text in the light of the Gospel, the theological center of the Bible. We must move from the analytic criticism of the scientific historian to the synthetic criticism of the theologian if the full intent of the text is to be comprehended. For a true understanding we must bring to the text "the mind of Christ" (I Cor. 2:16).

When the Reformers contended that Scripture interprets itself, they meant that the inner meaning of the text must be revealed to the interpreter of Scripture, who must then formulate it as best he can. Karl Barth has put it this way:

The door of the Bible texts can be opened only from within. It is another thing whether we wait at this door or leave it for other doors, whether we want to enter and knock or sit idly facing it. The existence of the biblical texts summons us to persistence in waiting and knocking.[83]

Luther, too, saw that human reason cannot penetrate the spiritual significance of the biblical text: "Those who presume to grasp Holy Scripture and the Law of God with their own intellect and to understand them by their own effort are exceedingly in error."[84] Instead of bringing our own understanding to the reading of Scripture, he warned, we "ought to come bringing nothing, but seeking to carry away thoughts from the Scriptures."[85]

To be sure, the interpreter of Scripture must do all within his power to ascertain the spiritual and theological significance of the text in question, but in the process he must be open to the guidance and illumination of the Spirit. He should have not only a critical but also a prayerful attitude born of the recognition that the matter of the text is the property only of Jesus Christ. Barth observes: "The Holy Scriptures will interpret themselves in spite of all our human limitations. . . . The Bible unfolds to us as we are met, guided, drawn on, and made to grow by the grace of God."[86]

We must take care, of course, not to read our own thoughts and imagination into the text in question. Our aim should be to discover as best we can what was in the mind of the writer, that is to say, the original or literal sense. If the writer intended to convey a figurative meaning, then we must by no means interpret the text literalistically. At the same time we wish to discover what was in the mind of the Holy Spirit, and not simply the mind of the writer, and what the Holy Spirit would have us hear today in and through this text. This is not pneumatic exegesis, which ignores or devalues the meaning of the written word, but theological exegesis which tries to relate the original meaning to the central message of Scripture. In theological exegesis the original meaning is both fulfilled and transcended in that the biblical writer only partially grasped what the Spirit was teaching him to see (1 Pet. 1:10, 11). There is definitely a place for typological exegesis so long as events and insights in the Old Testament are related to the self-revelation of Jesus Christ and not to events that are only on the margin of biblical history or even outside its scope. What the Reformers objected to in the exegetical methods of the fathers and medieval scholastics was that the literal or original sense was too often bypassed in favor of a purely subjective or mystical interpretation. We cannot remain with the natural or literal sense, but this must be our point of departure, the basis on which we make our synthetic judgments.

This is not to imply that one must consciously go through these various stages in hermeneutics before one can hear God's Word in the Bible. The simplest believer who comes to the Bible emptied of his own understanding and truly seeking the will of God for his life will discover what the Bible is really saying more quickly than an exegete trained in the latest biblical scholarship who nevertheless tenaciously clings to his own preconceptions. There is no doubt that the tools of historical criticism and research can be most helpful in understanding the linguistic history and cultural and religious background of any given text. They can enable one to see the text in a broader perspective. Yet it is not simply a knowledge of the cultural and historical setting of the text that is the goal of true Bible study; our preeminent concern is to uncover the intention of the text, but this is only possible when one has moved beyond criticism to a state of receptivity in which one is open to the guidance and direction of the Holy Spirit.

MISCONCEPTIONS IN MODERN EVANGELICALISM

With the rise of scholastic orthodoxy in the two centuries following the Reformation, the Bible became increasingly identified with divine revelation itself, and inspiration came to be interpreted in terms of mechanical dictation. M. Flacius in the sixteenth century resisted this trend and sought to maintain a dynamic view of both revelation and inspiration.[87] It was asserted by many Protestant scholastics that the Scriptures not only do not err but cannot err. "No error, even in unimportant matters," said Calovius, "no defect of memory, not to say untruth, can have any place in all the Holy Scriptures."[88] Barth makes this trenchant observation:

The Bible was now grounded upon itself apart from the mystery of Christ and the Holy Ghost. It became a "paper Pope," and unlike the living Pope in Rome it was wholly given up into the hands of its interpreters. It was no longer a free and spiritual force, but an instrument of human power.[89]

In modern fundamentalism, which signifies a synthesis of the old orthodoxy and evangelical pietism, the humanity of the Bible is virtually denied or ignored and the truth of the Bible is held to be directly accessible to human reason. Criswell reflects this docetic view of Scripture: "For this Volume is the writing of the Living God. Each sentence was dictated by God's Holy Spirit. . . . Everywhere in the Bible we find God speaking. It is God's voice, not man's."[90] Gordon Clark speaks of the Bible as a verbal revelation, thereby unwittingly calling into question the dual authorship of Scripture. Both Clark and John Warwick

Montgomery refer to the univocal language of Scripture concerning God, which contravenes the position of most theological luminaries of the past who held that human language concerning God is either metaphorical or at the most analogical.[91] This is to say, such language points beyond itself to a supernatural reality that transcends the compass of man's cognitive faculties (1 Cor. 2:7 ff.; Eph. 3:19). We take issue with Clark in his assertion that man's statements concerning God are to be taken literally or that man's logic and knowledge are identical with God's.[92] Through the gift of faith there can be a partial correspondence between man's knowledge and God's but not an equation, since God remains hidden *(deus absconditus)* even in his revelation.

It is well to note that Benjamin Warfield, who from our standpoint can be faulted for underplaying the human element in the Bible, never made the mistake of denying this side of Scripture. He candidly recognized its dual authorship and acknowledged that "inspiration is not the most fundamental of Christian doctrines, nor even the first thing we prove about the Scriptures."[93] He was careful not to make all Christian doctrines rest upon the single doctrine of biblical inerrancy, but he had absolute confidence in the trustworthiness of the biblical writers "as teachers of doctrine."[94] Both Warfield and Hodge conceded that the biblical writers were at times "dependent for their information upon sources and methods in themselves fallible, their personal knowledge and judgment were in many matters hesitating and defective or even wrong."[95]

Our main difference from Warfield is that while he affirms the Bible as a divine product through the instrumentality of men, he is reluctant and often unwilling to affirm the other side of the paradox—that the Bible is at the same time an incontestably human witness to divine truth, a witness that ipso facto bears the marks of historical conditioning. While we grant that in one sense the Bible is the revelation of God to man, this revelation is in the form of human witness and is, therefore, to a degree hidden from sight and understanding. Warfield refers to the "inscripturation" of the divine Word in Scripture, and we too can speak in this fashion, though this must not be taken to mean that the words of the Bible are now divine words but rather that the eternal divine Word is given in and through these very human words, which to be sure have been elected or inspired by the Spirit of God.[96]

The bane of much of modern evangelicalism is rationalism which presupposes that the Word of God is directly available to human reason. It is fashionable to refer to the biblical revelation as propositional, and in one sense this is true in that the divine revelation is communicated through verbal concepts and models. It signifies that revelation has a noetic as well as a personal dimension, that it is conceptual as well as experiential.[97] Revelation includes both the events of divine self-disclosure in biblical history and their prophetic and apostolic interpretation. At the same time we must not infer that the propositional statements in the Bible are themselves revealed, since this makes the Bible the same kind of book as the Koran which purports to be exclusively divine. It also seems to imply a transubstantiation of the human word into the divine word.[98] The Bible is not directly the revelation of God but indirectly in that God's Word comes to us through the mode of human instrumentality.[99]

Revelation is better spoken of as polydimensional rather than propositional in the strict sense, in that it connotes the event of God speaking as well as the truth of what is spoken: this truth, moreover, takes various linguistic forms including the propositional.[100] Objective intelligible truth is revealed (though not exhaustively),[101] but the formulation in the Bible is one step removed from this truth even while standing in continuity with it. The truth of revelation can be apprehended through the medium of the human language which attests it but only by the action of the Spirit. Those who reduce the content of revelation to declarative statements in the Bible overlook the elements of mystery, transcendence, and dynamism in revelation.

Karl Barth warns against this rationalistic approach to Scripture:

> The irremediable danger of consulting Holy Scripture apart from the centre, and in such a way that the question of Jesus Christ ceases to be the controlling and comprehensive question and simply becomes one amongst others, consists primarily in the fact that . . . Scripture is thought of and used as though the message of revelation . . . could be extracted from it in the same way as the message of other truth or reality can be extracted from other sources of knowledge. . . .[102]

Another earmark of Christian rationalism is the attempt to prove the credibility of Scripture by arguments and evidences. The fascination of many evangelicals with the current effort to unearth Noah's Ark is a reflection of a rationalistic temper. Calvin was amazingly forthright in his condemnation of rationalistic apologetics: "Scripture carrying its own evidence along with it, deigns not to submit to proofs and arguments, but owes the full conviction with which we ought to receive it to the testimony of the Spirit."[103] And again: "Therefore Scripture will ultimately suffice for a saving knowledge of God only when its certainty is founded upon the inward persuasion of the Holy

Spirit. . . . Those who wish to prove to unbelievers that Scripture is the Word of God are acting foolishly, for only by faith can this be known."[104]

Helmut Thielicke claims that an apologetics which seeks "to show a historical symmetry between prophecy and fulfillment, or to use historical miracles as a ground of faith, or to argue . . . that the resurrection of Christ is the best-attested event in all antiquity" actually destroys faith by giving it a foundation in something that is generally valid. It takes away the wonder of the salvation event and reduces faith to a purely "practical obedience in which I actively confess demonstrable supernatural facts."[105] It creates the illusion that "God's action is restricted to purely historical facts when in reality it also embraces illumination by the Holy Spirit, i.e., the granting of access to these facts, the opening of the eyes and ears, and the overcoming of hardness of heart."[106]

Like Barth Thielicke warns against positing a direct identity between divine revelation and the scriptural writing. We must avoid the "confusion of the Word of God with an aggregate of letters and sounds. Naturally the Word does take the form of letters and sounds. But these are only a medium. They are only a mode of manifestation which helps it to be perceived. Its true essence lies in what it says, from whom it comes, and to whom it is directed."[107]

One must remember that the basis of faith is not the trustworthiness of the manuscripts (though this is to be gratefully acknowledged) but the saving act of God in Jesus Christ and the inward testimony of his Spirit. The historical events of the Bible, which are accessible to sense perception, are the occasion but not the foundation of faith. The disciples knew Jesus according to the flesh, but they did not perceive his Messianic identity until they were granted illumination by the Spirit (Matt. 16:17; Luke 24:31). With Calvin we contend that in order to attain the knowledge of God "the human mind must exceed and rise above itself."[108] The Bible is a means through which God unveils himself, but he unveils himself only to the eyes of faith, not to natural reason (cf. Ps. 119:18).

In fundamentalism and much of the older orthodoxy the Bible offers no surprises. Too often it is used to support a dogmatic system—whether this be Lutheranism, Calvinism, Arminianism, or some other ism—instead of being treated as a vehicle of the Holy Spirit who uproots our man-made systems and confounds the vanity of our reason. We must remember that the Word of God is not fettered (2 Tim. 2:9). It leaps and runs and is not even bound to the means of grace—the

Bible, the sermon, the sacraments—though we are so bound. We need to recover the biblical concepts of the freedom of the Word and the unpredictability of the Word. We should remember with the Puritan father John Robinson that "the Lord has more light and truth yet to break forth out of his holy Word."

In his noted work on the Lutheran Confessions Edmund Schlink maintains that authentic orthodoxy posits a higher criterion than Scripture, namely, the Gospel. "This intense concern with the Gospel," he declares, "suggests that the Gospel is the norm in Scripture and Scripture is the norm for the sake of the Gospel."[109] Yet we must also avoid the error present in some neo-orthodox circles of separating the Gospel from the Law and treating only the Gospel as the Word of God. While acknowledging the priority of the Gospel over the Law, we must avoid a simple Gospel reductionism and a love monism, both of which disregard complementary truths and insights that are also testified to in Scripture.

Evangelical theology in its most authentic sense will indeed be a theology of the Word of God. We assert this against Rahner's call for reconceptualization and Bultmann's call for demythologization. As theologians we are bound to the concepts of Scripture as well as to its mythical imagery. Though we are constrained to put the message of faith in new forms and imagery, we must always return to what Barth terms "the language of Canaan" and the "language of Zion." Barth warns that it is "nonobligatory, uncommissioned, and perilous" to use words that are "at a distance from the vocabulary of Scripture."[110] Where the church "does not venture to confess in its own language, it usually does not confess at all."[111] Even Tillich, who sought to translate the language of the Bible into contemporary categories, confessed that no term or concept could take the place of the biblical term *sin,* which contains nuances of meaning that *alienation* and *estrangement,* for example, simply do not encompass.

At the same time evangelical theology will be a theology under the Word of God. Our theological systems as well as our confessions of faith must forever be reexamined and purified in the light of the Word of God. An authentic evangelical theology will be a theology forever in the process of reformation *(semper reformanda).* It will acknowledge that God is still free to remold and purify his church through his holy Word which, in its role as an instrument of the Spirit, remains in every age a thoroughly sound and relevant standard and guide.

NOTES

1. The terms *docetic* and *ebionite* are derived from heresies in the early church relating to the person of Christ. The docetists did not give full weight to the humanity of Christ and emphasized only the divinity, whereas the ebionites in their stress on the humanity lost sight of his essential divinity. See infra, p. 134 f.

2. H. Bavinck, *Our Reasonable Faith* (Grand Rapids: Eerdmans, 1956), p. 95.

3. Karl Barth, *The Preaching of the Gospel,* trans. B. E. Hooke (Philadelphia: Westminster Press, 1963), p. 64.

4. G. C. Berkouwer, *Holy Scripture,* trans. Jack Rogers (Grand Rapids: Eerdmans, 1975), pp. 165–166.

5. Karl Barth, *Church Dogmatics* I, 2, eds. G. W. Bromiley and T. F. Torrance (Edinburgh: T. & T. Clark, 1956), p. 463.

6. *Ibid.,* p. 501. It should be noted that in his *Church Dogmatics* I and II Barth reflects a neo-Calvinist sacramentalism by which Scripture, sermon, and sacraments are seen as means of grace having a human form but a divine content. In his later writings Barth tends to return to his earlier position of speaking of Jesus Christ as the one Word of God and the Bible (as well as the sermon and rites of the church) as only a human witness to this Word. See especially *Church Dogmatics* IV, 3, trans. G. W. Bromiley (Edinburgh: T. & T. Clark, 1961), pp. 3–165. He here is inclined to underplay the sacramental character of Scripture as both divine and human.

7. It is a mistake to aver, as do David Kelsey and Carl Henry, that Barth sees the authority of the Bible in purely functional terms. It is more proper to say that he views biblical authority in relational terms—in the light of its divine center, the cross and resurrection of Christ. In this position the authority, infallibility, and power of the Scriptures to convict and save lie not in what they are in themselves but in their incommensurable relationship to Jesus Christ.

8. *Sermons on Luke 24:13 f.* Quoted in Karl Barth, *Church Dogmatics* I, 2, p. 508.

9. *Luther's Works,* vol. 29, ed. Jaroslav Pelikan (St. Louis: Concordia Publishing House, 1968), p. 83.

10. John Calvin, *Commentary on Galatians 1:12, 13, Corpus Reformatorum, Calv. 50,* p. 177.

11. Conrad Cherry, *The Theology of Jonathan Edwards* (Garden City, N.Y.: Doubleday Anchor Books, 1966), p. 48.

12. James Packer, "Taking Stock in Theology" in *Evangelicals Today,* ed. John C. King (London: Lutterworth Press, 1973), [pp. 15–30], p. 21.

13. Carl Henry, *Personal Christian Ethics* (Grand Rapids: Eerdmans, 1957), p. 360.

14. Our position is in accord with the biblical understanding of revelation where it is depicted primarily, though not exclusively, in dynamic terms. Albrecht Oepke declares: "Revelation is not understood in terms of a fixed historical or eschatological objectivism." The making known of what God reveals "is itself part of the act of revelation." And again: "Revelation is not a material possession which we have in black and white. It is a divine act, the unveiling

of what is hidden." *Theological Dictionary of the New Testament,* ed. Gerhard Kittel, trans. G. W. Bromiley, vol. 3 (Grand Rapids: Eerdmans, 1965), pp. 581, 583. For an informative discussion of the meaning of revelation as this relates to various biblical words, see C. F. D. Moule, "Revelation" in *Interpreter's Dictionary of the Bible* IV (New York: Abingdon Press, 1962), pp. 54–58; and Dewey M. Beegle, *Scripture, Tradition and Infallibility* (Grand Rapids: Eerdmans, 1973), pp. 15–52. Both these authors recognize that revelation includes the communication of conceptual knowledge as well as communion and confrontation with God, but Beegle is better in holding objective and subjective dimensions of revelation in balance.

15. Benjamin Warfield, *The Inspiration and Authority of the Bible,* ed. Samuel G. Craig. Introduction by Cornelius Van Til (Philadelphia: Presbyterian and Reformed Publishing Co., 1948), pp. 158, 162. For a balanced appraisal of Warfield's doctrine of inspiration see David H. Kelsey, *The Uses of Scripture in Recent Theology* (Philadelphia: Fortress Press, 1975), pp. 17–24. For Kelsey, Scripture is authoritative only in a functional sense.

16. We are here using *formal* in the Aristotelian sense which denotes *goal* or *criterion.*

17. Inspiration, like revelation, can be conceived of as continuing in a qualified sense, but the meaning is that the Spirit is constantly acting to safeguard the original witness from corruption. Just as we can distinguish between original and dependent revelation, so we can distinguish between original inspiration and the providential preservation of the Spirit in assuring these writings as the divinely appointed channel of revelation.

18. Julius Wellhausen in the later nineteenth century formulated a philosophy of Israel's history which traced this history in terms of religious evolution with the prophets and exile being the high point. Elizabeth Achtemeier caustically comments: "In this view everything that was earliest in Israel's history was automatically labeled as primitive and put at the bottom of the scale of development as having minimal worth." See her *The Old Testament and the Proclamation of the Gospel* (Philadelphia: Westminster Press, 1973), p. 28.

19. It should be recognized that Jesus' ultimate criterion was not Scripture by itself but the Scripture and the Spirit together. He said that the Sadducees erred because they knew "neither the scriptures nor the power of God" (Mark 12:24; cf. Jn. 5:39, 40; 14:15–17).

20. See George Tavard, *Holy Writ or Holy Church* (New York: Harper & Row, 1959), p. 22 f.

21. Thomas Aquinas, *Summa Theologica* I, 1, 8.

22. See Heiko Oberman, *The Harvest of Medieval Theology* (Grand Rapids: Eerdmans, 1967), p. 406 f. Also see his "The Tridentine Decree on Justification in the Light of Late Medieval Theology" in Robert W. Funk, ed., *Journal for Theology and Church,* vol. 3 (New York: Harper & Row, 1967), pp. 28–54.

R. J. Geiselmann argues that Trent really did not have anything to say about the relationship between Scripture and tradition. He says that Trent did not mean to teach a theory of two sources of revelation. The final report of Trent read: "Scripture *and* tradition"; the original reading was "partly Scripture . . . partly tradition." See Geiselmann, *Die Heilige Schrift und die Tradition* (Freiburg: Herder, 1962).

Lennerz argues against Geiselmann that the alteration did not represent a material revision of the original report. But many Catholic scholars including Karl Rahner and Hans Küng are now speaking of only one source of revelation, sacred Scripture.

For an illuminating account of the recent discussion in Catholic theology see G. C. Berkouwer, *The Second Vatican Council and the New Catholicism,* trans. Lewis B. Smedes (Grand Rapids: Eerdmans, 1965), p. 89 f.

23. Quoted in Lev Shestov, *Athens and Jerusalem,* trans. Bernard Martin (Athens, Ohio: Ohio University Press, 1966), p. 298.

24. Yves Congar, *La Tradition et les traditions* II (Paris: Artheme Fayard, 1963), p. 176.

25. Luther, *Werke,* W. A., 30, II, p. 420.

26. Augustine, "St. Augustin: The Writings Against the Manichaeans and Against the Donatists" in *A Select Library of the Nicene and Post-Nicene Fathers,* ed. Philip Schaff, vol. 4 (Grand Rapids: Eerdmans, 1956), p. 131.

27. John Calvin, *Institutes of the Christian Religion,* ed. John T. McNeill, trans. Ford Lewis Battles (Philadelphia: Westminster Press, 1960), I, 7, 3, pp. 76–78.

28. *Luther's Works,* ed. E. Theodore Bachman, vol. 35 (Philadelphia: Muhlenberg Press, 1960), p. 151.

29. S. M. Jackson, ed., *Selected Works of Huldreich Zwingli* (Philadelphia: University of Pennsylvania, 1901), pp. 85–86.

30. Luther, *Werke* W. A. 51, p. 518.

31. The Christocentric orientation of the Reformation doctrine of Scripture is ably delineated in J. K. S. Reid, *The Authority of Scripture* (New York: Harper & Row, 1957), pp. 29–72.

32. In Heinrich Schmid, ed., *Doctrinal Theology of the Evangelical Lutheran Church,* 3d ed. rev. (Minneapolis: Augsburg Publishing House, 1961), p. 73.

33. In L. Bruce Van Voorst, "Follow-up on the Küng-Rahner Feud," *The Christian Century* (Aug. 25, 1971), [pp. 997–1000], p. 999.

34. Avery Dulles, *Models of the Church* (Garden City, N.Y.: Doubleday, 1974), p. 81.

35. Karl Barth, *Church Dogmatics* I, 2, p. 682.

36. Karl Barth, *Church Dogmatics* II, 2, p. 647.

37. Dietrich Bonhoeffer, *The Cost of Discipleship,* rev. and unabridged ed. trans. R. H. Fuller (London: SCM Press Ltd., 1959), p. 225.

38. Kilian McDonnell, *John Calvin, the Church, and the Eucharist* (Princeton, N.J.: Princeton University Press, 1967), p. 358.

39. Martin Luther, *Luther's Works,* vol. 26 ed. Jaroslav Pelikan (St. Louis: Concordia Publishing House, 1963), p. 387.

40. P. T. Forsyth, *The Gospel and Authority* ed. Marvin Anderson (Minneapolis: Augsburg Publishing House, 1971), p. 172.

41. P. T. Forsyth, *The Principle of Authority* (London: Independent Press Ltd., 1952), p. 335.

42. Though some of these groups uphold the infallibility of Scripture they regard continuing revelation through the gift of prophecy as on a par with Scripture if not superseding Scripture.

43. *Luther's Works,* vol. 32 ed. George W. Forell (Philadelphia: Muhlenberg Press, 1958), p. 96.

44. Watchman Nee, *The Ministry of God's Word* (New York: Christian Fellowship Publishers, 1971), p. 67.

45. P. T. Forsyth, *The Principle of Authority,* p. 396.

46. P. T. Forsyth, *The Gospel and Authority,* p. 25.

47. Another pertinent illustration is the church as the lamp, the Bible as the light bulb, and Christ as the light. The light comes to us only through the vehicles of the light bulb and lamp, but apart from the light these have little value.

48. *Ibid.,* p. 17.

49. It should be borne in mind that the voice of the living Christ cannot be divorced from either the Scriptures or the church. This voice is none other than the Word of God in the Scriptures which speaks to and through the church in every age.

50. This is not to be construed as an error, however, since Malachi is in all probability referring to a spiritual Elijah. Here, as in many other places, it is more proper to speak of "difficulties" rather than "errors" in Scripture.

51. William Gouge, *The Whole-armour of God,* (1616), p. 308. Quoted in Gerald R. Cragg, *Freedom and Authority* (Philadelphia: Westminster Press, 1975), p. 142.

52. See John R. W. Stott, *The Lausanne Covenant: An Exposition and Commentary* (Minneapolis: Worldwide Publications, 1975), p. 10.

53. *Luther's Works,* vol. 32, p. 11.

54. *Luther's Works,* vol. 54, ed. & trans. Theodore G. Tappert (Philadelphia: Fortress Press, 1967), p. 452.

55. *Ibid.,* pp. 79, 80.

56. He also cast doubt upon the value of Esther and Revelation.

57. In Willem Jan Kooiman, *Luther and the Bible,* trans. John Schmidt (Philadelphia: Muhlenberg Press, 1961), p. 227. For Kooiman's discussion of Luther's view of the inspiration and inerrancy of Scripture, see pp. 225–239. Also cf. J. K. S. Reid, *The Authority of Scripture,* pp. 56–72.

58. Martin Luther, *A Commentary on St. Paul's Epistle to the Galatians,* ed. Philip Watson (London: James Clarke & Co., 1953), p. 260.

59. Luther, *Werke* W. A. 39 I, 47.

60. John Calvin, *Commentary on the Book of Psalms,* vol. II, 58:4. trans. James Anderson (Edinburgh: Calvin Translation Society, 1846), p. 372.

61. We do not dispute the fact that notions of total or absolute inerrancy have appeared in the church from the first centuries onward, but these ideas were not given systematic formulation until the rise of evangelical orthodoxy and fundamentalism. See Jack Rogers, ed., *Biblical Authority* (Word Books, 1977), pp. 15–46.

62. Recent works that tend to give support to the doctrine of total inerrancy are John Warwick Montgomery, ed., *God's Inerrant Word* (Minneapolis: Bethany Fellowship, 1974), and Harold Lindsell, *The Battle for the Bible* (Grand Rapids: Zondervan, 1976). One reviewer has these critical comments on the first book: "The authors . . . are right about the Bible being a perfect book but are wrong in the way they define perfection. They demand that we must have a Bible that is perfectly accurate in all matters of religion, morals, history, geography, arithmetic, astronomy, biology. They are defining *perfect* the way

a mathematician or scientist would define it; they are not defining *perfect* the way the cross of Jesus Christ defines it." Robert H. Smith in *Lutheran Forum* (May 1975), p. 38. In our opinion these remarks do not apply to the essays by Packer and Pinnock, but the book as a whole creates this overall impression.

Harold Lindsell's book is an informative historical survey on how denial of biblical infallibility and inerrancy finally leads to apostasy (though not all of his examples stand up under scrutiny). In our estimation Lindsell would have strengthened his case for the truthfulness of the biblical witness had he distinguished between the inerrancy of Scripture in its teaching authority and in its historical preciseness in the reporting of events. Lindsell does show that the Bible is amazingly accurate and that many of its alleged historical errors have no basis in actuality. Yet one should keep in mind that amazing accuracy, even in the areas of history and science, is not the same as perfect accuracy. The inerrancy of Scripture must not be made to rest upon consistency in detail or scientific exactness—norms which are derived from scientific empiricism; instead it should be based upon the faithfulness of God to communicate his word to his appointed spokesmen and to preserve their testimony as the vehicle for his continual revelation to his children.

63. See Dewey M. Beegle, *Scripture, Tradition and Infallibility* (Grand Rapids: Eerdmans, 1973); Stephen T. Davis, *The Debate About the Bible* (Westminster, 1977); and Richard J. Coleman, "Reconsidering 'Limited Inerrancy' " in *Journal of the Evangelical Theological Society* 17:4 (Fall 1974), pp. 207–214. Coleman says: "To impose upon all Christians the deduction that plenary inspiration automatically guarantees total inerrancy is unwarranted. The gift of inspiration was granted not to insure the infallibility of every word and thought, though it did accomplish this in particular instances, but to secure a written Word that would forever be the singular instrument by which man learns and is confronted by God's will" (p. 213).

64. Cults or sectarian movements that hold to biblical inerrancy are the Jehovah's Witnesses, the Christadelphians, the Mormons, and the Unitarian (Oneness) Pentecostals. Seventh-Day Adventism, which has a sectarian as well as an evangelical bent, also contends for biblical inerrancy. The Christadelphians in England occasionally hold public forums in defense of biblical inerrancy.

65. Pinnock sees several disadvantages in the use of the term "inerrancy": "First, inerrancy does not describe the Bible we actually use. It is so strict a term that it can refer only to the lost autographs. Second, because it points to a text we do not have, it fails to assert forcibly the authority of the text we do have. Third, by its very nature, inerrancy directs attention to small difficulties in the text rather than to the infallible truth of its intended proclamation. Finally, it has become the slogan of a given party and thus serves to exacerbate conflict and ill-feeling." Pinnock prefers the recent statement of the International Fellowship of Evangelical Students: "Scripture is entirely trustworthy in the sense that its message conveys the true knowledge of God and his works, especially the way of salvation." See Clark Pinnock, "Inspiration and Authority: A Truce Proposal" in *The Other Side* (May–June 1976), [pp. 61–65], p. 65. Also see Clark Pinnock, "Three Views of the Bible in Contemporary Theology" in Jack Rogers, ed. *Biblical Authority*, pp. 47–73.

66. Berkouwer, *Holy Scripture*, pp. 240 ff.

67. *Ibid.,* p. 245.

68. Francis Schaeffer, despite his adherence to biblical inerrancy in the narrow sense, recognizes that the genealogies in Scripture do not have perfect historical accuracy. "The Bible," he says, "does not invite us to use the genealogies in Scripture as a chronology." In his *No Final Conflict* (Downer's Grove, Ill.: InterVarsity Press, 1975), p. 40.

69. Küng, it should be noted, believes that *indefectibility* stands in basic continuity with the original meaning of *infallibility (infallibilitas),* which is dependability or trustworthiness rather than "immaculateness" or "faultlessness" *(Fehlerlosigkeit).* Küng's remarks relate primarily to ecclesiastical authority, but they also have bearing upon his understanding of Scriptural authority. The problem with Küng is that he creates the impression that the infallible truth of the Gospel can be conveyed through erroneous propositions, whereas we hold that the biblical propositions come to have an infallible character when they are illumined by the Spirit and thereby seen in their rightful context. Because the whole course of the origin, collecting, and transmission of the word is under the guidance and disposition of the Spirit, the biblical writings participate in the infallibility of the One whom they attest. While human propositions in themselves are always ambiguous, through the action of the Spirit they can genuinely reflect and communicate infallible truth. Küng maintains that the Scriptures do not possess any inherent propositional inerrancy, since only God is unconditionally and a priori free from error. While we are in basic agreement with him, this must not be taken to mean that the truth in the Bible is purely external to its composition and not also internal. The truth inheres not in the biblical proposition in and of itself but in the proposition in its relationship to Jesus Christ. See Hans Küng, *Infallible? An Inquiry,* trans. Edward Quinn (Garden City, N.Y.: Doubleday, 1971), pp. 139 ff., 181 ff.

70. We maintain that the authentic teaching of the Bible concerning man and the cosmos is as binding as its teaching on salvation and morals.

71. Rosemary Ruether, "Sexuality and Transcendence" in *The Christian Century,* 92:8 (March 1975), p. 230.

72. See R. P. C. Hanson, *The Attractiveness of God* (Richmond: John Knox Press, 1973), p. 22.

73. Abraham Kuyper, *Principles of Sacred Theology,* trans. J. Hendrik De Vries (Grand Rapids: Eerdmans, 1954), p. 479.

74. The husk, which here represents the cultural garment that encloses the kernel (the gospel), only becomes error when it is confused with the kernel. Though the husk is the servant form of the truth and not the truth itself, it is not superfluous but indeed indispensable for coming to know the truth.

75. John Macquarrie, *Thinking About God* (New York: Harper & Row, 1975), p. 42.

76. *Pascal's Pensées and Provincial Letters,* trans. W. F. Trotter and Thomas M'Crie (New York: Random House, Modern Library, 1941), p. 189.

77. Neither God nor Christ is exclusively or exhaustively rational, however, and it is well to pay heed to the reminder of Rudolf Otto in his *The Idea of the Holy* that God also has a nonrational side—dynamic will and energy, which Otto calls "the numinous." God's nonrational energy and majesty are integrally related to his reason, but they are not wholly subordinate or ancillary

to his reason. God wills the Good not simply because he thinks the Good but because he is the Good. Yet he is more than the Good: he is the "Holy" which includes as well as transcends the Good as an ethical category.

78. Quoted in Hans Zahrnt, *The Question of God* (New York: Harcourt, Brace & Jovanovich, 1970), p. 308.

79. Karl Barth, *The Preaching of the Gospel,* p. 61.

80. E. J. Young, *Thy Word is Truth* (Grand Rapids: Eerdmans, 1957), p. 219. Cf. Gerhard Maier, *The End of the Historical-Critical Method* trans. Edwin Leverenz & Rudolph Nordern (St. Louis: Concordia, 1977).

81. See George Eldon Ladd, *The New Testament and Criticism,* 2d printing (Grand Rapids: Eerdmans, 1971).

82. See Brevard Childs, *Biblical Theology in Crisis* (Philadelphia: Westminster Press, 1970), pp. 94, 102.

83. Karl Barth, *Church Dogmatics* I, 2, p. 533.

84. *Luther's Works,* vol. 29, p. 186.

85. Luther, *A Commentary on St. Paul's Epistle to the Galatians,* ed. Philip Watson, p. 465.

86. Karl Barth, *The Word of God and the Word of Man,* trans. Douglas Horton (New York: Harper & Row, 1957), p. 34.

87. J. K. S. Reid, *The Authority of Scripture,* pp. 89 ff.

88. Heinrich Schmid, ed., *The Doctrinal Theology of the Evangelical Lutheran Church,* p. 49.

89. Karl Barth, *Church Dogmatics* I, 2, p. 525.

90. W. A. Criswell, *Why I Preach That the Bible is Literally True* (Nashville: Broadman, 1969), p. 68.

91. For Clark's reservations on the use of analogy in theology see Ronald Nash, ed., *The Philosophy of Gordon Clark* (Philadelphia: Presbyterian & Reformed, 1968), pp. 77–79. According to Ronald Nash, Clark does not rule out analogical language altogether in reference to God but is insistent that every analogy must contain some univocal meaning. In a personal letter to this author dated Feb. 17, 1977. Note that Henry follows Clark in holding to univocal predication in our language about God. See Carl Henry's *God, Revelation and Authority,* vol. II (Waco: Word Books, 1976), p. 115. In our view the analogical knowledge of God derived from faith is real knowledge but nonetheless incomplete.

92. Nash, *op. cit.,* pp. 57 ff., 406, 407.

93. Benjamin B. Warfield, "The Real Problem of Inspiration" in *The Living God: Readings in Christian Theology,* ed. Millard J. Erickson (Grand Rapids: Baker Book House, 1973), [pp. 277–291], p. 279.

94. *Ibid.* On the significance of the article by A. A. Hodge and Warfield in which they extend the meaning of inerrancy to cover other matters as well, see Bernard Ramm's discussion in Jack Rogers, ed., *Biblical Authority,* pp. 109 ff.

95. Cited in Richard J. Coleman, "Biblical Inerrancy: Are We Going Anywhere?" in *Theology Today* 31:4 (Jan. 1975), [pp. 295–303], p. 299. This contrasts with the position of many of the church fathers, e.g., Irenaeus, who believed that the writers of Scripture "were filled with perfect knowledge on every subject." See Irenaeus, *Adv. Haer,* III, 1. Cf. III, 22. For a cogent exposition of the views of the church fathers on this matter see George Duncan Barry,

The Inspiration and Authority of Holy Scripture, A Study in the Literature of the First Five Centuries (New York: Macmillan, 1919).

96. Warfield can speak of the biblical words as the "immediate words of God." Benjamin B. Warfield, *The Inspiration and Authority of the Bible,* p. 149.

97. We can also assert that revelation is cognitive but only in a qualified sense. It is capable of being apprehended not by man's natural faculties as such but by the spiritual eyes of faith. Faith is knowledge as well as trust, but its object transcends the empirical and humanly rational: it concerns the "secret and hidden wisdom of God" (1 Cor. 2:7; cf. Isa. 55:8; Dan. 2:22). This wisdom can enter into the humanly rational but nevertheless remains distinct from all general wisdom.

Once illumined by the Spirit human reason plays a formative role in faith's quest for understanding, but even then the central mysteries of the faith defy rational comprehension and can be expressed only in symbolic and paradoxical language. Our position here differs from that of Carl Henry who affirms with Pannenberg that revelation can be grasped by the "normal powers of human apprehension" requiring "no special work of the Spirit." Carl Henry, *God, Revelation and Authority,* vol. II, p. 309; cf. vol. I, p. 229. We concur with Henry in his espousal of a supernatural world view and his contention that revelation includes ontological as well as personal truth.

98. Ray S. Anderson skirts the opposite danger when he speaks of a kenosis of the Word becoming Scripture analogous to the kenosis of the Word becoming man in Jesus Christ. If the kenotic theory is carried too far this means that the divine Word is transmuted into the human word of Scripture and is thereby emptied of its divine content. In our view the human words of Scripture are taken up into or united with the divine Word, but the divine Word does not literally change into the human word. The two natures of the Bible are inseparable but must not be confused. See Ray S. Anderson, *Historical Transcendence and the Reality of God* (Grand Rapids: Eerdmans, 1975), pp. 212 ff.

99. God speaks to us indirectly when we hear the good news from his appointed spokesmen, but he also speaks directly when he conjoins his Word with their word by his Spirit. Scripture is not immediate revelation, but revelation is mediated through Scripture as the Holy Spirit acts upon it.

100. Cf. Bernard Ramm, *Special Revelation and the Word of God* (Grand Rapids: Eerdmans, 1961), pp. 154 ff. Ramm contends that the term *propositional revelation,* while having some validity, is basically an "unhappy one" because "it fails to do justice to the literary, historical, and poetic elements of special revelation" (p. 155).

101. Revelation is primarily personal and only secondarily conceptual, since its principal object is Jesus Christ himself. Nonetheless, Christ not only makes himself known and sheds his love abroad in our hearts: he also tells us who he is and why he has come.

102. Karl Barth, *Church Dogmatics* IV, 1, eds. G. W. Bromiley and T. F. Torrance (Edinburgh: T. & T. Clark, 1956), p. 368.

103. John Calvin, *Institutes of the Christian Religion,* trans. Henry Beveridge (Edinburgh: Calvin Translation Society, 1845), I, 7, 5, p. 95.

104. Calvin, *Institutes* McNeill, ed. I, 8, 13, p. 92. Cf. Voetius: "As there is no objective certainty about the authority of Scripture, save as infused and

imbued by God the Author of Scripture, so we have no subjective certainty of it, no formal concept of the authority of Scripture, except from God's illuminating and convincing inwardly through the Holy Spirit." In Heinrich Heppe, ed. *Reformed Dogmatics* Trans. G. T. Thomson (London: George Allen & Unwin Ltd., 1950), p. 25.

105. Helmut Thielicke, *The Evangelical Faith,* vol. I trans. and ed. Geoffrey W. Bromiley (Grand Rapids: Eerdmans, 1974), pp. 269, 270.

106. *Ibid.,* p. 270.

107. *Ibid.,* p. 181. Thielicke's position is here in accord with such luminaries of Protestant Orthodoxy as Flacius, Voetius, and Gerhard.

108. Calvin, *Institutes of the Christian Religion,* trans. John Allen (Philadelphia: Presbyterian Board of Christian Education, 1936), 7th ed., III, 2, 14, p. 613.

109. Edmund Schlink, *Theology of the Lutheran Confessions* (Philadelphia: Fortress Press, 1961), p. 6.

110. Karl Barth, *Church Dogmatics* I, 1, pp. 396, 397.

111. Karl Barth, *Dogmatics in Outline,* trans. G. T. Thomson (New York: Harper & Row, 1954), p. 31.

V.

TOTAL DEPRAVITY

Sin lurks deep in the hearts of the wicked, forever urging them on to evil deeds.

Psalm 36:1 LB

The heart is deceitful above all things, and desperately corrupt; who can understand it?

Jeremiah 17:9

Oh this propensity to evil, how did it creep in to cover the earth with treachery?

Ecclesiasticus 37:3 NEB

Vanity is so anchored in the heart of man that . . . those who write against it want to have the glory of having written well; and those who read it desire the glory of having read it.

Blaise Pascal

Sin, understood in the Christian sense, is the rent which cuts through the whole of existence.

Emil Brunner

THE GRANDEUR AND MISERY OF MANKIND

The Bible clearly affirms the grandeur as well as the misery of man. He has been made a little lower than the angels and has been given dominion over the animals (Ps. 8:5–8 KJ). He is created in the image of God and endowed with freedom for service and fellowship. Yet he has squandered his inheritance by seeking to be as God. He has not been content to remain within his limitations: though he is finite he aspires to be infinite. Or he seeks to escape from the demands of his freedom in gross sensuality. Yet even when he descends to the level of the beast he remains superior to the beast, since he sins knowingly and willingly. He is not the victim of fate or the prey of natural impulses but remains responsible in his sin. His sin is inexcusable, because he knows the good but does not do it. His misery consists in his wilful defiance of the good that is his salvation.

Though man is hopelessly lost, he is not nothing. "Man is lost," says

Francis Schaeffer, "because he is separated from God, his true reference point, by true moral guilt. But he never will be nothing. Therein
lies the horror of his lostness. For man to be lost, in all his uniqueness
and wonder, is tragic."[1]

In Zen Buddhism "man enters the water and causes no ripples." In
the biblical view he causes ripples that never end. Man leaves behind
both good and bad marks in history, but he is not a zero (Francis
Schaeffer). He remains infinitely precious in God's sight despite his
folly and perversity.

Sartre referred to man as a "useless passion"; the Christian faith
sees him as a responsible being before God, though one who has lost his
way. His life has been given purpose and meaning though he himself
may not yet be aware of it. He is irrevocably included in God's redemptive plan, even though he may still exist in darkness and corruption.

Man in the technological society has been reduced to the level of a
machine. But a machine cannot sin, for sin means a rupture in a
personal relationship with God. The machine runs mechanistically,
but man is a free being endowed with infinite possibilities. The tragedy
is that he has misused his freedom and has thereby fallen into slavery
to his own lust for power. Yet even in his slavery he remains free,
though no longer to do the good but now to satisfy his selfish desires.
The greatness of man is apparent even in his wretchedness (Pascal).

In constructing a Christian anthropology we must not ignore the
basic nobility of man. He comes from the hand of God, though he is not
a part of God. He is essentially good, having been created in the image
of God. At the same time we must not minimize the gravity of his sin
against his Creator. His created nature is unblemished, but his existence in the world is fallen. There is a glaring contrast between what
man is truly and essentially and what he has become. Because man
lives in opposition to his own God-given nature, his present nature
signifies an existence in contradiction (Emil Brunner). We must not
close our eyes to man's original goodness, but we must also acknowledge that his whole being is now marred by a deep-rooted perversity.
Every part of his being is now corrupted by an insatiable desire for a
place in the sun, and this is what is meant by total depravity.

There is no longer any way from man to God, since sin has blinded
man's perception as well as shackled his will. He is now a creature
under the wrath and judgment of God, though he nevertheless remains
an object of God's solicitous care. Indeed, precisely because he is loved
by God, he is pursued by the righteous anger of God. But herein lies his
hope: God in his holy love will not let go of the prodigal son. The man

in sin cannot return to God by his own volition, but God can come to him, and God has done so in Jesus Christ. In Christ God has taken upon himself man's sin and guilt so that man might be restored to his inheritance, so that man's enslaved free will might be liberated for service in love. The good news is that man's free will enthralled by sin can be turned around by grace. But this good news is meaningful only against the background of mankind's tragic fall into sin.

TOTAL AND UNIVERSAL CORRUPTION

Reformed Christianity has been known for its emphasis on the total depravity of man, but properly understood this doctrine is integral to all Evangelical Protestantism, and it also includes a significant measure of support within Roman Catholicism. It is a doctrine that has been insufficiently grasped, and too often its proponents have only added confusion by their exaggerated versions of it. The erroneous impression is given that the *imago Dei* itself has been lost through sin so that the very substance of man is nothing but sin.[2]

In the perspective of biblical faith total depravity can be thought of as having four meanings, all of which are valid. First, it refers to the corruption at the very center of man's being, the heart, but this does not mean that man's humanity has ceased to exist. Second, it signifies the infection in every part of man's being, though this is not to infer that this infection is evenly distributed or that nothing good remains in man. Third, it denotes the total inability of sinful man to please God or come to him unless moved by grace, though this does not imply that man is not free in other areas of his life. Fourth, it includes the idea of the universal corruption of the human race, despite the fact that some peoples and cultures manifest this corruption much less than others.

The depth of the corruption of sin is testified to in Psalm 53:1, 3 (NEB): "How vile men are, how depraved and loathsome; not one does anything good! . . . All are unfaithful, all are rotten to the core. . . ." (cf. Pss. 14:1–3; 36:1–4; Jer. 17:9; Rom. 7:18; Eph. 2:3; 4:18.) The universality of sin is indicated in Second Isaiah: "All we like sheep have gone astray, we have turned every one to his own way" (Isa. 53:6a). A similar note is sounded by St. Paul: "None is righteous, no, not one. . . . All have sinned and fall short of the glory of God" (Rom. 3:10, 23).

It was Augustine who rediscovered the biblical doctrine of total depravity and gave it the recognition that it deserves. He spoke of "the entire mass of our nature" being "ruined beyond doubt" and falling "into the possession of its destroyer."[3] Unfortunately he was unable to avoid a philosophical determinism in his conception of inherited sin. By making sin a fatality due to natural causes and by seeing its eradication in the rite of baptism, he failed to do justice to personal responsibility in sin and to personal faith in the overcoming of sin.[4]

The total depravity of man was given strong emphasis in the Reformation. Calvin declared: "We are so entirely controlled by the power of sin, that the whole mind, the whole heart, and all our actions are under its influence."[5] Luther saw sin as permeating every part of man's being so that he is incapable of turning to God by his own volition. And in the words of the Reformed theologian Polan: "Original sin is in the whole man, soul and body: in the soul strictly as in its proper subject, in the body as in an instrument through which the soul acts."[6]

Total depravity does not mean that there is no natural goodness or freedom remaining in man. The *imago Dei* has been darkened but not destroyed. It is marred by sin, but it still exists. Man continues to reflect the glory of his Creator, even in his sin and defiance. Man, even in the state of sin, has natural talents, intelligence, and also a moral sense, though because of sin it cannot be regarded as a safe or sure guide.

Our Lord certainly acknowledged the remnant of goodness that exists in evil people: "If you then, who are evil, know how to give good gifts to your children, how much more will the heavenly Father give the Holy Spirit to those who ask him!" (Luke 11:13).

It is not only the *imago Dei* but also the common grace of God that accounts for sinful man's ability to arrive at a modicum of justice. Common grace is the grace of preservation by which man's rapacity is restrained. Indeed, if it were not for common grace, the world would fall into anarchy and disorder, but God preserves his created order out of his mercy so that people may hear the good news of redemption through Christ and turn to him and be delivered from their sins. Common grace, together with the reflection of the glory of God in created human nature, is responsible for the fragments of wisdom and truth that exist in the non-Christian religions and also in the moral codes of the great civilizations of pagan antiquity.

At the same time evangelical theology insists that though man in his sin can still attain a certain degree of moral virtue, all his good works are infected by a sinful motivation or purpose and are, therefore, unacceptable in the sight of God. Because our natural goodness is mixed with evil thoughts and desires, it can only be deemed repugnant by a holy God who is satisfied by nothing less than perfection. Before men our righteousness may elicit admiration but not before God *(coram Deo),* as Luther saw so well (cf. Ps. 130:3). Those who recognize their sin can only confess: "We have all become like one who is unclean, and all our righteous deeds are like a polluted garment. We all fade like a leaf, and our iniquities, like the wind, take us away" (Isa. 64:6).

Charles Hodge reveals a keen insight into the human situation: "Every man should bow down before God under the humiliating consciousness that he is a member of an apostate race; the son of a rebellious parent; born estranged from God, and exposed to his displeasure."[7]

THE MEANING OF SIN

Sin in the biblical perspective is positive rebellion, not simply a privation of goodness or being. The essence of sin is unbelief, which appears as both idolatry and hardness of heart. Luther described the man in sin as *incurvatus in se* (bent inwards upon himself) whereas the man in Christ looks away from himself towards God and his neighbor in love. According to Schoonenberg: "Sin is an aversion from and an unfaithfulness to Yahweh himself; hence it is placed in the heart rather than in the wrong deed."[8] Bitterness in the soul is the seething caldron from which all manner of evil proceeds. As our Lord declared, "Out of the heart come evil thoughts, murder, adultery, fornication, theft, false witness, slander" (Matt. 15:19; cf. Matt. 5:28; 12:34; Luke 16:15). To be sure human sin is not sheer defiance, since it is mixed with ignorance and weakness, but this does not take away from its devastating consequences. Sin has brought discord and misery to man (cf. Isa. 47:10, 11), but its source is a ruptured relationship with God.

Against the idealistic and mystical traditions we contend that sin is to be located not in the subrational vitalities of the self but rather in man's spirit. Though man's nature makes him vulnerable to temptation, sin itself is an act of the will. It signifies neither a necessity of man's nature nor an invariable concomitant of his finitude, but instead an abuse of his freedom.

In the thinking of Augustine on this subject both biblical and classical views can be discerned. While he often saw sin as a "defect" of the will and a lack of power to do the good, which reflects his neo-Platonism, he also realized that sin is a perversion of the will and an assault on the good. Though he associated sin with nonbeing, this only meant that it has no positive ontological standing before God, not that it has no reality. *Nonbeing* was interpreted as resistance to being and a perversion of being.

The neo-Platonic idea of evil as *privatio* has continued to make a deep impression on Christian thought, though it is often modified and held in tension with more biblical insights. Thomas Aquinas, while understanding sin as an omission of the good, perceived that it is the direct cause of the derangement in the powers of the soul. Abraham Kuyper sought to affirm both "sin's privative being" and "positive working." If he sometimes recognized that it is a deprivation he also acknowledged that it is "a positive evil and malignant power."[9] Though making use of the concept of *privatio,* Bavinck saw that this is an insufficient designation for sin, which is a cataclysmic and destructive power.

It should be acknowledged that sin entails both privation and positive rebellion, but the latter is prior to the former. "The origin of pride," says the prophet, "is to forsake the Lord, man's heart revolting against his Maker" (Ecclesiasticus 10:12 NEB). By turning away from God man finds himself deprived of the light and truth of God. Sin is not pure negation but a "positive negation" (Brunner). It is not simply discreativity but a mixture of creativity and discreativity. It is not merely the absence of good but an attack upon the good.

The Scriptures often portray sin as a positive force of destruction, sometimes as a power outside as well as inside man. Eve was pressed to eat of the tree of the knowledge of good and evil by the power of sin personified in the voice of the serpent (Gen. 3:1 f.). Cain is told by God that "sin is couching at the door; its desire is for you, but you must master it" (Gen. 4:7). Paul confessed that sin wrought in him "all kinds of covetousness" (Rom. 7:8). He also says that "sin, finding opportunity in the commandment, deceived me and by it killed me" (Rom. 7:11).

Sin, in the biblical perspective, is both an act and a state. It entails separation from God as well as a deliberate violation of his will. It signifies both a state of alienation or estrangement from God and a transgression of his law. It is a wrong direction as well as wrong acts. It is missing the mark, but even more profoundly it is a fatal sickness.

What should be borne in mind is that the bias of sin precedes the act of sin at least as far as man in history is concerned. Bad fruit can only come from a bad tree (Luther). Even before the act of sin man finds a propensity to sin within him. As the Psalmist declared: "Behold, I was brought forth in iniquity, and in sin did my mother conceive me" (Ps. 51:5). For Pelagius, the antagonist of Augustine, man is guilty only of actual sins, not of original sin. But this betrays a lack of insight into the precariousness of the human condition. Luther in particular under-lined the gravity of original sin: "Original sin, natural sin, or *personal sin* is the principal sin. If it did not exist, neither would there be any actual sin."[10]

On the question of the depth of the corruption of sin we see a pronounced difference between Roman Catholicism and Reformation Protestantism. In what came to be the official Catholic view human nature is only wounded and is susceptible to healing. Irenaeus precipi-tated an enduring line of thought on this subject by his distinction between the likeness of God *(similitudo)* and the image of God *(imago)* based on a faulty exegesis of Genesis 1:26. Through sin man has lost the likeness to God, which consists in the gift of supernatural commu-nion with God and original righteousness, but not the image, which represents the freedom and rationality of his nature. This formed the basis of the later Catholic distinction between *pura naturalia* and a *donum supernaturale,* a special gift in addition to his natural endow-ment. In the developing Catholic orthodoxy "original righteousness" is lost in the fall, but a natural justice remains. Man still retains some freedom to turn to God and some sense of his moral law.

The Reformers sharply criticized this view of the fall, since it did not seem to take seriously the actual defilement of man's nature by sin. For Luther man has lost not a supernature but his God-given nature. Sin represents a corruption of man's essential nature so that he is now "altogether sinful and wicked." Emil Brunner reflects the Reformation view when he says: "By sin the nature of man, not merely something in his nature, is changed and perverted."[11] In this perspective to quote Gustaf Aulén, "sin does not have reference to something external and peripheral in man, nor to something 'accidental'; it has its 'seat' in his inner being, in the inclination of the will, and applies, therefore, to man as a whole."[12]

Although they spoke of the utter defacement of the *imago Dei,* the Reformers believed that some vestige of the *Imago* remains, for other-wise man would not be man. A few of their followers went further, however, and defined original sin as the very substance of fallen man (e.g., Matthias Flacius).

Protestant Orthodoxy as it developed reacted against exaggerations of the corruption of man. The Lutheran theologian Quenstedt argued that sin is not the very substance or essence of man but that it inheres in man after the manner of an accident. It dwells in man, but just as an inhabitant or guest is not the same as the house, so sin is not the same as man. For Kuyper, not our being but our nature was corrupted by sin. *Being* is that which makes man what he is while *nature* refers to the character of his being and working.

Karl Barth maintains, in opposition to the Reformation emphasis, that man is basically good, since his created being comes from God.[13] This is why he describes sin as an "ontological impossibility," for it is not presupposed in man's original freedom. It happens as something irrational and inexplicable and thereby distorts man's nature and humanity.[14] Sin is to be regarded as inhuman and unnatural rather than natural. Yet sin infects every area of man's being, and his achievement is therefore "not only incomplete but perverted."[15] Barth can even describe man as "radically and totally evil";[16] yet the *imago Dei* is not eradicated but marred and obscured.

Emil Brunner seeks to correct what he sees as an imbalance in the Reformation doctrine by maintaining that man's relation with God is not sundered by sin but perverted. Man is still responsible before God, but he is no longer in "a state of being-in-love" but now finds himself in "a state of being-under-the law, a life under the wrath of God."[17] Brunner is concerned to maintain human responsibility in sin while at the same time avoiding any kind of Pelagianism or semi-Pelagianism.

Reinhold Niebuhr contends against the Catholic position that original righteousness remains in man, but that it is marred and distorted by sin. With the Reformers he avers that "sin is a corruption of man's true essence,"[18] but against the Manichaeism that sometimes intrudes into Reformation theology he insists that sin does not destroy man's true essence. Despite the corrupting influence of sin man retains the freedom of his will. Niebuhr also maintains against the Reformers and Barth that though there is an equality in sin, there is an inequality in guilt, which signifies the historical and objective consequences of sin, and "for which the sinner must be held responsible."[19]

In our view the essential nature of man is good, since it is created by God, but his existential nature, his being in the world is corrupted. Man's humanity remains just as the eye remains after a poisonous insect sting destroys its sight, though it is now deprived of its luster and checked in its moral activity (Abraham Kuyper). True human nature as we find it in Jesus Christ is without sin, and therefore sin is rightly seen as a deviation from human nature. It signifies the unnature of man, the abnormal which has now become natural. The *imago Dei*, the reflection of the being of God in man, is defaced, but it is not destroyed. Man is still responsible before God, though his freedom has been considerably impaired.

It is misleading to speak, as do some Quakers and mystics, of a pearl in the heart of every person, since this implies that there is a part of man not touched by sin. It is the whole man who is the pearl, since his entire being reflects the glory of his Creator, but he is a badly flawed pearl because he has turned away from his God to pursue his own ends. It is not the inner light that brings man into contact with God, since he already stands in the light of God. The tragedy is that he misconstrues this light or fails to see it at all because of his sin.

On the relation of sin and temptation, Schleiermacher has cogently observed that temptation presupposes sin, for man could not be seriously tempted unless the bias toward sin were in him (though Schleiermacher's understanding of this differs from ours). Reinhold Niebuhr concurs with Schleiermacher, but unlike the latter, he will not affirm the sinlessness of Jesus, since Jesus was tempted.[20] Here it is necessary to distinguish between two kinds of temptation—external and internal; only the second presupposes sin, since it indicates that the temptation has roots within man himself. Niebuhr will affirm an amazing coincidence between Jesus' internal purpose and his outward actions, but he does not think it possible for human nature as such to be without even the taint of sin. We here must ask whether Niebuhr, despite his attempt to do justice to the freedom of man, does not harbor a covert Manichaeism. More probably the trouble is in his Christology rather than his anthropology, since he does not really succeed in uniting the Christ of faith and the Jesus of history.[21]

The question of sin in the natural man leads inevitably to whether there is sin in the Christian. We are told that in regeneration our sin is washed away (John 13:10) and that in Christ we cannot sin (1 John 3:9). At the same time a bias toward sin lingers on even in the Christian, and this is why we must daily put off the old nature and put on the new (Eph. 4:22–32). We are acceptable to God because we are covered by the righteousness of Christ, but we need to grow toward this righteousness in our daily living so that we become righteous in fact. In Christ to be sure we cannot sin, but the sad truth is that we do not abide in Christ and thereby we fall into sin ever again. The good that we want, we do not do (Rom. 7:19) because we rely not on our Savior but on ourselves.[22]

It is only in Christ that we become aware of the depth and magnitude of our sin, since we do not really know ourselves until our eyes are opened by the illumination of the Holy Spirit. "The light of the Lord alone," says Calvin, "can open our eyes to behold the foulness which lies concealed in our flesh."[23] Luther described our corruption as so "deep and evil . . . that no reason understands it," and therefore "it must be believed from the revelation of the Scriptures."[24]

Our position is that the knowledge of sin comes through both the Law and the Gospel, the Law united with the Gospel. Indeed, sin can be defined in relation to both the Law and the Gospel: it is a transgression of the divine commandment and a violation of God's love as revealed in Christ. Through the Law alone we can arrive at a knowledge of our guilt, but we cannot have a true perception of our sin. We can be awakened to the burden of our guilt through the Law by itself, but we will not know the enormity of our sins until they are exposed in the light of the cross and resurrection of Jesus Christ. The Puritans made a useful distinction between legal and evangelical repentance. We can have sorrow over our guilt as we hear the harsh words of God's law, but we will not be convicted of our sin until we encounter Jesus Christ himself and discover that our sins cost his life. We will not truly repent and forsake our sins until our hearts are regenerated by the Holy Spirit as we hear the message of the Gospel.

MANIFESTATIONS AND CONSEQUENCES OF SIN

While the core of sin is unbelief, its chief manifestations are pride and sensuality. Collective pride, as Niebuhr has trenchantly observed, is probably the worst form of sin, since in this case whole peoples succumb to idolatrous pretension. Racism, sexism, classism, and nationalism are rightly seen as collective expressions of inward sin.

Other incontestable earmarks of sin are lovelessness, hostility, envy, alienation, fear, and cowardice. It can be said that sin excludes spiritual love *(agape)* and perverts natural love. Man's sexual yearnings degenerate into lust while his natural aspirations for the good are converted into the lust for power. Fearfulness too is a product of sin as attested in the Wisdom of Solomon: "For wickedness proves a cowardly thing when condemned by an inner witness, and in the grip of conscience gives way to forebodings of disaster" (17:11 NEB).

Doubt of God can be regarded as the intellectual form of sin. We do not subscribe to Tillich's view that doubt is included in faith. The man of God will doubt himself, his own goodness and worthiness, but he will not deny the promises of God nor the reality of his salvation as a gift of God. Such doubts will occur in his life, but their source is the sin that lingers within him, not the faith implanted in him by the Holy Spirit.

Religiosity is the spiritual form of sin and, indeed, one of its most subtle manifestations. It is well to remember that the polemic of the

Bible is directed not so much against godlessness or secularity as against human religion whereby man seeks to be God or to control God for his own ends. Brunner has made this apt observation: "Even in his worship of God man seeks himself, his own salvation; even in his surrender to the Deity he wants to find his own security."[25]

Biblical faith is very explicit concerning the penalties for sin: guilt, death, hell, moral servitude, and spiritual blindness. Man in sin forfeits his chance for happiness and becomes paralyzed by guilt and captive to forces and powers beyond his control. He faces a future that is dark and foreboding—death, and after death the judgment of God. Sin carries death with it and calls for death (Wisd. of Sol. 1:11–16; Prov. 8:36; John 8:24). "It was through one man," declared the apostle, "that sin entered the world, and through sin death, and thus death pervaded the whole human race, inasmuch as all men have sinned" (Rom. 5:12 NEB; cf. 6:23). But it is not simply physical death but eternal death that awaits the doomed sinner. The imprisonment and destruction of the soul, which is appropriately called hell, is the final outcome of the tragedy of sin.

It is appropriate at this point to give special attention to the maladies of moral servitude and spiritual blindness because of their far-reaching ecumenical implications. In exploring these particular consequences of sin we shall endeavor to bring to light traditional tensions and divisions in the church.

The bondage of the will is affirmed throughout Scripture as one of the principal hallmarks and penalties of sin. After sin man's will is no longer directed toward God but away from God. He finds himself in flight from God rather than in quest for God (Gen. 3:8; Isa. 65:1; Ps. 53:1–3; Rom. 3:11). In his sin he is not only unwilling but also unable to do the good and choose salvation. He may yearn for the good, but he is incapable of pursuing the good. Sinful man is like stubble, which the fire consumes, and he cannot deliver himself from the power of the flame (Isa. 47:14). "Can the Ethiopian change his skin," asks Jeremiah, "or the leopard his spots? Then also you can do good who are accustomed to do evil" (Jer. 13:23). John tells us that the man in sin loves darkness more than light because his deeds are evil; he "does not come to the light, lest his deeds should be exposed" (John 3:19, 20). Fallen man is said to have a "hard and impenitent heart" (Rom. 2:5) and is depicted as "captive to the law of sin" (Rom. 7:14, 23). Paul declares: "For the mind that is set on the flesh is hostile to God; it does not submit to God's law, indeed it *cannot*. . . ." (Rom. 8:7, italics mine).

This biblical conception of man in captivity to sin did not take hold in the church until the time of Augustine. The early apologists and church fathers, including Tertullian and Origen, testified to the freedom of man to choose good or evil. In the fifth century Pelagius went even further and denied the necessity of directly assisting grace for any true service of God on the part of man. He rejected the transmission of a fault or corruption in nature and held that grace was given to those who sought it. He even maintained that "man, if he pleases, can be perfectly free from sin," though he made clear that his reference was to the converted man. He acknowledged that one could never be free of temptation in this life and therefore must always be viligant. Pelagius' heresy was condemned at the Councils of Carthage (in 418) and Ephesus (in 431).

Because Pelagius' views had a certain innate appeal, semi-Pelagianism soon appeared in the church, and it has never been completely eradicated in either Catholicism or Protestantism. John Cassian held that in the renovation of the human will there are two efficient agencies—the will itself and divine grace. It was also his conviction that nature unaided may take the first step in its recovery. Semi-Pelagianism was refuted at the Second Council of Orange (529).

It was Augustine who stated the case for the *servum arbitrium* and thereby counteracted Pelagius' views. While acknowledging the reality of natural freedom in fallen man, he insisted that it is not a freedom to do good. "How then do miserable men dare to be proud of free will before they are liberated or of their own strength after they are liberated?" Free will exists, but it must be renewed or converted into Christian freedom by grace: "We shall then be made truly free when God fashions us . . . not as men, which He has already done, but as good men, which he now does by His grace, in order that we may be *a new creature in Christ.*"[26] While Adam's freedom included both the possibility to sin and to refrain from sinning, the true liberty which Christ brings is a freedom only for obedience.[27] Augustine also affirmed the irresistibility of grace, since the will, when it has true freedom restored to it, has no desire to resist the good.

Thomas Aquinas, whose views came to prevail in Roman Catholicism, believed that man's will is weakened but not enslaved to sin. "Reason remains in possession of its free choice, so as to turn away from God, or turn to Him."[28] Man's will needs to be assisted by grace, but it still retains some freedom to turn toward God. Man remains a free moral agent even in his sin. This view was reflected in the Council of Trent which affirmed that the fall of man does not deface the center of man's nature, his real being, but only curbs and weakens man's original freedom, his originally good will.

Augustine's theology was given prominence again by the Protestant

Reformers, though they appealed more directly to the Bible and sought to eschew philosophical explanations of evil and sin. Neither Luther nor Calvin denied man's natural freedom but were adamant on man's inability to free himself from his servitude to sin. Luther affirmed that man is free "in the realm of things below him" but not "toward God" or "in the kingdom of God."

In contrast to the mainline Reformation the Anabaptists were willing to allow man a certain measure of latitude in coming to salvation. Balthasar Hubmaier maintained that the fall primarily affects man's body and that the spirit of man, though now imprisoned in a fallen body, retains some of its original goodness and freedom. Most Anabaptists held to the view that man has a partial freedom before regeneration, a freedom that enables him to say yes to the call of the Word of God, and then a full freedom after regeneration.[29]

Among the Puritans Jonathan Edwards was noted for his emphasis on man's inability and unwillingness to come to God. Man through his own volition can seek for God, but the Holy Spirit must act in and through his seeking if it is to result in faith and repentance.[30] Edwards went so far as to state that the imagination of the natural man in matters pertaining to religious truth is "totally blind, deaf and senseless, yea dead."[31] Man can nonetheless be stirred to seek for salvation when confronted with the terror and dread of hell. Yet even here the Spirit is very likely present stimulating the natural powers of man, though the Spirit regenerates and indwells only those whom he chooses.

While maintaining that man is created for freedom, Karl Barth insists that true freedom, the freedom to believe and obey Jesus Christ, is outside man's grasp. In his view man "has no freedom for God. He cannot assert any such freedom over against God. He has no freedom in which he may will to help himself."[32] Barth has deep reservations concerning the Roman Catholic doctrine of the surviving *liberum arbitrium,* since it creates the illusion that man of himself can respond to God's grace. This doctrine, he says, "misunderstands and distorts in the most dangerous way the seriousness of sin and therefore the seriousness of the human situation in relation to God."[33]

The universal and inevitable sinfulness of man is staunchly affirmed by Reinhold Niebuhr, though he seeks to stay clear of any philosophical determinism. Because man stands at the boundary between nature and spirit, he is placed in a position where anxiety induces him either to assert himself in pride or lose himself in sensuality. Sin is "inevitable but not necessary." Anxiety is the internal precondition of sin, but with Kierkegaard Niebuhr acknowledges that sin presupposes itself.[34] Anxiety would not predispose man to sin unless there were already present within man a bias toward sin. Yet man sins in freedom, and "man is most free in the discovery that he is not free."[35] It is well to bear in mind that "the same freedom which tempts to anxiety also contains the ideal possibility of knowing God."[36] Niebuhr sees not only the paradox of sin but also the paradoxical character of salvation: though we decide for Christ in freedom, only divine grace working in us enables us to make such a decision. Niebuhr opposes the Reformation view that man is totally helpless until he is acted upon by grace. He wishes to affirm human responsibility as well as the inevitability of sin. We believe that Niebuhr is right that man sins in freedom, but we question whether man comes to God by means of his freedom, if the reference is to natural free will. In our view man must be given a new freedom by grace before he can truly hear and truly obey. It seems that for Niebuhr man has a capacity for faith as well as for sin whereas both faith and the condition to receive faith must be seen as coming from the hand of God.

At times Niebuhr does perceive the truth that man's freedom in coming to God is itself a gift of God's grace. Yet in his apologetics he appeals not to the inherent credibility of the Word of God or to the persuasive power of the Holy Spirit, but to man's uneasy conscience. He believes that we can prepare the way for faith by showing the incongruities and ambiguities in the secular way of life. The apologist can bring man to despair "where he is ripe for faith," though only the grace of God can transmute this into "creative despair" which leads to faith and repentance.[37]

In this whole discussion on freedom it is necessary to distinguish between a natural freedom (free will) and an acquired or renewed freedom (Christian liberty). Man's surrender and obedience to Christ are to be attributed not to his natural free will but to the new freedom created in him by the grace of God. It is not enough for man's will to be assisted or strengthened. It must be converted or turned in an altogether new direction; the whole orientation of man's life must be drastically changed. This indeed is the meaning of conversion.

The gravity of the human predicament is further attested by the impairment of man's reasoning by sin. Sin manifests itself not only in bondage but also in blindness. This is to say that it has serious noetic implications. When Jeremiah declares that "the heart is deceitful above all things" (17:9), he is referring to the root of man's thoughts and imagination (Gen. 6:5).[38] Paul declares that through sin people "became futile in their thinking and their senseless minds were darkened" (Rom. 1:21). Sin not only enslaves man's will but also blinds him to the truth about God and himself. Man in sin is not guided by the light of clear intelligence but gropes in the darkness of fear and resentment.

Any attempt to take the fall of man seriously will radically call into question the capacity of reason to discover or come to the truth. Niebuhr astutely observes that man's reason has become "a servant of the passions of nature within him and a victim of the caprices of nature about him."[39] The structure of man's reason is not impaired, but the way in which he reasons is surely distorted by sin. The Enlightenment ideal of a completely disinterested or impartial reason is a chimera, since the reasoning of the natural man is most assuredly in the service of the sinful craving for power. "The will-to-power," Niebuhr says, "uses reason, as kings use courtiers and chaplains to add grace to their enterprise."[40] In Emil Brunner's view the sinful distortion of reason is most apparent in the realm of the personal, in man's relationship to God. It is least obvious in the impersonal object-world, especially in the pure abstraction reflected in the discipline of mathematics.

Thomas Aquinas sought a synthesis of natural or rational wisdom and morality and the supernatural reality of grace. His position was that reason is disturbed but not blinded by sin. Man's natural powers remain intact though because of sin they are no longer in complete harmony with each other. Man, even fallen man, can still know some valid things about God and his moral law. Human philosophy can be a handmaid to theology, going before it to prepare the way, though it seems that it is an entirely trustworthy handmaid only when employed by the person of faith.[41] Grace does not contravene man's nature but instead builds upon it. Faith does not overthrow man's reason but rather complements and perfects it. This fulfillment of man's rational quest also entails its reorientation, since reason must necessarily be brought into accordance with the new light given by grace.

For Thomas only the miracle of grace permits the man of reason to apprehend the unfathomable mysteries of revelation and to enter into the fellowship of the blessed. Yet supernatural truth could find no lodging in the human soul unless man were enabled to receive it by virtue of his divinely given natural potentialities which are dimmed but not obliterated by sin.[42] Ernst Troeltsch observes: "The morality of reason and the natural-social world is the preparation for grace, with which it is united through the common procession of both from God, through the Divinely ordered continuous ascent from reason and nature to Grace."[43] One must not, of course, lose sight of the fact that in the Thomistic schema there is a discontinuity as well as a continuity between nature and grace and that a leap is required in order to advance from one stage to the other. Moreover, this leap is made possible only by power sacramentally bestowed from above.

The scholastic asseveration that "the natural powers are unimpaired by sin" came under severe criticism by the Reformers. It was their contention that through sin man is completely alienated from God so that it is impossible for him to think correctly in matters that affect his spiritual and moral status before God. Luther put this very emphatically: "Human reason as well as the will has been blinded and turned away from the good and the true."[44] This means that man's natural and social morality are not just transcended by grace but drastically altered if not negated. The Reformers, however, did not always follow through the logic of their position and continued to allude to a universal moral code.

Reformed theology has traditionally affirmed the possibility of a natural knowledge of God and morality on the basis of general revelation and common grace. Yet because of sin this general revelation does not lead man to God or give him a true picture of God; instead it renders man without excuse. The general revelation is the wrath of God that is revealed from heaven against "all ungodliness and wickedness of men who by their wickedness suppress the truth" (Rom. 1:18). This general awareness of God does not prepare man for a special revelation but condemns him to perdition.

THE STORY OF THE FALL

Several reasons can be advanced as to why the story of the fall of Adam and Eve in Genesis 3 is no longer credible to many people today. First a literalistic interpretation has created tensions with the sciences of paleontology and paleethnology, whose findings appear to contradict certain elements in the story. Besides cultural obscurantism, a false determinism has intruded itself in the circles of orthodoxy by which original sin is interpreted as a biological inheritance. Sin comes to be viewed as a genetic deformity, and sex is seen as the locus of sin. This Manichaean strand in theology overlooks the truth that sin is basically a spiritual not a natural defilement, though its infection extends to every part of man's nature. In opposition to this kind of theology Berkouwer prefers to speak of "the guilt character of all sin" rather than of a sin "originally inherited."[45] Moreover, to make sin a necessity of nature is to render it excusable whereas it is totally inexcusable and basically inexplicable.

Another strand in Protestant orthodoxy sees the sin of Adam imputed to his descendants by virtue of the fact that he is the Representative of the human race. This position, known as the federal theory, tends to make man a victim of destiny rather than a willing accomplice in sin. Man's condemnation is made to rest upon the guilt of his first parents. Such a view subverts human responsibility from another angle than the determinist position mentioned above.[46]

Emil Brunner contends that the Genesis account has been given more weight by the church than is warranted by Scripture. According to him this story is not a major formative influence in the scriptural doctrine of the fall.

Yet we must not underestimate the penetrating theological insights in the Genesis story, nor should we disregard the truth that it is inspired by the Holy Spirit of God. Reinhold Niebuhr has astutely remarked that this story must be taken seriously but not literally. In his view it is a myth that accurately reveals the existential situation in which man finds himself in the world. Myth for Niebuhr does not mean a story of mythological deities that dramatizes a universal truth about nature (as in the history of religions school), but a spiritually profound attempt to relate the biblical view of life to the meaningfulness of history.

Karl Barth prefers the term *saga* to myth in this connection, since saga refers to a poetic tale that describes real encounters between God and man. It is a pictorial elaboration of what has occurred in the past. While it is anchored in history, its significance is not limited to a particular history. It has reference to realities that are inaccessible to historical science.

At this point it is important to establish the correct hermeneutical procedure for understanding the "myth" of the fall. In order to discover what the author really intended we must take into consideration the literary genre of the narrative. In this way the literal sense is not less but more respected. The historical critical method throws light upon this tale, as it does upon the creation stories, the stories of the flood, the story of the Tower of Babel, and so on, especially when these are compared to similar tales in other religions of the ancient Middle East. This method cannot give us the theological significance of the account, but it can show that the language or terminology employed is, for the most part, symbolic or mythopoetic rather than univocal. To affirm that there are mythical and legendary elements in the Scripture is not to detract from its divine inspiration nor from its historical basis but to attest that the Holy Spirit has made use of various kinds of language and imagery to convey divine truth.

Paul Tillich sees in the biblical accounts the myth of a transcendent or ontological fall as well as an immanent fall. For Tillich sin is presupposed in the actualization of finite freedom. The fall signifies the transition from essence to existence, essence being understood as an undifferentiated unity out of which all things come. I concur with Niebuhr that this view smacks more of neo-Platonism than of a careful exegesis of Scripture.[47] In the Tillichian perspective the fall is treated no longer as historical guilt but instead as an ontological fate.

Against Tillich Niebuhr affirms the myth of an historical fall, but this does not mean that he sees a literal fall at the beginning of history. The perfection symbolized in the Garden of Eden is the perfection before the act of sin. Man is never in a state of dreaming innocence, since being both free and finite he is always anxious. The Genesis story reveals how man is moved to prideful self-assertion in order to allay his anxiety.

While agreeing with Niebuhr on the symbolic nature of this story we diverge from his interpretation at several major points. First was Adam in a state of anxiety or in a state of communion with God? Does not the fall indicate a passage from communion to a break rather than a transition from anxiety to prideful self-affirmation? Moreover, it is our conviction that this story indicates a first fall before recorded history as well as a universal fall.

Another line of interpretation which extends from Irenaeus to Hegel, and which includes representatives on the contemporary scene, is that Adam represents the childhood of the race. The Garden of Eden is a prehistoric state of primeval innocence out of which both historic virtue and evil emerge. For Hegel the fall is the prerequisite of virtue, since through sinful self-assertion man comes to self-consciousness. In Hegel's view the eating from the tree of knowledge signifies the rise rather than the fall of man.

On the modern scene Gordon Kaufman is one who manifests an affinity with this general position.[48] The fall is an historical process by which primitive man emerges "from a pre-human level of existence" characterized by "innocent spontaneity" to "self-centered autonomy."[49] "Despite the lack of direct historical documentation," he declares, "the fall should be regarded as a genuinely historical event or process; for *we cannot understand the continuing historical processes, filled as they are with hatred and disharmony, guilt and distrust, without presupposing an earlier one through which these came to be what they are.*"[50] In contradistinction to orthodoxy Kaufman rejects the notion that Adam fell as a mature and fully responsible self. At the same time he sees the fall as having more historicity than do Tillich and liberal theologians generally.

Bernard Ramm makes a valiant effort to reconcile the Genesis account with modern paleontology and anthropology by positing an original paradise in a restricted area of the world.[51] He likens it to an oasis in which man was tested but outside of which existed disease and death. While recognizing that great parts of this story are symbolic, he wishes to give it more historical concreteness than does neo-orthodoxy. The origin of man and all other creatures is explained in terms of progressive creationism or creation in stages; he sees the root-species created by divine fiat but allows for modification or development within these parameters.[52] Ramm acknowledges that evolution may be entertained by a biblical Christian as a possible secondary cause in biological science "but to raise it to a metaphysical principle or as the all embracing key or category or scheme of Reality and to cancel out the metaphysical worth of all other possible clues is improper science and doggerel philosophy."[53] Though agreeing with much of what Ramm says on creation and evolution, I have these reservations concerning his position: he does not see demonic sin prior to Adamic sin in the Genesis account; this account nowhere implies that nature was disrupted outside the Garden of Eden.[54]

We see the fall of man as an event that happens in both prehistory *(Urgeschichte)* and universal history. The tale in Genesis concerns not only a first fall and first man but a universal fall and universal man. Adam is not so much a private person as the head of the human race. He is generic as well as first man. He is Everyman and therefore Representative Man. He is the representative of both our original parents and of all humankind, and Paul sometimes combines these two motifs.[55] It is human nature which sins in the Genesis narrative and not simply the first man.

We agree with Brunner that the relation of the primal sin *(Ur-Sünde)* to the many particular sins is not the relation of cause to its effects, or of a law to its manifestations, "but a relation *sui generis,* which has absolutely no analogies at all."[56] Sin is not a natural necessity but a historical inevitability. The sinner can avoid any particular sin, but he cannot escape the taint of sin in all his actions. Kierkegaard, who sought to do justice to the paradox of responsibility and inevitability in sin, affirmed the reality of both original sin and human freedom. One interpreter of Kierkegaard puts it this way: "We come in a sinful context and bring ever new sin to birth, for there is in sin an inscrutable combination of conscious volition and inability to act otherwise."[57]

Original sin is not a biological taint but a spiritual contagion which is nevertheless, in some inexplicable way, passed on through biological generation. Yet it does not become rooted in man until he assents to it and allows it to dominate his whole being.

The fall is not the transition from essence to existence (as in Tillich) but a turning away from God in the life of every person within history. It is not simply "being in the world" (M. Heidegger) that is the cause of man's predicament but being caught up in a rebellion against his Creator, one that was already in effect at the beginning of the race. With Reinhold Niebuhr we affirm not an ontological or transcendent fall but a historical fall.

Yet this does not mean that the story of Adam and Eve as presented in Genesis is itself exact, literal history. Not only Niebuhr but also Jacques Ellul, Paul Althaus, Karl Barth, Raymond Abba, C. S. Lewis, and many other evangelically oriented scholars would concur. Lewis sees this as belonging to the fabulous element in the Bible.[58] James Orr suggests that the Genesis narrative is "old tradition clothed in oriental allegorical dress," but he insists in line with the older orthodoxy that it refers to a fall from an original state of purity.[59] H. M. Kuitert of the Free University of Amsterdam also disputes the literal historicity of the Genesis narrative and maintains that in order to do justice to what the Scriptures intend to teach about man it is not necessary to assume an original created couple in a paradisaical garden.[60]

It seems, however, that the story of the fall does assume that mankind has a common ancestor or ancestors who forfeited earthly happiness by falling into sin. The story has a dual focus: it points not only to generic man but to primal man. Its message holds true in both cases: man is not created a sinner but becomes a sinner through a tragic misuse of his freedom. We also maintain that if the symbolism of both Genesis 2 and 3 is to be taken seriously, the emergence of man is to be attributed to a special divine act of creation and not to blind, cosmic evolution.[61]

The lost paradise is not simply a state of dreaming innocence before the act of sin (as in Hegel and Tillich) nor a utopia in the past (as in some strands of the older orthodoxy) but an unrealized possibility that was removed from man by sin.[62] It represents not an idyllic age at the dawn of history but a state of blessedness or communion with God which has been given to the first man and all men at their creation but which is irremediably forfeited by sin.[63]

We should take care not to make Adam responsible for our sin, as is the danger when Genesis 2 and 3 are interpreted in an exclusively or fundamentally historical sense. But let us not err on the other side by seeing Adam as only a symbol of undeveloped mankind. The fall indicates a passage from communion to a rupture, not a development from innocence to self-actualization and independence.

The story of the fall, like the parable of the stewards who wanted to be masters (Matt. 21:33 f.) and the parable of the prodigal son (Luke 15:11 f.), reveals that sin in its essence is prideful defiance, rebellion against God, seeking to be God. It is not the omission of being but the presumptuous attempt to be like divine being.

Karl Barth has thrown additional light on the status of Adam in his asseveration, which has biblical support, that Christ, not Adam, is the first or true man.[64] It is well to remind ourselves that Jesus Christ is the "image of the invisible God" and the "first-born of all creation" (Col. 1:15). All things were created in him and through him (Col. 1:16). Barth affirms that Adam representing universal man is created in the image of Jesus Christ. Adam's nature is only "a *provisional copy* of the real humanity that is in Christ."[65] Barth is not simply affirming the preexistence of the Word of God but the preexistence of the humanity of Jesus Christ which is latent in the Word. The incarnation was feasible because flesh was not foreign to the nature of the Word or Son of God. This position tends to be corroborated by such passages as 2 Corinthians 8:9, John 8:58, and Revelation 1:8, though at first glance it appears to be contradicted in 1 Corinthians 15 and Romans 5. On the plane of history Adam, to be sure, can be seen as the first man, but in the perspective of eternity it can be argued that Christ is prior to Adam. Paul says that the second man is from heaven (1 Cor. 15:47), and eternity antedates earthly history, since it is the source and ground of historical time. I do not go along with Barth, however, in his conviction that all people are in Christ by virtue of his universal atonement. We are certainly created in his image, but we are restored to his image only through faith.

It may also be asked whether Adam is even the first sinner. The church has always insisted that the sin of angels predates the sin of man. In Genesis 3 the serpent is the symbol of prehuman sin. The myth of the fallen angels is solidly anchored in the biblical witness, and in this sense it is possible to speak of a transcendent fall.[66] Barth rejects this idea as belonging to the marginal area of Scripture, but it is a theme that runs throughout Scripture (cf. Gen. 6:2; Isa. 14:12; Job 4:18; Ezek. 28:14, 15; Jude 6; 2 Pet. 2:4; Matt. 25:41; Luke 10:18; Rev. 12:7–9). Luther was fond of quoting the Wisdom of Solomon 2:24: "Through the devil's envy death entered the world." We must not, however, make the mistake of some well-meaning churchmen in blaming the devil for man's predicament, since man suffers the penalty of death through his own sin (Gen. 3:17–19). At the same time we should not underestimate or deny the reality and power of the demonic hosts of wickedness who entice human beings to sin and who thereby gain control of the destinies of whole peoples and nations. Bondage to sin means captivity to an anti-god power, the prince of darkness. This power is inferior to God but superior to man, and man can only gain freedom from this spiritual force of wickedness through faith in Jesus Christ. The devil goes under many different names in Scripture, and it is well to note that in Revelation 20:2 the devil, Satan, the dragon, and the serpent are all equated.

MODERN OPTIMISM

The Enlightenment of the eighteenth century successfully challenged the Reformation view of man and the world. Not the depravity of man but his natural goodness and perfectibility were affirmed. Sin came to be understood as reason's imperfect mastery of lower impulses or ignorance of man's unique status in the universe. Revelation was seen no longer as a divine intervention into human history but as a continuous unfolding of the truth that is within.[67] Also included in the Enlightenment perspective were man's inevitable progress and the sufficiency of reason to solve the world's problems. It was said that man had come of age (Kant) and need no longer rely upon outmoded, external authorities such as the Bible and the church. The autonomy of man was championed against the heteronomy of orthodox Catholicism and Protestantism. The Kantian axiom "I ought, therefore I can" reflected the growing faith in man's natural powers and resources.

Though basically a child of the Enlightenment Immanuel Kant diverged from the optimism of his age in his conception of radical evil, an inborn evil propensity that is inexplicable to reason. Kant's discovery of this malignant force within man is perhaps to be attributed to the Lutheran Pietistic influence in his upbringing, since it certainly contradicts the prevailing mood of his day as well as the presuppositions of his own philosophy. He was aware that he was faced with a paradox of impenetrable mystery. It should be recognized, however, that Kant did not speak of sin, opposition to God, but of evil which contradicts the abstract law of reason. He also contended in the same work that there remains hope for man because of his naturally good will. Even while gazing into the abyss of darkness that threatens man, Kant would not affirm, as did Calvin and Luther, that man apart from the redeeming grace of God is helpless to help himself in a moral or spiritual sense.

Schleiermacher too represents a departure from at least some aspects of the Enlightenment mentality, especially in his emphasis on feeling over reason. Yet he remained within the basic framework of the new optimism and felt that the era which the Western world was entering gave much hope for peace and progress. Sin is a blocking or arresting of the forward movement of the spirit. He even saw sin as a necessary preparation for grace, as a gateway to the good. Salvation is a continuous strengthening of God-consciousness and a corresponding diminishing of the consciousness of sin. In his thought the kingdom of God is unequivocally identical with the advance of civilization. Belief in a continuing kingdom of Satan would weaken Christian courage and hope. He saw new epochs of humanity which would represent "a palingenesis of Christianity" and awaken its spirit in new and more beautiful forms.[68]

Albrecht Ritschl rejected the doctrine of inherited guilt in order to do justice to human responsibility. At the same time he did not wish to deny or minimize the reality of sin. He spoke of the "indescribable entanglement of sinful acts" and of a "realm of sin" or "kingdom of evil." Yet in his view sin is only a failure to realize ethical values, a seeking after things of inferior rank, an upsetting of the scale of things. He saw evil imbedded in human society and thereby explained sin as a social infection. Sin threatens but does not really bind the freedom of man, since man remains free to resist the evil influences of the world (the kingdom of sin) and also to adopt the higher values of the kingdom of God. Justification is revealed by Christ, but it is made effective only in reconciliation which is a work of man. Barth observes that Ritschl saw only "active or concrete sins"; he did not see the "being of man in sin, in enmity against God."[69] He could speak of the development of an evil character in man, but not of an evil inclination which precedes the evil act.

In Ritschl's thought the kingdom of God is progressively realized in history. It is essentially an ethical ideal, a kingdom of love, which can be partially attained through benevolent action. He saw the human race as being "educatively prepared for the Kingdom of

God."[70] The forward movement of humanity was interpreted as a progression toward this ideal of universal love.

How different is Reinhold Niebuhr's view of culture and history in relation to the kingdom of God. For Niebuhr the kingdom is essentially beyond history, but it impinges on history as the judgment of God on human sin and vanity. The creative achievements of man may signify technical but not moral progress. They are a potent testimony to man's creativity, to the breadth of his knowledge, and may open up new channels for alleviating the misery and oppression in the world. At the same time they are a monument to man's *hybris* or idolatrous pretension and consequently invite new disasters upon the human race. Niebuhr saw that "every higher principle of order to which the soul might attach itself, in the effort to rescue meaning from chaos, is discovered, upon analysis, to have new possibilities of evil in it."[71]

The Social Gospel movement that followed Ritschl pressed his position to its logical conclusion by envisioning a kingdom on earth that can be established through human engineering. The grace of God, it was assumed, would assist man in bringing in the kingdom. The transcendent dimensions of the kingdom were largely disregarded as was the testimony of the Gospels that the kingdom is wholly a gift of grace and would come unexpectedly.

Walter Rauschenbusch, who had a keen sensitivity to the social evils of his time, saw the coming of the kingdom in the "ethical and spiritual progress of mankind."[72] For him sin is transmitted essentially through social tradition. Sin was equated with selfishness and especially corporate selfishness. He believed that sin can be overcome through love and even entertained the hope of "a progressive reign of love in human affairs."[73] While Ritschl still retained some idea of the kingdom as a supramundane reality, Rauschenbusch envisaged the kingdom as a historical force now at work in humanity and destined to include the whole world. The kingdom of God is a new society "in which the brotherhood of man will be expressed in the common possession of the economic resources of society. . . ."[74] It signifies not the destruction of the present social order but the redemption of the "permanent institutions of society." He perceived that the kingdom would not come simply or essentially by human effort, since it is and will remain God's kingdom. Moreover, it will not be finally established apart from a great struggle with the kingdom of evil.

The new Social Gospel of our day mirrors the optimism of the earlier movement, but there is a more ready endorsement of political coercion and violence to insure a just and equitable social order. Harvey Cox sees the secular city as the dawning of the kingdom of God.[75] Locating the essence of sin in slothfulness, he calls upon churchmen to unite with other people of good will and become involved in the cause of social righteousness, for the social revolution that will bring in the new age is already upon us. Richard Shaull, Rubem Alves, and Gustavo Gutierrez urge the violent overthrow of existing orders of oppression so that the kingdom of God can be manifested in the realization of man's hopes for liberation.

While Marx's influence can be detected in the new Social Gospel, Freud's shadow is evident in the pastoral psychology movement. In the view of psychoanalysis and its religious offspring, sin and guilt are experiential, not ontological. Guilt is a feeling that can be overcome by knowledge, not a broken relationship that is restored by divine forgiveness. Man's problem is sickness, not sin; and his greatest need is therapy, not atonement. Paul Tillich has challenged the psychoanalytic view in his contention that while psychotherapy can remove compulsive forms of anxiety by the resolution of inner conflicts, it cannot remove the deeper ontological anxiety, since it cannot change the structure of finitude or the existential situation of man. Pathological anxiety, he says, is amenable to medical healing, while existential anxiety is an object of priestly help. Yet Tillich's stress is on the experience of the power of acceptance and self-affirmation more than on divine forgiveness and atonement.[76]

The New Catholicism also reflects the optimism of a resurgent Enlightenment and thereby shows its distance from an Augustine or a Pascal. For Teilhard de Chardin the human race is surging forward and upward toward an Omega point when Christ will be all in all. An evolutionary stance is indicated in this remark of Andrew Greeley's: "As the world grows ever so slowly toward more love (and hence more order and justice) God grows too in the sense that His immanent loving goodness, still partially chained by the forces of fear and hatred and disorder, is more and more liberated. As man is liberated, God is also liberated."[77] Karl Rahner speaks of all humanity being encompassed by God's grace and of the spirit of Christ indwelling people of all religions so long as they respond to this grace.

For Thomas O'Meara, who leans on both Rahner and Teilhard, this is a "B-minus world," since despite their sin all persons are "surrounded" by God and are beneficiaries of implicit faith.[78] All are on the way to salvation, though they may and do resist the urgings and promptings of grace. Luther on the contrary (and Augustine would agree) would label this an F world, since it is universally corrupted by sin and stands under the wrath of God. At the same time those in Christ would probably be given the mark of A, since his perfect righteousness hides our sinfulness.

In modern evangelicalism a this-worldly optimism is also apparent, despite the fact that it continues to affirm original sin. The historicity of Adam is defended, but the confession that everyone is in Adam is not given its due weight. An undercurrent of semi-Pelagianism is certainly present in the circles of evangelical revivalism where it is assumed that man is free to decide for salvation on his own, though he needs the assistance of grace to carry through his decision. This is not the theoretical position of Billy Graham, whose Calvinism is more evident, though he is sometimes equivocal in this area. In fundamentalism it is widely held that man's will is perverted but that man's reason is only relatively impaired; therefore, reason can prepare the way for faith and even make the truth of faith credible to the unbeliever. Os Guinness, who has broken with fundamentalism at many points, can nevertheless describe faith as "a reasonable decision after rational reflection."[79] Both Guinness and Francis Schaeffer adhere to a theological methodology that is closer to Thomas Aquinas than to Luther or Calvin.

In some circles, particularly in the Holiness tradition, it is sometimes alleged that man can arrive at a state of sanctity that is free from the ambiguity of sin. The continuing sin in the Christian is minimized or denied. What exists in the sanctified Christian, it is said, are faults, not sins. As in Pelagius and Ritschl, sin is defined more in terms of deeds than as a state of estrangement. John Wesley saw that even in the sanctified there is a corruptibility and vulnerability to sin, but he preferred not to call this sin.

The Catholic tradition, including Augustine, refers to an inclination within man that tends to sin called *concupiscence*. Augustine saw concupiscence in the Christian as a spur to sin but not as sin itself. The Reformers in a break with this tradition insisted that not only sinful acts but concuspiscence itself is always sin. It connotes not simply the weakness of the flesh but the opposition of the entire man to God. Luther and Calvin maintained that we can never be free from the presence of sin, but we can be free from its controlling power. Their emphasis was on the struggle against sin, not the victory over sin, and perhaps in their preoccupation with the continuing sinfulness of the Christian they did not do justice to the triumph of grace in the life of the Christian. Some of their followers admittedly exaggerated the helplessness and depravity of man, even the man under grace. The way was thereby prepared for the reaction of Pietism and Wesleyanism which rightly saw that man can overcome in and through grace. But an optimism based on grace must be sharply distinguished from an optimism based on man's resources, the kind of optimism that is reflected in the Enlightenment and the new theology.

NOTES

1. Francis Schaeffer, *Escape From Reason* (Downers Grove, Ill.: InterVarsity Press, 1972,) p. 90.

2. Because of the misunderstandings associated with the phrase *total depravity* Roger Nicole prefers the term *pervasive evil* as more faithful to the Reformed heritage. See Roger R. Nicole, "A Call to Great Preaching" in *Presbyterian Communique* 8:4 (Aug 1975), pp. 1, 2.

3. Augustine, *On Original Sin,* chap. 34. In *Basic Writings of Saint Augustine,* vol. 1, ed. Whitney J. Oates (New York: Random House, 1948), p. 644.

4. For a poignant critique of Augustine's determinism by two contemporary evangelical theologians see Roger T. Forster and V. Paul Marston, *God's Strategy in Human History* (Wheaton, Ill.: Tyndale House, 1974). This book is slightly marred, however, by a palpable bias against Augustine; the authors fail to show where evangelicals can and should appreciate him.

5. John Calvin, *Commentaries on the Epistle of Paul the Apostle to the Romans,* trans. & ed. John Owen (Edinburgh: Calvin Translation Society, 1849), p. 261.

6. Heinrich Heppe, *Reformed Dogmatics,* p. 336.

7. Charles Hodge, *A Commentary on the Epistle to the Romans.* Abridged. (Philadelphia: Perkins & Purves, 1843), p. 137.

8. Piet Schoonenberg, *Man and Sin,* trans. Joseph Donceel. (Notre Dame, Ind.: University of Notre Dame Press, 1965), p. 8. The wrong deed, of course, belongs to the domain of sin, just as bad fruit belongs to a bad tree (and Schoonenberg here would agree).

9. Abraham Kuyper, *The Work of the Holy Spirit,* trans. Henri De Vries (Grand Rapids: Eerdmans, 1900), p. 263.

10. Luther, *Werke* W. A. 10, I, 1, 508.

11. Emil Brunner, *Man in Revolt,* trans. Olive Wyon (New York: Scribner's, 1939), p. 137.

12. Gustaf Aulén, *The Faith of the Christian Church,* trans. Eric H. Wahlstrom and G. Everett Arden (Philadelphia: Muhlenberg Press, 1948), pp. 272, 273.

13. Barth has problems with the Heidelberg Catechism's view that man is inclined by nature to hate God and his neighbor (part I, question 5). See his *Church Dogmatics* IV, 2 (Edinburgh: T. & T. Clark, 1958), p. 441. He also has reservations in speaking of the "poisoned" nature of fallen man as does the Heidelberg Catechism in part I, question 7. Instead he prefers to speak of man poisoning himself in his pride. *Church Dogmatics* IV, 1 (Edinburgh: T. & T. Clark, 1956), p. 494.

14. Barth's stress on the irrationality of sin is paralleled by Berkouwer's emphasis on the absurdity of sin. See G. C. Berkouwer, *Sin,* trans. Philip C. Holtrop (Grand Rapids: Eerdmans, 1971), pp. 130–135, 141–144, 536 f.

15. Karl Barth, *The Word of God and the Word of Man,* p. 170.

16. Karl Barth, *Church Dogmatics* IV, 1, p. 500.

17. Emil Brunner, *Man in Revolt,* p. 105.

18. Reinhold Niebuhr, *The Nature and Destiny of Man,* vol. 1 (N.Y.: Scribner's, 1951), p. 269.

19. *Ibid.,* p. 222.

20. Note that Schleiermacher denies the reality of the temptations of Jesus but affirms his sinlessness. Niebuhr affirms the reality of these temptations but denies the sinlessness of Jesus.

21. This indeed is Alan Richardson's criticism of Niebuhr. See Charles W. Kegley and Robert W. Bretall, eds. *Reinhold Niebuhr: His Religious, Social, and Political Thought* (New York: Macmillan, 1956), pp. 226, 227.

22. We here side with Luther, Calvin, Nygren, and Barth over Origen, Augustine, Brunner, and Bultmann in interpreting Romans 7 as referring to the Christian life and not merely to the pre-Christian experience of Paul.

23. John Calvin, *The Epistles of Paul the Apostle to the Romans and Thessalonians,* eds. David W. and Thomas F. Torrance, trans. Ross Mackenzie (Grand Rapids: Eerdmans, 1961), p. 135.

24. Luther, *Werke* W. A. 50, 221. Cf.: "Through sin we are completely turned away from God, so that we do not think correctly about God. . . . What remains, therefore, is that only through divine revelation in the Word can we know that we are sinners and that God is righteous." *Luther's Works,* vol. 12, ed. Jaroslav Pelikan (St. Louis: Concordia Publishing House, 1955), pp. 309, 341.

25. Emil Brunner, *Revelation and Reason,* trans. Olive Wyon (Philadelphia: Westminster Press, 1946), p. 266.

26. *St. Augustine: Faith Hope and Charity,* trans. Louis A. Arand (Westminster, Maryland: Newman Press, 1963), p. 39.

27. Cf. Augustine: "This is what constitutes true liberty—the joy experienced in doing what is right." *Ibid.,* p. 38.

28. Thomas Aquinas, *Summa Theologica* (first part of the second part, Q. 77, Art. 8. In *Basic Writings of Saint Thomas Aquinas,* vol. 2, ed. Anton C. Pegis (New York: Random House, 1944), p. 643.

29. See Kenneth Ronald Davis, *Anabaptism and Asceticism* (Scottdale, Pa.: Herald Press, 1974), p. 149 f.

30. Edwards affirmed both man's natural ability to seek salvation and his moral inability to find it. For an illuminating study of the meaning of conversion and salvation in Jonathan Edwards see John H. Gerstner, *Steps to Salvation* (Philadelphia: Westminster Press, 1960).

31. Jonathan Edwards, *A Treatise Concerning Religious Affections,* ed. John E. Smith, (New Haven, Conn.: Yale University Press, 1959), p. 274.

32. Karl Barth, *Church Dogmatics* II, 2, p. 29.

33. *Ibid.,* p. 532.

34. Reinhold Niebuhr, *The Nature and Destiny of Man,* vol. I, p. 251.

35. *Ibid.,* p. 260.

36. *Ibid.,* p. 252.

37. *Ibid.*, vol. II, p. 207. Cf. Reinhold Niebuhr, *Faith and History* (New York: Scribner's, 1949), pp. 154–155.

38. Note that *heart* in the Bible means the seat of the intellect as well as the ground of the will and emotions. See Alan Richardson, ed., *A Theological Word Book of the Bible* (London: SCM Press Ltd., 1950), pp. 144–146. See also Johannes Behm's discussion of *kardia* in Gerhard Kittel, ed., *Theological Dictionary of the New Testament,* vol. III (Grand Rapids: Eerdmans, 1965) pp. 605–614.

39. Reinhold Niebuhr, *Beyond Tragedy* (New York: Scribner's, 1937), p. 102.

40. Reinhold Niebuhr, *Moral Man and Immoral Society* (New York: Scribner's, 1932), p. 44

41. "Hence, it is impossible," Thomas says, "for items that belong to philosophy to be contrary to those that pertain to faith; but the former may be defective in comparison with the latter. Yet, they contain some likenesses and some prolegomena to the latter, just as nature is a preamble to grace. If any point among the statements of the philosophers is found contrary to faith, this is not philosophy but rather an abuse of philosophy, resulting from a defect in reasoning." Thomas Aquinas, *Exposition of Boethius on the Trinity,* II, 3, c. In Vernon J. Bourke, ed., *The Pocket Aquinas* (New York: Washington Square Press, 1960), pp. 292, 293.

42. According to Windelband, Thomas understands the relation of natural and revealed theology "as a relation of different stages of development, and sees accordingly, in philosophical knowledge, a possibility given in man's natural endowment, which is brought to full and entire realisation only by the grace active in revelation." Wilhelm Windelband, *A History of Philosophy,* trans. James H. Tufts, vol. I (New York: Harper Torchbooks, 1958), p. 321.

Cf. Henri Bouillard: "The possibility of natural knowledge of God is the transcendental condition for the knowledge of faith." In his "A Dialogue with Barth: The Problem of Natural Theology" in *Cross Currents* 18:2 (Spring 1968), [pp. 203–226] p. 226.

43. Ernst Troeltsch, *The Social Teachings of the Christian Churches,* 3d imp. trans. Olive Wyon (London: George Allen & Unwin Ltd., 1950), p. 268.

44. *Luther's Works,* vol. 12, p. 342. Cf. Calvin: "The light of reason which God imparted to men has been so darkened by sin that scarcely a few meagre sparks still shine unquenched in this intense darkness or rather dreadful ignorance and abyss of errors." John Calvin, *The Gospel According to St. John,* Part I trans. T. H. L. Parker; eds. David W. Torrance and Thomas F. Torrance. (Grand Rapids: Eerdmans, 1959), p. 15.

45. G. C. Berkouwer, *Sin,* p. 530.

46. For an able defense of the Federal theory see A. A. Hodge, *The Atonement* (Grand Rapids: Baker Book House, 1974).

47. See Reinhold Niebuhr, "Biblical Thought and Ontological Speculation in Tillich's Theology" in Charles W. Kegley and Robert W. Bretall, eds., *The Theology of Paul Tillich* (New York: Macmillan Co., 1952), pp. 216–229.

48. See Gordon D. Kaufman, *Systematic Theology: A Historicist Perspective* (New York: Charles Scribner's Sons, 1968). Brunner and Tillich have also been attracted to this position, though both combine it with other perspectives.

49. *Ibid.,* pp. 359, 360.

50. *Ibid.,* p. 353.

51. See Bernard Ramm, *The Christian View of Science and Scripture* (Grand Rapids: Eerdmans, 1954).

52. Ramm's position is close to Carnell's "threshold evolution" which allows for a wide possibility of change within the "kinds" originally created by God.

53. Ramm, *The Christian View of Science and Scripture,* p. 280.

54. We definitely admit the idea that death and corruption were already in the world prior to the creation of our first parents, but this does not necessarily imply that there was a geographical area (the Garden of Eden) that was immune from the curse of death. At the same time we are not closed to this possibility either, though the Genesis account is by itself not a sufficient basis for this kind of speculation.

C. S. Lewis set forth the view that Satan ruled the earth before the creation and that his rebellion against God caused the earth to be disoriented, to become, as he expressed it, "the silent planet." Francis Schaeffer indicates a marked openness to this theory and sees Isaiah 14:16–17 as giving it possible support. See his *No Final Conflict* (Downers Grove, Ill.: InterVarsity Press, 1975), pp. 26–28. As it is stated, the fall of Lucifer "made the earth to tremble" and "made the world as a wilderness" (KJ). According to Schaeffer the Garden of Eden would then be thought of as a prepared garden in a spoiled world, and man was created in order to "have dominion" (Gen. 1:28) in a world that had fallen into chaos. It is debatable whether this is proper exegesis, but the thesis is nonetheless interesting and certainly merits consideration.

55. It is quite clear that Paul, who here reflects his Rabbinic training, uses Adam as a pedagogical example or teaching model. In 1 Corinthians 15:22 Adam is depicted as both the first man and representative man. In Romans 5:12 ff. it is essential to Paul's argument that Adam be the first sinner, though Genesis pictures Eve as the first sinner. In 1 Timothy 2:14 Paul argues that Eve and not Adam was the first sinner again in order to make a pedagogical point.

56. Emil Brunner, *The Christian Doctrine of Creation and Redemption,* trans. Olive Wyon (Philadelphia: Westminster Press, 1952), p. 109.

57. H. R. Mackintosh, *Types of Modern Theology,* 6th printing (London: Nisbet & Co., Ltd., 1949), p. 237.

58. C. S. Lewis regards the story of Adam and Eve as paradigmatic of the fall of Paradisal man, who may have included several persons. "We do not know how many of these creatures God made," he says, "nor how long they continued in the Paradisal state. But sooner or later they fell." In his *The Problem of Pain* (New York: Macmillan, 1962), p. 79.

59. James Orr, *The Christian View of God and the World* (Grand Rapids: Eerdmans, 1948), p. 185. Orr can speak of the tradition of Eden as "mythical," but he sharply distinguishes "myth" in this case from mythology, the stories of the gods rooted in nature-phenomena. He says, "From this element . . . the Biblical religion seems entirely free." In his *The Problem of the Old Testament* (New York: Scribner's, 1906), p. 486.

60. H. M. Kuitert, *Do You Understand What You Read?* (Grand Rapids: Eerdmans, 1970), pp. 35 ff.

61. We are open to the view of Karl Rahner that the first authentic hominisation (coming into being of man) happened only once—in a single couple. Yet

it would not contradict Christian faith "to assume several hominisations [pre-Adamites] which quickly perished in the struggle for existence and made no contribution to the one real saving history of mankind. . . ." In Karl Rahner and Herbert Vorgrimler, *Theological Dictionary,* 3d ed., ed. Cornelius Ernst; trans. Richard Strachan (New York: Herder & Herder, 1968), p. 292.

62. This is not to say that the conditions of paradise were not present at any place in the world. The meaning rather is that paradise could not take permanent root in the world because of man's sin.

63. In the case of our original parents it appears from the Genesis account that there was a certain though very brief time span between their creation and their fall into sin, but let us not be misled into seeing their situation as entirely or substantially different from ours. It seems that the fall occurs in connection with man's coming into the world and gaining self-awareness, but this itself is not a sin nor does it make sin necessary. Inexplicably but indisputably the urge to domination invariably takes control as man finds himself in the world as a responsible being. We can, therefore, say that the original state of blessedness or communion with God is immediately or almost immediately forfeited by sin, and this is true of the first man as well as of all others. We, too, are created as free beings, and we, too, inexcusably fall into sin. Our freedom *in* God and *for* God is irrevocably perverted into a freedom *from* God; as a result we too are plagued with the guilt of a paradise lost. Adam's sin should consequently be seen as typifying the fall of man in general.

64. See Karl Barth, *Christ and Adam,* trans. T. A. Smail (New York: Harper & Row, 1956).

65. *Ibid.,* p. 35.

66. Whether the fall of the angels predates the creation of the world was a matter of debate in nineteenth century German theology. Lange held that the fall of the devil occurred on one of the days of the creative week. Kurtz and others held that the formless and void chaos of the world (Gen. 1:2) was the result of Satan's fall. In historical orthodoxy it is generally agreed that the fall of the angels preceded the creation of man.

67. Cf. Lessing: "Education is revelation coming to the individual man; and revelation is education which has come, and is still coming, to the human race." Gotthold Ephraim Lessing, *Education of the Human Race.* In Henry Chadwick, ed., *Lessing's Theological Writings* (London: Adam & Charles Black, 1956), p. 83.

68. Friedrich Schleiermacher, *On Religion,* trans. John Oman (New York: Harper & Row, 1958), p. 251.

69. Karl Barth, *Church Dogmatics* IV, 1, p. 382.

70. Albrecht Ritschl, *The Christian Doctrine of Justification and Reconciliation,* 3d ed., trans. H. R. Mackintosh and A. B. Macaulay (New York: Scribner's, 1900), p. 304.

71. Reinhold Niebuhr, *An Interpretation of Christian Ethics* (New York: Harper & Row, 1935), p. 68.

72. Walter Rauschenbusch, *A Theology for the Social Gospel* (New York: Macmillan, 1917), p. 225.

73. *Ibid.,* p. 142.

74. *Ibid.,* p. 224.

75. Harvey Cox, *The Secular City* (New York: Macmillan, 1965).

76. See Paul Tillich, *The Courage to Be* (London: Nisbet & Co., Ltd., 1952), pp. 163 ff.

77. Andrew Greeley, *The New Agenda* (Garden City, N.Y.: Doubleday, 1973), p. 127.

78. Thomas O'Meara, *Loose in the World* (New York: Paulist Press, 1974), pp. 68 ff., 119.

79. Os Guinness, *The Dust of Death* (Downers Grove, Ill.: InterVarsity Press, 1973), p. 358. In his *In Two Minds* Guinness speaks of the need for "sure and sufficient reasons for believing" (InterVarsity, 1976), p. 114.

VI.
THE DEITY OF JESUS CHRIST

For to us a child is born, to us a son is given . . . and his name will be
called "Wonderful Counselor, Mighty God, Everlasting Father, Prince of
Peace."

Isaiah 9:6

For in Christ all the fullness of the Deity lives in bodily form. . . .
Colossians 2:9 NIV

Jesus whom I know as my Redeemer cannot be less than God!
Athanasius

You should point to the whole man Jesus and say, "That is God."
Martin Luther

The most pressing question on the problem of faith is whether a man, as
a civilized being . . . can believe in the divinity of the Son of God, Jesus
Christ, for therein rests the whole of our faith.

Fedor Dostoevsky

This Man Jesus Christ . . . does not only live through God and with God.
He is Himself God.

Karl Barth

THE STRUGGLE WITH LIBERALISM

Evangelical theology has been compelled to emphasize the deity of
Christ in its struggle against neo-Protestantism, and today we would
add neo-Catholicism. Against theological liberalism Evangelicals have
insisted that Jesus was not simply a great teacher, a spiritual master,
or a prophet but a divine Savior. In liberalism the significance of Jesus
lies in his teachings or in his unique experience of God, but not in his
Person. Much more attention is given to the life he lived and the
principles he enunciated than to his atoning death and resurrection.
Adolf Harnack contrasted the religion of Jesus, which is an ethical
message, with the religion about Jesus, which supposedly represents
the Pauline distortion of the original Gospel.[1] He saw the Christological dogma as an intrusion of Greek metaphysics into primitive Christi-

120

anity. In the view of David Strauss the true God-Man is not just one person but humanity as a whole. For him Jesus was the first to perceive the essential unity between God and man. Alois Emmanuel Biedermann (d. 1885), Professor of Theology at Zurich, maintained that the church must ascribe redemption to man's religious self-consciousness, not to a mythological God-Man. For Schleiermacher Jesus was not a divine being who assumed human nature but a prophetic figure who fully realized the divine nature that is in all men. He is to be distinguished from other men by "the constant potency of his God-consciousness."[2] In Ritschl's conception Jesus was not one in essence with God, but he was perfectly united and harmonious with God in will. Instead of "the Word made flesh," he was the bearer of a religio-ethical ideal. Troeltsch saw Jesus as a great religious personality, the one who pierces to the highest truth of the spirit and who in this sense has primacy.

The emergence of higher criticism in the church drew attention to the Jesus of history, the famed man from Galilee whose life and personality could be objectively delineated by historical science; yet the pictures that resulted proved to be quite different from the Christ of traditional faith.[3] Martin Kähler convincingly argued that it is neither proper nor possible to go behind the apostolic testimony concerning the Christ in order to reconstruct a scientific picture of Jesus as he really was.[4] Historical criticism can tell us about *Historie* (objective history) but not *Geschichte* (the inner significance of history). Some existentialist theologians (e.g., Bultmann, Käsemann) have seized on this distinction in maintaining that decisive events of salvation like the resurrection and ascension have happened not in objective history but only in personal, existential history. Against both strands of liberalism we contend that the church must begin neither with the Jesus of history nor the Christ of faith but with the historical Jesus Christ of the Scriptures whose identity can only be perceived by faith. We further maintain that the picture that faith gives is identical with the true perception of the historical reality of Jesus.

Among those who effectively challenged the presuppositions of liberal theology and philosophy was Soren Kierkegaard, whose significance was not generally discovered until the 1920s. Kierkegaard particularly reacted against the Hegelian distortion of Christianity as this was reflected in philosophical theology. Whereas liberal and philosophical theologians contended that the object of faith is the most universal, Kierkegaard maintained that it is the absolutely singular as this appears in history. "The object of faith," he says, "is thus God's reality in existence as a particular individual, the fact that God has existed as an individual human being."[5] The Incarnation is not a cosmic process whereby the Absolute goes out of itself and then returns to itself. Rather it is a decisive event in history whereby Eternity enters into time. Such an event is an "absolute paradox" to reason and can only be believed against the understanding. The paradox is not simply that God became man or that the Word of God became historical but that "Christ came into the world *in order to suffer.*"[6] This indeed calls into question the whole classical philosophical tradition whose God is static and impassible.

According to Kierkegaard the teachings of philosophical theology rest on the Socratic method whereby the role of the teacher is to be a midwife, bringing to birth what is already latent within the self.[7] But Kierkegaard maintains that because of sin the truth is not in man and consequently must be given to him from without. The teacher must therefore be a Savior, one who not only embodies the truth but also grants the condition to receive the truth. We are saved not by a teaching that is universally accessible to the mind of man but by a Teacher who converts the will of man.

For Kierkegaard Christianity is not a doctrine about God that can be accepted or rejected, but Jesus Christ himself entering time, confronting man in his sin and calling him to decision. Kierkegaard's challenge to liberalism was therefore more radical and far-reaching than that of Abraham Kuyper, Charles Hodge, and J. Gresham Machen in that he demonstrated the fallacy of viewing Christianity as a static deposit of truth, as a doctrine amenable to rational appropriation. Yet Christianity certainly entails doctrine, and perhaps his existentialism did not do justice to the intellectual dimension of the faith. At the same time he cogently showed that Christianity understood as the entry of the living God into human history demands the passionate response of faith, which would not be the case if it were essentially a doctrine or teaching. Kierkegaard reflects the aversion of Pietism to speculative or philosophical theology.

P. T. Forsyth was another effective spokesman for evangelical Christianity. He too perceived the deleterious effects of Hegelian and other types of philosophy upon Christian thought. He particularly objected to the ideas that the incarnation is a universal process rather than a decisive event in time and that Jesus is simply the sign or mirror of divine love which is everywhere present.

It is of course rather a serious thing to think of the Incarnation as the consummation of a process whether within God, or within the world, or both;

a process whose composure is affected but not fatally perturbed by sin, in which sin is not utterly damning and damnable, only deplorable and dreadful; a process which moves on to a growing but hardly redemptive reconciliation, of a more or less ideal cast. It all tends to make the agony of the Cross gratuitous, the judgment in it but collateral, the wrath of God a metaphor, and the horror in the guilty conscience overdone.[8]

The dialectic theology associated with the names of Karl Barth and Emil Brunner also signalized a powerful countermovement to theological liberalism and modernism. Bernard Ramm has correctly observed that the older liberal theology was not forced into retreat until the emergence of neo-orthodoxy.[9] While Brunner's views on the Person of Christ are not altogether adequate, Karl Barth has given a powerful affirmation of the divine Personhood and twofold nature of our Lord: "As very man Jesus Himself is the Son of God and therefore of divine essence, God by nature."[10] The early Barth, like Kierkegaard, perhaps went too far in asserting that history does not really tell us anything of significance about Jesus Christ. At the same time he reminds us that the object of our faith is not Jesus after the flesh, the man of Galilee who can be directly perceived as such, but the heavenly Son of God, who was incarnate in Jesus and whose identity can only be known by faith. Barth's espousal of the preexistence of Christ, the virgin birth, and the bodily resurrection of our Lord mark his Christology as orthodox and biblical in the best sense of these words.

THE NEW TESTAMENT WITNESS

The core of Christological doctrine as developed in the church is to be found in the Scriptures and particularly the New Testament. The New Testament is unequivocal in asserting the deity of Christ. Paul declares in Colossians 2:9: "For in him the whole fulness of deity dwells bodily. . . ." (cf. Col. 1:19). In Titus 2:13 Jesus is referred to as "our great God and Savior" (cf. Matt. 4:7; John 20:28; 2 Pet. 1:1). The author of Hebrews describes Christ as "the effulgence of God's splendour and the stamp of God's very being," the one who "sustains the universe by his word of power" (1:3 NEB). In verse 8 Christ is addressed by an angel echoing one of the Messianic Psalms (45:6): "Thy throne, O God, is for ever and ever, the righteous scepter is the scepter of thy kingdom."

Bruce Metzger convincingly argues that Romans 9:5 gives a clear affirmation of the deity of Christ, though the Revised Standard Version reflects another interpretation.[11] This controversial verse is translated in the Jerusalem Bible this way: "They are descended from the patriarchs and from their flesh and blood came Christ who is above all, God for ever blessed!" The New International Version gives this rendering: "Theirs are the patriarchs, and from them is traced the human ancestry of Christ, who is God over all, forever praised!" In verses such as this where the precise meaning is in doubt, one must consider not only the immediate context but also the wider context, which in this case means the whole Pauline corpus.[12]

The prologue of the Fourth Gospel is the touchstone of orthodox Christology. "In the beginning was the Word," declared John, "and the Word was with God, and the Word was God" (1:1; cf. 5:26). It is this Word that assumed human flesh and "dwelt among us, full of grace and truth" (1:14). Unlike Philo and those in the general stream of Gnosticism, all of whom regarded the Logos as an intermediary between God and man, John sees the Logos as on a par with deity or as deity itself.

Moreover, it can be shown that the title Lord (kúrios) when applied to Christ generally indicates divinity, and in the Pauline Epistles this is always the case.[13] Paul speaks of the one whom he variously calls "the Lord Jesus Christ," "the Lord Christ," and "the Lord Jesus" as being in "the likeness of God" (2 Cor. 4:4) and "the form of God" (Phil. 2:6). The glory of this Lord is equivalent to and indeed surpasses the divine glory that shone on the face of Moses (2 Cor. 3:7, 8). Paul virtually equates the risen Lord Jesus with "the Spirit" as well as intimating that the Spirit proceeds from the Lord (2 Cor. 3:17, 18). The "Lord Jesus Christ" is even more closely identified with the "beloved Son" (Col. 1:13) who is "before all things" and through whom "all things were created" (1:16, 17). In 1 Cor. 2:8 Christ even in his humiliation is called "the Lord of glory" because he possessed the divine splendor of light (doxa) and was able to bestow this on men. A parallelism between Lord, Spirit, and God is drawn in Ephesians 4:4–6 where Paul links the unity of Christ, as the one Lord of Christian worship, with the unity of God the Father and the unity of the Spirit. In the mind of the apostle "the whole majesty of Christ" lies in the predicate Lord.[14] Wherever Christ is depicted by Paul as subordinate to God, this should be understood as referring to the mode of his redemptive activity, not to his trinitarian being.[15] The "divine nature was his from the first" (Phil. 2:6 NEB), but he let go of his essential equality with the Father in order to identify himself with the misery and guilt of a fallen race.

In the Synoptic Gospels it is not always clear whether the title Lord when applied to Jesus indicates Messianic divine glory as well as formal authority and jurisdiction, but the former is evident in many passages. In Luke 2:11 the angelic annunciation to the shepherds that a "Savior" is born "who is Christ the Lord" definitely carries the connotation of divinity. That the evangelists apply to Jesus the incommunicable name of *Yahweh* (Jehovah) from Isaiah 40:3 in discussing the mission of John the Baptist as the forerunner of the Lord indicates that they understand Christ as divine (Mark 1:3; Matt. 3:3; Luke 3:4). In his discussion of David's words in the 110th Psalm, Jesus, with obvious reference to himself, argues that the Messianic Lord has a dignity very much greater than could belong to him simply as David's son (Mark 12:36, 37).

In Acts Jesus is depicted as the one who has been exalted to the right hand of God in heaven (2:33; 7:56), the one who has thereby been made "Lord and Christ" (2:36). He is both the giver of eternal life and the Lord of life (3:15; 5:31). It is often difficult to determine in this book whether by "Lord" Jesus or God is meant. Peter designates Christ as "Lord of all" (10:36), a phrase that recalls to mind Paul's declaration in Romans 9:5 that he is "God over all" (NIV).

The Messianic title *Lord* reappears in the Book of Revelation as well as comparable titles *Son of Man* and *Word of God,* which likewise connote divinity. This book does not apply to Christ the simple title of "God," but he is represented emphatically as God himself, as the living one (1:18), eternal (1:8), omniscient (1:14; 2:18; 19:12), in whose hands are the keys of death and hell (1:18). In Revelation 19:16 he is portrayed as the "King of Kings" and "Lord of Lords." The one who is called the "Lord Jesus" is represented as saying: "I am the Alpha and the Omega, the first and the last, the beginning and the end" (22:13; cf. 1:17, 18; 2:8; 21:6).

The phrase *Son of Man,* which frequently occurs in the Gospels, can signify either a prophet called by God (as in Ezekiel) or the Messianic messenger from heaven, who carries the aura of divinity. In the latter sense it is derived from Daniel 7:13, 14 and some Jewish apocalyptic writings not found in the Old Testament. In the Similitudes of the Book of Enoch this Messianic figure is called variously "the Elect One, "the Anointed One" and "the Son of Man." Jesus frequently uses this term of himself to describe not only his earthly mission but also his ultimate triumph as Redeemer and Judge (Matt. 16:27 f., 19:28; 24:30; 25:31; Luke 12:8–10; 18:8; John 5:27; 8:28; 13:31). In Acts Stephen at his martyrdom is given a glimpse of coming glory: " 'Behold, I see the heavens opened, and the Son of man standing at the right hand of God' " (Acts 7:56). In the Book of Revelation Jesus is said to be "like unto the Son of man" (1:13; 14:14 KJ) thereby again recalling the Danielic vision of a Messianic emissary of God. Jesus adopts the apocalyptic title *Son of Man* but gives it a connotation of his own, since he identifies himself with the "suffering servant" of Isaiah 53 pointing out that "the Son of man came not to be served but to serve, and to give his life as a ransom for many" (Matt. 20:28).

Finally we would do well to consider the title *Son of God.*[16] In the Scriptures this term has a variety of meanings, but it is applied to Jesus Christ in a special and unique sense. His sonship is natural (John 16:28) whereas the sonship of his followers is acquired (John 17:22; Gal. 4:5). He is the unique Son (John 1:18) who has made all the other sons of God possible. His sonship is rooted in his fundamental nature as un-created and eternal. In Jewish thought at the time of Christ the phrase *Son of God,* like *Son of Man,* was a Messianic title indicating the function of deliverer (cf. Matt. 26:63; Luke 4:41; John 11:27). The voice from heaven at his baptism announcing "This is my beloved Son" was taken by Jesus as a revelation of his Messiahship. With the resurrec-tion there came on his part a complete awareness of his divine Sonship (Matt. 28:18–20).

At the same time the New Testament is equally adamant that Jesus Christ existed as a real man. Paul declares that he was "born of woman, born under the law" (Gal. 4:4; cf. Phil. 2:7). He shared in the same "flesh and blood" as fallen humanity (Heb. 2:14). In the days of his flesh he "offered up prayers and supplications, with loud cries and tears. . . ." (Heb. 5:7; cf. Matt. 26:36–46). He advanced "in wisdom and stature" and in the favor of God and man (Luke 2:40, 52 KJ). He pointed his hearers not to himself but to God, the one who alone is good (Matt. 19:17). He "became obedient unto death, even death on a cross" (Phil. 2:8). The Apostles' Creed declares on the basis of the New Testament witness that he was "crucified, dead and buried." After his resurrection his humanity was still intact and indeed still visible (Luke 24:39).

The picture of Christ that the New Testament presents is incontest-ably enigmatic and paradoxical. He was a man born in a stable of lowly parentage, and yet he was begotten of the Father from all eternity (John 1:14 KJ; 8:42). He had physical needs and desires including hun-ger and thirst and such genuinely human passions as anger, pity, and sorrow; yet in his innermost being he was united with the eternal Father in heaven (John 10:30, 38). He was tempted to despair in the Garden of Gethsemane (Mark 14:32–37) and again at Calvary (Mark 15:34), and yet because of his indissoluble unity with God he triumphed over death by rising from the grave. He predicted his future death and resurrection as well as his coming again at the end of history, but at the same time he confessed that he did not know the day or the hour when the eschatological event would take place (Matt. 24:36; Mark 13:32).

To construct a purely scientific picture of the historical Jesus that ignores this central paradox and mystery is to miss the reality of Jesus as the Christ. To do justice to his Messianic identity and mission means to develop a Christology in which the faith of the church plays as decisive a role as historical investigation. In this enterprise philosophical terminology will necessarily be employed, though such terms will inevitably be transformed in the light of the Word of God as they are used in the service of his glory.

JESUS CHRIST—TRUE GOD AND TRUE MAN

On the basis of its fidelity to the scriptural witness the church has declared that Jesus Christ is true God and true Man in One Person. As the Creed of Chalcedon (451) so powerfully enunciates, he is consubstantial with the Father according to his divinity and consubstantial with us men (except for sin) according to his humanity. He is both the Revealing God and Representative Man. He is invisible as true God and visible as true Man (K. Barth).

The early church fathers generally sought to affirm the true humanity as well as the full deity of Jesus Christ, though the Christology of the church was only decided on after often fierce theological battles resulting in the Councils of Nicaea and Chalcedon among others. While professing a fidelity to the Scriptures many of the early fathers, nonetheless, tended to underplay the humanity of Christ in favor of his divinity. The influence of Hellenistic philosophy, which denigrated the world of matter, was certainly a significant contributing factor. Clement of Alexandria remarked, "It would be ridiculous to imagine that the body of the Redeemer, in order to exist, had the usual needs of man."[17] Too often the fathers fled from the manhood of Christ to the Godhead with the plea that the flesh profits nothing.

The Protestant Reformers countered this trend by stressing the humanity of Jesus but viewing it as inseparable from his divinity. It was said that the deity of Christ can be known only in his humanity. In Luther's words: "I have no God whether in heaven or in earth, and I know of none, outside the flesh that lies in the bosom of the Virgin Mary. For elsewhere God is utterly incomprehensible, but comprehensible in the flesh of Christ alone."[18]

One must be careful not to confuse the incarnation with a metamorphosis. God did not change into a man, as in Greek mythology. Instead the Son of God adopted human nature and united it with his divine nature in the unity of one person. As the Athanasian Creed expresses it: "He is one not by conversion of the Godhead into flesh, but by taking of the manhood into God" (Art. 35). Christ in his incarnation did not cease to be God, but he chose to meet us on our level in the garb of human flesh.[19]

In formulating its Christology the early church had to guard against certain heretical or mistaken notions. Arius saw Jesus Christ as an angelic being created by God and therefore less than God but higher than man. Apollinaris averred that Christ had a human body but a divine soul, a position that tended to call into question both his full divinity and his humanity. In the view of Paul of Samosata Jesus was adopted into union with God through the grace of God. For him the Logos existed in Jesus not personally or essentially but only as a quality. The Monophysites held that the human nature merged into the divine. Nestorius on the contrary affirmed both natures but refused to give them any substantial unity. The two natures were loosely associated, not organically related, and therefore it seemed that Jesus had two different personalities. The impression is given that the Word of God never actually became incarnated but simply joined himself to a human nature.

Against the Monophysites the Chalcedonian creed affirmed two natures "without confusion and without change." The two natures coexist in Jesus Christ; they do not merge into one another. Against the Nestorians, Chalcedon stated that the two natures exist "without division and without separation." While its latter day critics have accused Chalcedon of intellectualizing the faith, it actually succeeded in safeguarding the fundamental mystery and paradox of the faith. Thielicke comments that it focused attention not on "the intellectual difficulties in the foreground" but "on the kerygmatic core, on the person of Christ himself."[20]

In Jesus we do not have a perfect blending of deity and humanity. There is no absorption of the humanity into deity. We cannot go along with Gregory of Nyssa (d. 400) who likened the human nature of Christ to a drop of vinegar which is completely encompassed and absorbed in the vastness of the ocean. Nor is there merely a reflection of deity in his humanity. Every part of his being is indwelt by deity, and yet no part is bereft of humanity.

There is no simple equation of God and Jesus, but neither can there be any separation.[21] God has united himself with the manhood of Jesus, and yet deity remains forever distinct from humanity. We affirm not the transmutation of God into the man Jesus but the coinherence of God and man in Jesus Christ (John 14:11). This must be taken to mean not that Jesus Christ is a third being between God and man but that he is the One who is fully God and truly man. He is not God alongside of man but God *in* man.[22] There is an identity of God the Son and the Person of Jesus, but this identity is veiled by Jesus' true humanity. The perfect manhood of Jesus was not assimilated into deity but instead was made its chosen vessel.

Jesus is humanly personal but has no independent human existence, since the center of his being is the Word of God, the second Person of the Trinity.[23] His human nature is personalized in the divine Logos who assumes it.[24] Jesus Christ must not be thought of as being autonomous or self-existent. God is the acting subject, and the manhood of Jesus is the predicate of the Godhead. This means that Jesus Christ differs from other men in kind and not simply in degree. He is set apart from the human race in that his origin is in heaven. Yet he has assumed human nature in order to identify with the trials and tribulations of mankind. He lived among us and died as one of us, and yet he was qualitatively different from us.

The union of the two natures in Christ is to be regarded as unique and incomparable. It is both a personal (or hypostatic) and an ontological union. Thomas Aquinas rightly observed that this union is neither accidental nor essential (as we find between the persons of the Trinity) but profoundly personal, since the two natures coexist in One Person. It does not signify a union whereby humanity is mingled with deity so that a third entity results; instead it entails the intimate and perpetual conjunction of two natures into unity with one person, with each nature retaining its distinctive properties (Heppe). It is more fundamental than a union of grace, though it is effected by grace. It means a union so personal and intimate that human being, even under the conditions of estrangement, is virtually transparent to divine being, though this can be grasped only by the eyes of faith. The hypostatic union represents an ontological union, since human being at the deepest level participates in and is directed by divine being. Yet the humanity of Christ is never displaced by his divinity; both natures remain intact without any confusion or conversion of one into the other.

Calvin compared the two natures of Christ to the two eyes of man: "Each eye can have its vision separately; but when we are looking at anything . . . our vision, which in itself is divided, joins up and unites in order to give itself as a whole to the object that is put before it."[25]

The deity of Christ necessarily entails his sinlessness, for God cannot sin. He was truly tempted, but he never yielded to temptation (Heb. 2:18; 4:15). He is portrayed as the lamb "without blemish or spot" (1 Pet. 1:19). He "committed no sin; no guile was found on his lips" (1 Pet. 2:22; cf. 2 Cor. 5:21). The reason he appeared was to take away sins (1 John 3:5), so he himself had to be victorious over sin.

Jesus spoke of God alone as good (Matt. 19:17) because the people could then accept him only as a teacher or prophet. Their eyes had not yet been opened to his Messianic identity, for he was not yet risen nor had the Holy Spirit been given. It is consequently only faith in the risen Christ that perceives the perfection of Jesus in the ambiguity of his humanity.

Barth contends with some biblical support that Christ assumed fallen human nature and not simply human nature (cf. 2 Cor. 5:21; Heb. 2:14, 17, 18). The implication which he intends, however, is not that Christ became a sinner but rather that he identified himself completely with fallen humankind in its frailty and dereliction. In bearing our guilt and shame our Lord did not in any way contribute to human apostasy. He was by no means an unwitting accomplice in man's sin but instead a vicarious sin-bearer. His sinlessness was not an innocence that is sheltered from evil but a perfect love that enters into evil and transforms it.

To uphold the deity of Jesus Christ also means to affirm his preexistence. Paul referred to this when he declared: "Though he [Christ Jesus] was in the form of God," he "did not count equality with God a thing to be grasped, but emptied himself, taking the form of a servant. . . . " (Phil. 2:6,7; cf. 1 Cor. 15:47; 2 Cor. 8:9; Col. 1:15–17). The preexistence of Jesus is indicated in this prayer of his: "Glorify thou me in thy own presence with the glory which I had with thee before the world was made" (John 17:5; cf. 1:1–3). We affirm not the preexistence of the flesh but the preexistence of the Word of God and the humanity that was latent in the Word.[26]

The full meaning of the incarnation is likewise tied to the Virgin Birth of Christ. It is important to understand that the Virgin Birth signified the conception not of an independent human personhood (personalitas) but of a human nature. Jesus Christ united human flesh with his divine Person. The doctrine of the Virgin Birth safeguards and communicates the significance of the event of the incarnation. It does not prove the incarnation but serves to convey the reality of the incarnation from one generation to another. This doctrine is not necessary for one's salvation, but it is necessary for the preservation of the integrity of the faith. Karl Barth maintains that the Virgin Birth marks off the origin of Christ from the human race just as his end is marked off by the resurrection.

We do not discount certain legendary elements in the Virgin Birth stories as contained in Luke and Matthew, but it is to be remembered that these stories form part of the authentic New Testament witness and were overwhelmingly accepted by the apostolic church.[27] Containing the ring of truth they are assuredly self-authenticating. We dispute the view of Niebuhr and Brunner that they were later additions made for the purpose of apologetics. They contain too many discrepancies and unanswered questions to be of apologetic value.

We also take issue with Brunner's allegation that the Johannine Prologue was quite probably placed in opposition to the doctrine of the Virgin Birth. Several scholars including C. C. Torrey, Theodor Zahn, and Oscar Cullmann regard the singular "who was born" in John 1:13 as the original reading, and this would mean that John is actually affirming the Virgin Birth. Whatever the case it cannot be doubted that the Virgin Birth is a type of the new birth that must happen to every Christian.

Against some fundamentalists we contend that the Virgin Birth of Christ is not proved by Old Testament prophecy, but we do believe that it is genuinely witnessed to in Isaiah 7:14, since this text is quoted in support of the Virgin Birth in Matthew 1:23. The prophet in Isaiah 7 was not only promising deliverance to Judah in the then near future but was also looking forward to the wondrous birth of Immanuel ("God with us") who would bring deliverance to all peoples.[28] Whether the Hebrew word *almah* must be translated as *virgin* in this case, and whether the prophet himself expressly had in mind the Virgin Birth of Christ are probably open to question, but that his prophecy firmly points to this birth, that it finds its spiritual fulfillment in the miraculous coming of Christ into human history is incontrovertible.[29]

The Virgin Birth of Christ itself is not the central mystery of faith, but like the empty tomb it is a sign that serves to communicate this mystery. It is not itself the stumbling block, but it is a potent witness to the real stumbling block of faith—the Son of God becoming man and taking upon himself the sin and guilt of humankind.

Finally, in our discussion of orthodox Christology it is incumbent upon us to affirm the eternal incarnation of Jesus Christ. On the third day the humanity of Jesus was resurrected from the grave and continues to coexist with his deity throughout eternity. The Shorter Westminster Catechism states that Christ "being the eternal Son of God, became man, and so was and continueth to be, God and man in two distinct natures and one person for ever" (question 21). As Donald Baillie points out: "If we believe in the Incarnation, we cannot possibly say that Jesus ceased to be human when He departed from this world."[30] Cyprian proclaimed that the Savior Jesus Christ "who once conquered death for us, is continually conquering it in us."[31] The same Jesus who rose from the dead now intercedes for us at the right hand of God in heaven and also comforts and strengthens us by his indwelling Spirit.

AREAS OF TENSION WITHIN THE CHRISTIAN FAMILY

Although both endorse the Chalcedonian definition concerning Christ, Roman Catholic and Reformed Christologies diverge at several important points. First the well-known Catholic (and Eastern Orthodox) concept of the interpenetration of the two natures causes some problems. In this idea the human nature is elevated to its culmination point. Reformed theology sees the danger of the altering or transfiguration of the human nature. The question can be posed as to whether Rome does justice to the full reality of the human nature of Christ. Reformed theology insists that all that is truly human, including limitation and growth, is found in Christ. Calvin's conception of two distinct natures united in One Person would seem to guard against any downplaying of the humanity of Christ. In Reformed (and Lutheran) theology Christ takes on our weakened humanity in all its imperfections and limitations. Roman Catholic Christology historically sees Christ's human nature as an elevated and glorified human nature.

This Monophysite tendency in Catholic thought is apparent in Thomas Aquinas. For Thomas, the person of the God-Man is completely perfected from the Virgin Birth onwards. In Christ there exists neither faith nor hope, since both are excluded by his perfect vision of God. Thomas teaches that the Logos takes impersonal humanity *(anhypostasia)* upon himself, but it seems that there is no real union between the two natures, since only man *becomes* and not God. The divine Logos does not really enter into the suffering and travail of the human nature, but the human nature on the other hand is elevated or transfigured by the divine nature. It seems that the union is real only in the human nature, since divinity remains unaffected. H. R. Mackintosh suggests that this is, at bottom, a Monophysite view.[32]

In contemporary Catholic thought voices can be heard that warn against the danger of Monophysitism. Yves Congar holds that a Monophysite tendency is definitely present in much popular Catholic preaching, teaching and devotion.[33] Too often, he says, Christ is thought of as not having a true or complete human nature. It sometimes appears that God is only making use of a human body.

The notions of Mary as co-mediatrix and co-redemptrix also tend to betray a Monophysite point of view. The logic of this position is that Mary provides the human side of salvation while Christ provides the divine side. Both Schillebeeckx and Rahner see Monophysite tendencies in the co-redemptrix idea.

Luther and Calvin both affirmed the reality of suffering and struggle in the life of Christ as well as a growth toward a deeper maturity and fidelity. This seems definitely in accord with the Epistle to the Hebrews where it is said that Jesus "learned obedience through what he suffered" and was "heard for his godly fear" (Heb. 5:7, 8). Luther assented to the impassibility of the Godhead as an abstract proposition but confessed on the basis of Scripture that God at the same time shared in the anguish and searchings of Jesus Christ: "For if I believe that the human nature alone suffered for me, then is Christ worse than no Savior to me."[34]

Another area of difference is that Catholic theology (Roman, Greek, and Anglo-Catholic) tends to view the incarnation as a cosmic principle working from the union of God and man apart from the cross of humiliation.[35] Reformation theology on the other hand subordinates the incarnation to the atonement and, therefore, stresses its historical particularity. The accent is not on a process of divinization begun in the incarnation of Christ but on the removal of the penalty of sin by the death of Christ. In Reformed thought the incarnation has significance primarily because of its relation to the vicarious sacrifice of Christ on Calvary. What is of crucial importance for us is not simply that the Word of God appeared in human flesh but that "God was in Christ reconciling the world to himself" (2 Cor. 5:19). It is not the incarnation of the Word as such that is the content of our preaching but rather the "Lamb of God, who takes away the sin of the world" (John 1:29). Luther put it this way:

Christ is not called Christ because He has two natures. What is that to me? That He is by nature God and man is for Himself. But what gives me comfort and blessing is that He so applies His office and pours forth His love and becomes my Saviour and Redeemer.[36]

Certain points of divergence can also be discerned between Reformed and Lutheran Christologies. Lutheran theology has emphasized the *communicatio idiomatum,* the mutual participation and exchange of the properties of the individual natures. The Formula of Concord asserts not a transfusion but a perpetual communication of the qualities of one nature into the other. The Reformed view has been governed by the principle of *finitum non capax infiniti* (the finite is not capable of receiving the infinite). Karl Barth reflects this orientation in his assertion that the Word does not become but assumes flesh. The unity between the two natures in classical Reformed theology is an indirect one—through the Person or the Spirit who unites Jesus and Christ. In Lutheran Christology the divine nature totally governs the human nature. Reformed theology must forever be on guard against Nestorianism. Its position on the union of the two natures has been likened, perhaps unfairly, to two planks united by glue at one end. Lutheran theology on the other hand must resist the temptation to Monophysitism and docetism, though it seeks to maintain the humanity of Christ intact.

TWO TYPES OF CHRISTOLOGICAL HERESY

Two general types of Christological heresy can be discerned, and virtually every erroneous notion concerning the person of Christ can be subsumed under one of these headings. The first is the ebionite type of heresy, derived from the Christian Jewish sect of the same name which denied the full divinity of Christ. Jesus is here thought of as a religious genius, the greatest of the prophets, a spiritual master, a guru, but not the very God himself. The docetic type of heresy affirms the divinity of Christ but does not do justice to his humanity. It is said that Christ only appeared in the flesh of Jesus or that he only seemed to die. While the ebionite type of heresy begins with the humanity of Jesus and seeks to relate this to his deity, the docetic type begins with the deity of Christ but never truly arrives at his humanity. Both these aberrations have their source in the attempt to rationalize or resolve the Christological paradox—that Jesus was truly God and truly man in one Person. In both we see the attempt to exalt one nature at the expense of the other. Both are unable to unite the Jesus of history and the Christ of faith. Whereas the ebionite view has an affinity with Nestorianism and Arianism the docetic view is allied with Monophysitism and Apollinarianism.

In the ebionite perspective Jesus is a divinized or Spirit-filled man. In some circles he becomes a superhuman being but not quite a divine being. Schleiermacher saw Jesus as "Elder Brother" and "Archetypal Man," but not as the divine Savior from sin. His Christology also contains an even more marked docetic strand, as will be shown later. In Ritschl's theology Jesus is the prophet and foremost representative of the kingdom of God, the new humanity inspired by the ideal of love.[37] Tolstoy regarded Jesus as the greatest of all ethical teachers. In the view of Rauschenbusch Jesus was the "perfect religious personality, a spiritual life completely filled by the realization of a God who is love."[38] Donald Baillie can also be criticized for ebionite tendencies in that he understands the union between Jesus and Christ in terms of the paradox of grace and freedom and not as an ontological union. It is sometimes said that Jesus was adopted as the Son of God at his baptism, but this denies his preexistence. We must not say that Jesus *becomes* the Christ but that he *is* the Christ by virtue of being united from his conception with the Eternal Word of God. Current theology, which sees Jesus as liberator and political revolutionary, also has a disturbing ebionite cast.[39]

In the docetic type of heresy the eternal core is not the person of Jesus Christ but an overarching pattern or truth that is exemplified in Christ. Christ becomes an eternal principle, a pattern for life, a divine force or Absolute Spirit. But he is not the Concrete Absolute, God existing in human form in a particular time and place. He is the Word as timeless truth but not the Word as living address. In Apollinarianism God takes a temporary human disguise. William Blake saw Christ as the unifying principle of all immortal beings. For Schleiermacher Jesus is the creative type of the new life and of freedom. He is the *Urbild*, the perfect ideal of religious truth. What is crucial is not his Person but the ideal that he actualized.[40] Tillich rejects the doctrine of the two natures and following Hegel contends that in Jesus the "eternal unity of God and man has become historical reality."[41] He says that we should pray not to Jesus but to the Christ Spirit, to the New Being that was manifested in Jesus. As Schleiermacher spoke of the *Urbild*, so Tillich speaks of the biblical picture of Christ which would be valid even if Jesus as a man had not existed. Emil Brunner, despite his opposition to docetism, also disputes the doctrine of the two natures and refers to the "human disguise" or "historical mask" of Christ. It would be unfair to label Brunner a docetist, but it seems that he never quite succeeds in bringing together the Jesus of history and the Christ of faith.

In our view Jesus is not an appearance of God or a mask of God. Neither is he a product of "creative emergence" or human evolution.

He represents not the maturation of the human spirit but the condescension of the holy God. Yet through this condescension manhood is
exalted by being brought into union with Godhood. With keen insight
Barth describes him as "the Lord humbled for communion with man
and likewise the Servant exalted to communion with God."[42]

Charles Whiston, veteran missionary to China, has shared with this
author that in his student days at Harvard the standard introduction
to prayer in the University Chapel was, "O Jesus Our Great Teacher
and Companion." This, of course, reflects an ebionitic or ethical-
humanistic outlook, which was a formative influence on Whiston's own
life of devotion. It was not until he was on the mission field many years
later that it suddenly dawned upon him that Jesus was more than a
teacher or prophet: He was the Savior of the world, the Lord of glory.
He was then moved for the first time to address Christ with the words,
"O Jesus Lord and Savior." He was thereafter poignantly reminded of
Paul's words in 1 Corinthians 12:3: "No one can say 'Jesus is Lord'
except by the Holy Spirit." It is only the Spirit who can reveal to us the
Messianic identity of Jesus (cf. Matt. 16:17). Apart from the Spirit we
lapse into either ebionitism or docetism.

KENOTIC CHRISTOLOGY

One strand within historical evangelicalism has sought to do justice
to the humanity of Christ by a development of the concept of *kenosis,*
the self-emptying of Christ based on Philippians 2:6 f. and 2 Corinthians 8:9. The kenotic theory has also found support in Eastern Orthodoxy. Among Evangelicals who have subscribed to this theory in
some form or other are Zinzendorf, Johann von Hofmann, Thomasius,
Gess, A. M. Fairbairn, Bishop Gore, P. T. Forsyth, and H. R. Mackintosh. More recently Vincent Taylor, Malcolm Furness, Geddes McGreggor, and Jürgen Moltmann have come to the defense of a moderate
kenotic theory.[43]

The controversy over the kenosis of Christ first erupted in post-
Reformation Lutheranism where the kenoticists (Chemnitz, Mentzer),
who argued that Christ in his humiliation temporarily divested himself
of certain of his divine attributes, were arrayed against the Cryptics
(Brenz, Hafeneffler), who contended that these attributes were merely
concealed by Christ. In the nineteenth century the controversy was
revived by the German theologians Thomasius and Gess who unlike
the older kenoticists maintained that the subject of humiliation was

not the incarnate God-man but the preincarnate Son. Whereas the kenoticists betrayed a slight tendency toward ebionitism since they spoke of the man Christ regaining his divine glory, the Cryptics sometimes gave the impression of holding to a docetic position.

Kenoticism has generally been criticized for viewing the incarnation as the abdication of deity rather than the assumption of humanity by deity. Many kenoticists tend to forget that Jesus is both God *and* man, not God *as* man, understood in a reductionist sense.[44] In some of its forms there is no doubt that kenoticism is heretical. If the divine attributes were renounced by Christ when he became man, as many kenoticists hold, it is difficult to see how he can still be regarded as God. If the humiliated One is not the very same as the Exalted One, then Jesus becomes little more than a demigod who lives on earth. The Calvinist Gess went so far as to contend that Christ laid aside all his divine attributes and that the Logos became a human soul. The divine consciousness was said to be totally absent at the incarnation, though Christ regained it in the course of time. P. T. Forsyth presents an interpretation of kenosis that is more in keeping with orthodoxy. He sees the divine attributes not as renounced at the incarnation but as retracted from the actual to the potential. The kenosis is accompanied by a plerosis by which Jesus Christ, through genuine moral effort, regains the mode of being that he had voluntarily laid aside.

The main difficulty with kenoticism is that it too often signifies still another attempt to overcome the paradox of the two natures of Christ by seeking to make the incarnation and humiliation credible to human reason.[45] A Nestorian tendency is evident in that the two natures no longer seem organically related. We must not lose sight of the fact that Christ even in his weakness and humiliation remained God, though he was God incognito and therefore God only for faith. Bonhoeffer grasped the import of this when he remarked: "If Jesus Christ is to be described as God, then we may not speak of . . . his omnipotence and his omniscience, but we must speak of this weak man among sinners, of his cradle and his cross."[46] Barth censures the kenoticists for failing to recognize that it is precisely in the humiliation of Christ that his divinity is manifested and demonstrated.

In our view the kenosis must be affirmed since it is solidly biblical, but kenoticism as it has developed should be treated with a certain amount of caution and reserve.[47] Kenotic Christology is to be appreciated for its earnest attempt to take seriously the reality of suffering and struggle in the life of Christ. It quite rightly seeks to stay clear of an incipient docetism that sees the humanity of Christ as only a transparent envelope for deity. At the same time we must beware of that version of kenoticism in which the transmutation of God into a man takes the place of genuine incarnation. With Barth we contend that kenosis means the renunciation by Christ not of his divinity but of his being in the form of God alone.[48] The divine attributes were not discarded by Christ but were now concealed in the weakness of human flesh. They were always available to our Lord, but either he did not generally choose to draw upon them, or he exercised them in a new way.[49] He could have summoned a host of angels to his defense (Matt. 26:53), but instead he chose the way of nonresistance which led to the cross. He imposed a definite limitation upon himself not only when he became man but also on his earthly pilgrimage. He ventured into the far country where his heavenly glory was only dimly reflected, where his majesty was no longer immediately evident (Barth). He remained fully God, but his divinity was hidden in his humanity and remains hidden except to the eyes of faith.

THE CONTEMPORARY SCENE

A confusing picture of the person of Christ emerges as we turn to the contemporary scene. Docetism and ebionitism are both very much present, but the latter is dominant. Pannenberg, in jettisoning the doctrine of the two natures, maintains that Jesus was a real man who lived completely in and for the future, that is, in and for God. He begins not with the incarnation of our Lord but with his resurrection and avers that this event gives us the clue to the status of Jesus—as the One who anticipates and embodies the future of world-history.[50] J. A. T. Robinson affirms the full humanity of Jesus but not his deity except in a functional sense.[51] Jesus represents God to man. He is but the parable or sign by which it is possible to recognize the Christ in others. Ellen Flesseman, a Dutch theologian, in her book *Believing Today* has a similar view: "The Son Jesus Christ is not God, but a man who was so one with God that in Him I meet God."[52] Thomas O'Meara regards Jesus as "the climax of man," the culminating point in human evolution. He is "not the creator of salvation but its prophet."[53] For Ernst Fuchs Jesus should be considered "a man who dares to act in God's stead."[54] In Schoonenberg's Christology Jesus is basically a human person who embodies and reveals the presence of God rather than a divine person who assumes human nature.[55] Hans Küng depicts Jesus as "God's advocate and deputy," the man who by his words and deeds attests God's love for us.[56] The impact of positivistic historicism is clearly evident in his attempt to show what can be believed and what can be discarded in the life of Jesus.[57] John Cobb rejects the traditional idea of Jesus Christ as a supernatural being in human form and contends instead that he was an extraordinary prophetic figure who fully realized the divine creative urge to fulfillment within him.[58]

While the mainstream of contemporary liberal theology seeks in some sense to maintain the uniqueness of Jesus there is a tendency in many circles to call even this into question. It is now commonplace to see Christ-Figures in other religions.[59] Rosemary Ruether speaks of the need for a "relativizing of the identification of Jesus as the Christ" and refers to Jesus as the "messianic experience for us."[60] Radhakrishnan echoes the views of many Christians who have embraced a syncretistic form of mysticism:

> What is possible for a Gautama or a Jesus is possible for every human being. The nature of man receives its fulfillment in them. In us, ordinary human beings, God-consciousness is darkened, enfeebled, imperfectly developed. In Jesus it is absolutely powerful; the image of God is in full radiance.[61]

Against an immanentalist mysticism and evolutionary monism, evident in J. A. T. Robinson, Teilhard de Chardin, John Cobb, David Griffin, Bernard Meland, and others, we contend that Jesus' divinity is not a mutation in the evolutionary process but the incursion of the eternal Word of God into human time and history. In Jesus we see not "the breakthrough of cosmic consciousness" (Robinson) but the descent of the heavenly Son of God into the human cosmos. Jesus is not the symbol of transformed personal identity under the impact of the divine but the divine Word himself in human garb (Phil. 2:7). In him we see not simply a development of God-consciousness but the living God himself who forms human consciousness in his image and who guides and directs the human will.

The heresies of today like the heresies of yesterday begin not with the God-Man, the Absolute Paradox, but with Jesus as a historical personage or with the Christ Spirit who transcends time and space. We reject both a Christology from below and one from above and affirm instead a Christology of the center. The object of our faith is neither Jesus as the Christ nor the New Being manifested in Jesus but the Jesus Christ of biblical faith who is in himself very God and very man. Barth is indubitably correct that the theological approach is neither idealistic nor materialistic but unionistic, since it takes for its point of departure the union of spirit and matter in Jesus Christ. We proceed not from an idea towards its humanization (as in docetism) nor with human personality towards its divinization (as in ebionitism) but with the Word incarnate in human flesh. This is why Christian faith is more aptly termed "theanthropocentric" (Brunner) than either theocentric or anthropocentric.

Modern evangelicalism has for the most part successfully avoided the heresies that we have been discussing, but even here there are dangers. Too many Evangelicals see the incarnation as a theophany, the visible appearance of God in human form, and therefore the divinity of Christ as something self-evident. But we have to remember that God was in Christ incognito, that deity is hidden in his humanity. The "personality" of Jesus as an observable historical phenomenon must not be confused with his "Person" which is a suprahistorical reality. The object of our faith is not Jesus after the flesh but the Son of God who assumed human nature. The deity of Christ can only be grasped by the inwardness of faith and not by historical investigation. If there could be a direct recognition of Jesus as God, this would then make Jesus a mythological being, as Kierkegaard has so trenchantly observed.

Other danger signals can also be mentioned. The fact that in popular evangelical piety the omniscience of Jesus is practically taken for granted betrays a Monophysite tendency. We are inclined to forget that real incarnation means that Jesus entered into our historical and cultural limitations, though he also transcended the times in which he lived and indeed all historical time in the message that he embodied. That most evangelicals today will not affirm the *theotokos* (Mary as Mother of God) indicates a possible Nestorian bent,[62] since the two natures are presumably not seen as inseparably related.[63] The fear of Mariolatry is, of course, also a factor that weighs heavily in evangelical disinclination to identify with this dogmatic formula.

Christomonism is another perennial temptation in evangelical Protestantism, particularly in its sectarian guises. This heresy is very much apparent in the "Jesus Only" variety of Pentecostalism in which Jesus is equated with Jehovah of the Old Testament.[64] Similarly the Local Church sect of Witness Lee, which supposedly carries on the work of Watchman Nee, speaks of only one person in the Godhead—Jesus Christ, who expresses himself in three stages. Zinzendorf verged toward Christomonism in his view that Jesus Christ is the Creator and Sustainer of the Universe as well as Redeemer and that God is our Father only indirectly—through faith in Christ. For Swedenborg, who departed from evangelicalism at many key points, "God is Jesus Christ, who is the Lord Jehovah, from eternity Creator, in time Redeemer and to eternity Regenerator."[65] Swedenborg saw the Trinity as "three modes of manifestation" rather than crucial ontological distinctions within the being of God.[66]

We have already alluded to Barth's quasi-Christomonism in which Christ is depicted as the center of every man's being, and a virtual equation is made between the providential grace of God and the redemptive activity of Christ.[67] Emil Brunner has given a timely warning against the absolute identification of God and Christ, for this invariably results in universalism and the obscuring of the truth that outside of Christ God is wrathful and judgmental. Brunner contends against Barth that only God the Father is the Elector and Christ is the mediator of election. Yet Brunner's arguments may also betray a kind of subordinationism in which the equality in the Trinity is disregarded.

Again modern evangelicalism can be accused of trying to make the divinity of Christ palatable to reason. Much is made of the miracles of Christ, and especially his Virgin Birth and bodily resurrection, as confirming his Messiahship.[68] Kierkegaard rightly warned against basing the claims of faith upon the humanly rational, for the paradox of faith is then dissolved into a self-evident axiom of reason. "The proofs which Scripture presents for Christ's divinity," he declared, "His miracles, His Resurrection from the dead, His Ascension into heaven—are therefore only for faith, that is, they are not 'proofs,' they have no intention of proving that all this agrees perfectly with reason; on the contrary they would prove that it conflicts with reason and therefore is an object of faith."[69] Pascal too saw that the miracles of Christ are not the cause of saving faith in Christ. They may be helpful to those who earnestly desire and seek salvation, but it is only the cross that makes people believe. The miracles and prophecies in the Bible must not be disregarded, since they bear witness to the Messianic identity and saving work of Jesus Christ, but the content of our preaching can only be Jesus Christ and him crucified, since the message of the cross authenticates itself by bringing conviction of sin and assurance of salvation (cf. 1 Cor. 1:17–25).

Both Bonhoeffer and Barth have maintained that Christology is the touchstone of theology, since how one regards the person of Christ determines every other facet of theology. We regard the meaning of the cross as the pivotal doctrine in Christian theology,[70] but there is no doubt that the work of Christ is indissolubly united with his person. Each of us needs again to confess with Luther in his *Small Catechism* that "Jesus Christ, true God, begotten of the Father from eternity, and also true man, born of the Virgin Mary, is my Lord."[71] The one who overcomes the world is "he who believes that Jesus is the Son of God" (1 John 5:5). May we be bold to uphold the deity of Jesus Christ in a time when he is regarded only as the flower of humanity or the apex of human spirituality; but may we at the same time never lose sight of his bona fide humanity lest we succumb again to the perennial temptations of docetism and gnosticism by seeing him only as the symbol of an eternal truth or as the master key that unlocks the secrets of the kingdom.

NOTES

1. Adolf Harnack, *What Is Christianity?*, trans. Thomas Bailey Saunders (New York: Harper & Row, 1957), pp. 183–186.

2. Friedrich Schleiermacher, *The Christian Faith*, vol. 2, eds. H. R. Mackintosh and J. S. Stewart (New York: Harper Torchbooks, 1963), p. 385.

3. Through his historical investigation Albert Schweitzer concluded that Jesus was an apocalyptic visionary whose prophecies concerning the end of time were mistaken. Our faith and hope should therefore rest not on the historical Jesus but on the eternal Spirit which goes forth from him. See Albert Schweitzer, *The Quest of the Historical Jesus*, trans. W. Montgomery (New York: Macmillan, 1959), p. 401.

4. Martin Kähler, *The So-Called Historical Jesus and the Historic Biblical Christ*, trans. and ed. Carl E. Braaten. Foreword by Paul Tillich (Philadelphia: Fortress Press, 1964).

5. Soren Kierkegaard, *Concluding Unscientific Postscript*, trans. David F. Swenson (Princeton, N.J.: Princeton University Press, 1941), p. 290.

6. *Ibid.*, p. 529.

7. Soren Kierkegaard, *Philosophical Fragments*, trans. David Swenson (Princeton, N.J.: Princeton University Press, 1962), pp. 28–45.

8. P. T. Forsyth, *The Justification of God* (London: Independent Press Ltd., 1948), p. 145.

9. Bernard Ramm, *The Evangelical Heritage* (Waco, Texas: Word Books, 1973), pp. 103, 104.

10. Karl Barth, *Church Dogmatics* IV, 2, p. 71. Cf.: "This Man Jesus Christ is identical with God because the Word became flesh. . . . He does not only live through God and with God. He is Himself God." *Church Dogmatics* I, 2, p. 162.

11. Bruce Metzger, "The Punctuation of Rom. 9:5" in Barnabas Lindars and Stephen S. Smalley, *Christ and Spirit in the New Testament* (Cambridge: Cambridge University Press, 1973), pp. 95–112.

12. Another controversial verse that divides liberal and conservative exegetes is 1 John 5: 20. I am persuaded after careful examination that the conservative rendering is probably more true to the original meaning of this verse. The New International Version gives this reading: "And we are in him

who is true—even in his Son Jesus Christ. He is the true God and eternal life."

13. See Quell and Foerster, *"Kúrios"* in Gerhard Kittel, ed., *Theological Dictionary of the New Testament,* vol. 3, trans. and ed. Geoffrey W. Bromiley (Grand Rapids: Eerdmans, 1965), pp. 1039 ff. The authors hold that Paul did not make any basic distinction between *theos* and *kúrios* as though the latter were an intermediary god. Their contention is that the name *kúrios* "implies a position equal to that of God." It is well to note that *Yahweh* was translated by the Jews as *kúrios* in the Septuagint.

14. See Benjamin B. Warfield, *The Lord of Glory,* reprint ed. (Grand Rapids: Baker Book House, 1974), p. 225.

15. *Ibid.,* pp. 232–238. Also cf. Benjamin Warfield, *The Person and Work of Christ,* ed. Samuel G. Craig (Philadelphia: Presbyterian & Reformed Publishing, 1950), pp. 37–90.

16. For an intriguing comparative study of the metaphor "Son of God" in the New Testament writings, the early church, ancient Judaism, and Hellenistic religion, see Martin Hengel, *The Son of God,* trans. John Bowden (Philadelphia: Fortress Press, 1976).

17. Clement of Alexandria, *Stromata* VI, 9 in *Patrologia Graeca,* (ed. Migne, 9:291–292c

18. In H. R. Mackintosh, *The Doctrine of the Person of Jesus Christ,* (Edinburgh: T. & T. Clark, 1962), p. 231.

19. Cf. Calvin: "It follows that when He became man Christ did not cease to be what He was before and that nothing was changed in that eternal essence of God which assumed flesh. In short, the Son of God began to be man in such a way that He is still that eternal Word who had no temporal beginning." John Calvin, *The Gospel According to St. John* (Eerdmans, 1959) 1: 14, pp. 20, 21.

20. Helmut Thielicke, *The Evangelical Faith,* vol. 2, trans. G. W. Bromiley (Grand Rapids: Eerdmans, 1977), p. 324. Cf. Bonhoeffer: "The Chalcedonian Definition is an objective, but living, statement which bursts through all thought-forms." Dietrich Bonhoeffer, *Christ the Center,* trans. John Bowden (New York: Harper & Row, 1966), p. 92.

21. We can say that Jesus, i.e., Jesus Christ, is not God in himself apart from man but God *for* man and *in* man, God in human flesh. He is also in a qualified sense God *as* man in that in his mode of existence as man he remained fully God.

22. We do not mean to imply that God was only manifest in man; on the contrary he was fully incarnate in man. In order to guard against such a misunderstanding Athanasius declared: "He became man and did not just come into man." *Contra Arianos* III, 30.

23. For Barth this is the classical meaning of *anhypostasia.* See his *Church Dogmatics* I, 2, pp. 163–165.

24. This idea *enhypostasia* was propounded by Leontius of Byzantium and John of Damascus. The meaning is that the human nature of Christ is not impersonal (as implied in *anhypostasia*) but *in*personal. For further discussion see Donald Baillie, *God Was in Christ* (New York: Scribner's, 1948), pp. 90–91; F. Pieper, *Christian Dogmatics,* vol. 2 (St. Louis: Concordia Publishing House, 1951), pp. 79–84; and, G. C. Berkouwer, *The Person of Christ* (Grand Rapids: Eerdmans, 1955), pp. 305–326.

25. From *Corpus Reformatorum,* Calv. 53. 326, Sermon 27, *Sur la Première à Timothée.* Cited in François Wendel, *Calvin,* trans. Philip Mairet (London Collins, 1963), p. 220.

26. Compare Barth: "We do not have here a dual, but the one Jesus Christ, who as such is of both divine and human essence, and therefore the one Reconciler, Saviour and Lord. He preexisted as such in the divine counsel." *Church Dogmatics* IV, 2, p. 64. Cf. *Church Dogmatics* II, 2, pp. 108, 116; IV, 1, p. 53. Note that for Barth the historical flesh did not preexist but was prefigured in the Word.

27. We are familiar with Raymond Brown's allegation that the Virgin Birth stories have a dubious historicity and that a literal Virgin Birth is extraneous to the New Testament witness (R. Brown, *The Virginal Conception and the Bodily Resurrection of Jesus* [New York: Paulist Press, 1973]). We believe that this position is effectively countered by Manuel Miguens, *The Virgin Birth: An Evaluation of Scriptural Evidence* (Westminster, Md.: Christian Classics, 1975).

28. Machen contends that this prophecy has a double meaning—one that has an immediate reference to a child born at that time and then an eschatological or Messianic reference to Jesus Christ: "So, in our passage, the prophet, when he placed before the rebellious Ahaz that strange picture of the mother and the child, was not merely promising deliverance to Judah in the period before a child then born should know how to refuse the evil and choose the good, but also, moved by the Spirit of God, was looking forward, as in a dim and mysterious vision, to the day when the true Immanuel, the mighty God and Prince of Peace, should lie as a little babe in a virgin's arms." J. Gresham Machen, *The Virgin Birth of Christ* (New York: Harper & Row, 1930), p. 293. Some conservative scholars, e.g., Hengstenberg, James Orr, Edward Young, and Robert Gromacki see Isaiah 7:14 as referring exclusively to Jesus Christ.

For an illuminating scholarly defense of the traditionalist interpretation of Isaiah 7:14 see Edward J. Young, *The Book of Isaiah,* vol. 1 (Eerdmans, 1965), pp. 277–299. Also see Robert Glenn Gromacki, *The Virgin Birth* (Nashville: Thomas Nelson, 1974), pp. 140–149.

Our position is that the prophecy in verse 14 should be seen as primarily Messianic, since it entails a wondrous birth and seems to be addressed not simply to Ahaz but to the nation. One can presume that the prophet had only a fragmentary vision of the coming of the Messiah (cf. Dan. 12:8; 1 Pet. 1:10–12), but it is indisputable that his prophecy points to and was fulfilled in the wondrous birth of the Christ child.

One should bear in mind that the context of this verse indicates not simply a sign but a miraculous sign, a sign of the overwhelming power of God. The fact that the prophet later gives Immanuel supernatural attributes (Isa. 9:6) further attests the Messianic nature of his prophecy. Hugo Gressmann contends that this text should be interpreted in the light of the expectation widespread in the ancient world that a divine mother would give birth to a redeemer babe who would supplant the reigning king (in his *Der Messias* [Göttingen: Vandenhoeck & Ruprecht, 1929], pp. 235–242). Micah 5:2, 3 can be cited to support the view that such a belief was entertained in some Judean prophetic circles.

29. The Hebrew word *almah* basically denotes a maiden who is

unmarried and who is or is justly supposed to be a virgin, though its primary meaning is not spotless virginity. While sympathizing with the conservative argument that *virgin* is an appropriate translation for *almah* in this particular case, we maintain that the concluding decision on this matter cannot be made on the basis of historical-grammatical exegesis alone; it is finally a matter of theological exegesis whereby the text is seen in its wider theological context.

30. Donald M. Baillie, *God Was in Christ,* p. 152.

31. In Jaroslav Pelikan, *The Emergence of the Catholic Tradition* (Chicago: University of Chicago Press, 1971), p. 154.

32. H. R. Mackintosh, *The Doctrine of the Person of Jesus Christ,* p. 228.

33. See Peter W. Bartholome et al., *Christians in Conversation* (Westminster, Md.: Newman Press, 1962), p. 41.

34. In H. R. Mackintosh, *The Doctrine of the Person of Jesus Christ,* pp. 233, 234.

35. Teilhard de Chardin goes so far as to see the whole of the spiritualizing evolution of the universe as one great, continuous incarnation. The birth of Christ is a supreme incident or symbol of the cosmic evolution.

36. Cited in Mackintosh, *The Doctrine of the Person of Jesus Christ,* p. 236. See Theodosius Harnack, *Luthers Theologie* (Erlangen: Verlag von Andreas Deichert, 1886), XVI, 244.

37. It can also be legitimately argued that Ritschl's position, like Schleiermacher's, verges even more toward docetism, since he sees Jesus as the paradigm or model of the victory of spirit over nature. What is primarily important is not His person but the abiding values which He manifests and personifies, namely, mastery over nature and fidelity in vocation.

38. Walter Rauschenbusch, *A Theology for the Social Gospel,* pp. 154, 155.

39. Cf. Glenn Bucher who depicts Christ as "the full historical exemplar" of the human potential for liberation. In his "Liberation, Male and White: Initial Reflections" in *The Christian Century* 91:11 (March 20, 1974), [pp. 312–316], p. 315.

40. Schleiermacher writes that the "truly divine element" in Jesus "is the glorious clearness to which the great idea He came to exhibit attained in His soul." Friedrich Schleiermacher, *On Religion,* p. 246.

41. Paul Tillich, *Systematic Theology,* vol. 2 (Chicago: University of Chicago Press, 1957), p. 148.

42. Karl Barth, *The Humanity of God,* trans. Thomas Wieser and John Newton Thomas (Richmond: John Knox Press, 1964), p. 46.

43. Vincent Taylor, *The Person of Christ in New Testament Teaching* (London: Macmillan, 1958), pp. 260–276; Malcolm Furness, *Vital Doctrines of the Faith* (Grand Rapids: Eerdmans, 1973), pp. 21–24; Geddes McGreggor, *He Who Lets Us Be* (New York: Seabury Press, 1975), pp. 59–110; Jürgen Moltmann, *The Crucified God,* trans. R. A. Wilson and John Bowden (New York: Harper & Row, 1974), pp. 205–207; and, Ray Sherman Anderson, *Historical Transcendence and the Reality of God,* pp. 146–168.

44. One may indeed affirm that Jesus is God as man but not as the kenoticists understand this (see footnote 21). For the dominant strand within kenoticism the Logos was changed into a man by reducing Himself, either wholly or in part, to the dimensions of a man.

45. See Dietrich Bonhoeffer, *Christ the Center,* pp. 98–102; and G. C. Berkouwer, *The Person of Christ,* pp. 27–31.

46. Dietrich Bonhoeffer, *Christ the Center,* p. 108.

47. Our position here differs from that of the conservative Lutheran scholar R. C. H. Lenski who sees no merit whatever in kenoticism. See his *Interpretation of St. Paul's Epistles to the Galatians to the Ephesians and to the Philippians* (Columbus, Ohio: Wartburg Press, 1946), pp. 772–787.

48. Karl Barth, *Church Dogmatics* IV, 1, p. 180.

49. Barth writes concerning the self-emptying of the Son of God: "It does not consist in ceasing to be Himself as man, but in taking it upon Himself to be Himself in a way quite other than that which corresponds and belongs to His form as God, His being equal with God." *Ibid.*

50. See Wolfhart Pannenberg, *Jesus—God and Man* (Philadelphia: Westminster Press, 1968).

51. J. A. T. Robinson, *The Human Face of God* (Philadelphia: Westminster Press, 1973).

52. Ellen Flesseman-Van Leer, *Geloven vandaag* (Nijkerk: Callenbach, 1972). Cited in *Christianity Today* 18:7 (Jan. 4, 1974), p. 6.

53. Thomas O'Meara, *Loose in the World,* pp. 62, 71.

54. Ernst Fuchs, *Studies of the Historical Jesus,* trans. Andrew Scobie (Naperville, Ill.: Alec R. Allenson, 1964), p. 22.

55. Piet Schoonenberg, *The Christ,* trans. Della Couling (New York: Herder & Herder, 1969). Schoonenberg terms his position a "christological humanism." Similar views are expressed in John Hick, ed, *The Myth of God Incarnate* (Phil.: Westminster Press, 1977). Chalcedonian Christology is ably defended by Catholic theologian Walter Kasper in his *Jesus the Christ* (N.Y.: Paulist Press, 1976).

56. Hans Küng, *On Being a Christian,* p. 449. Like Schoonenberg and Pannenberg he affirms a "Christology from below," i.e., one that begins with the humanity of Jesus.

57. Küng frankly doubts the historicity of the virgin birth and empty tomb as well as the "mythology" of Jesus Christ's preexistence in heaven. The miracles of Jesus are interpreted in such a way as to deny all supernatural intervention into nature and history.

58. Cobb maintains that all humanity includes in some measure the immanent Logos, which he identifies with the Whiteheadian "lure for feeling," the "eternal urge of desire," and the "divine Eros." John B. Cobb, Jr., *Christ in a Pluralistic Age* (Philadelphia: Westminster Press, 1975), pp. 225–229, 246–257, 264. Yet in Jesus there was an optimum realization of this creative urge toward novelty. "The more fully the lure is responded to," Cobb says, "the more fully the human potential is actualized. The optimum realization would occur when human existence constituted itself in unity with the lure, as in the case of Jesus" (p. 171). Jesus is unique because he was fully open to the "creative transformation" which is at work everywhere and in every person. In Cobb's view we cannot rule out a priori the possibility that others too may have actualized their full human potential in union with the indwelling Logos.

59. For a penetrating critique of syncretistic and humanistic religion in the area of Christology see Russell F. Aldwinckle, *More Than Man: A Study in*

Christology (Grand Rapids: Eerdmans, 1976). See especially the chapter "Jesus or Gotama", pp. 211–246. Aldwinckle also gives a cogent rebuttal of process Christology (pp. 270–293).

60. Rosemary Ruether, *Liberation Theology* (New York: Paulist Press, 1972), p. 92.

61. Sarvepalli Radhakrishnan, *Recovery of Faith* (London: Allen & Unwin, 1956), p. 179.

62. Nestorius refused to affirm the *theotokos*. For him and his followers the man Christ was not God but the God-bearer *(theophoros)*.

63. For a current criticism of the *theotokos* by an evangelical see Robert Glenn Gromacki, *The Virgin Birth,* pp. 88, 89.

64. See John Miller, *Is God A Trinity?,* reprint. (Hazelwood, Mo.: Word Aflame Press, 1975). Note that one of Miller's chief charges against the doctrine of the Trinity is that it contradicts reason.

65. Emanuel Swedenborg, *The True Christian Religion,* vol. 1 (New York: Houghton, Mifflin, 1907), p. 42. Swedenborg's thought should probably be categorized as a trinal monism rather than a Christomonism, since Father, Son, and Spirit often appear to be interchangeable terms in his theology. At the same time a certain centrality tends to be accorded to Christ.

66. Despite the fact that he was a devout student of the Scriptures, Swedenborg was more mystical and speculative than evangelical; at the same time some genuinely biblical notions derived partly from his Lutheran upbringing survived in his thinking. Swedenborg had a marked influence on the German Pietist Friedrich Christoph Oetinger.

67. Barth is very much aware of the charge of Christomonism and seeks to guard against it. See his *Church Dogmatics* IV, 4, ed. G. W. Bromiley and T. F. Torrance (Edinburgh: T. & T. Clark, 1969), pp. 19–23.

68. See, for example, Floyd E. Hamilton, *The Basis of Christian Faith* (New York: Harper & Row, 1933); and John H. Gerstner, *Reasons for Faith* (New York: Harper & Row, 1960).

69. Robert Bretall, ed., *A Kierkegaard Anthology* (Princeton, N.J.: Princeton University Press, 1946), p. 389.

70. Compare Martin Kähler, "Without the cross there is no Christology, and there is not any feature in Christology which would not have to show its justification in the cross." In M. Kähler, *Schriften zu Christologie und Mission* (München: Chr. Kaiser Verlag, 1971), p. 302.

71. *Luther's Small Catechism* in Philip Schaff, ed., *The Creeds of Christendom,* vol. 3, 4th ed. (New York: Harper & Row, 1919), p. 79.

VII.
THE SUBSTITUTIONARY ATONEMENT

For our sake he made him to be sin who knew no sin, so that in him we might become the righteousness of God.

2 Corinthians 5:21

But Christ without guilt . . . took upon himself our punishment, in order that he might thus expiate our guilt, and do away with our punishment.

Augustine

When we say that grace is procured for us by the merit of Christ, we intend, that we have been purified by his blood, and that his death was an expiation for our sins.

John Calvin

This is the mystery of the riches of divine grace for sinners; for by a wonderful exchange our sins are now not ours but Christ's, and Christ's righteousness is not Christ's but ours.

Martin Luther

Our position is such that we can be rescued from eternal death and translated into life only by total and unceasing substitution, the substitution which God Himself undertakes on our behalf.

Karl Barth

THE BIBLICAL UNDERSTANDING

Evangelical theology contends that there is a consistent biblical witness to the atonement of Jesus Christ, though no one theological position is completely dominant. Most objective scholars will agree that the theme of vicarious, substitutionary atonement runs through the entire Bible. The prophet Isaiah portrays Christ as "an offering for sin" (53:10), as the one who "has borne our griefs and carried our sorrows" (53:4). The Psalmist reminds us that no man can ransom himself, but God himself will ransom our souls from the powers of darkness (Ps. 49:7–9, 15). The heart of the doctrine of the atonement is summed up in Paul: "For there is no distinction; since all have sinned and fall short

148

of the glory of God, they are justified by his grace as a gift, through the redemption which is in Christ Jesus, whom God put forward as an expiation by his blood, to be received by faith" (Rom. 3:22–25). In the words of the author of Hebrews, Christ "offered for all time a single sacrifice for sins" and "by a single offering he has perfected for all time those who are sanctified" (Heb. 10:12, 14). The doctrine of vicarious atonement is also clearly affirmed in the Epistles of John: "Herein is love, not that we loved God, but that he loved us, and sent his Son to be the propitiation for our sins" (1 John 4:10 KJ). 1 Peter expresses it this way: "For Christ also died for sins once for all, the righteous for the unrighteous, that he might bring us to God. . . ." (3:18).

The biblical witness in its fuller perspective is brought out in an examination of certain key words in the area of the doctrine of salvation. One of these is *redemption.* This term bears a close relation to *liberation, deliverance,* and *ransom.* Here we find the idea of a struggle between God and the hostile powers of darkness which enslave mankind. The root meaning of *redemption (apolutrōsis)* is to be brought out of slavery into the freedom of the new life. As Redeemer Jesus Christ breaks the power of sin and creates a new and obedient heart. He came to deliver us from sin, guilt, death, and the devil. We might add he also frees us from the curse of the Law and the wrath of God. Jesus came to release the captives, to set at liberty those who are oppressed (Luke 4:18). The people of God are constantly portrayed as those who have been bought with a price—ransomed (Isa. 35:10; 51:11; 62:12; 1 Cor. 6:20; 7:23; 1 Tim. 2:6).

Reconciliation (katallagē) is another crucial term in the doctrine of the atonement. It basically means to be brought out of our alienation into a state of peace and harmony with God. As Reconciler Jesus Christ heals the breach created by sin and restablishes communion between God and man. Reconciliation is not a process by which we become ever more acceptable to God but an act by which we are delivered from the condition of estrangement and restored to fellowship with God. It consists not only in a change of attitude on the part of man but also in a change of attitude on the part of God.[1] Because of the atoning sacrifice of Christ God has chosen to treat the man in sin as a son rather than a transgressor. The integral relation between reconciliation and redemption is brought to light in Colossians 1 which asserts that we are reconciled "by the blood of his cross" and redeemed from "the dominion of darkness" and transferred into "the kingdom of his beloved Son" (Col. 1:13, 14, 20).

A word which perhaps comes even closer to the meaning of atonement is *propitiation (hilasmos)*. J. I. Packer sees propitiation as the nucleus and focal point of the whole New Testament idea of the saving work of Christ.[2] In Isaiah the Messiah figure is depicted as "an offering for sin" (53:10). In 1 John we read: "And he is the propitiation for our sins: and not for our's only, but also for the sins of the whole world" (2:2 KJ; cf. 4:10; Rom. 3:25). Some scholars (e.g., C. H. Dodd and Alan Richardson) have objected to the translating of this word as *propitiation;* their preference is *expiation*. In some cases to be sure the latter may be the more appropriate translation, but both words are solidly biblical.[3] As A. A. Hodge puts it: "Propitiation has reference to the bearing or effect of satisfaction upon God. Expiation has reference to the bearing of the same satisfaction upon the guilt of sin."[4] Whereas God's wrath is propitiated or turned away, man's guilt is expiated or annulled. Both terms are organically related to the sacrificial system of the Old Testament, though they both transcend the meaning of ritual sacrifice. Expiation is especially evident in Isaiah 43:25 where the prophet says that God "blots out your transgressions" and "will not remember your sins."

The integral relationship between the two terms is underlined by D. Martyn Lloyd-Jones:

Surely the very idea of expiation in and of itself leads to propitiation! If there must be expiation, why must there be propitiation? There is only one answer —that there cannot be a true relationship between God and man until that sin has been expiated. But that is just another way of saying *propitiation*.[5]

Propitiation can only be understood in the light of the wrath of God, the severity of the reaction of God's holiness to man's sin. God's inviolable holiness needs to be satisfied, and man's transgressions need to be removed. This is realized when God himself takes upon himself in the person of his Son our sin and guilt so that his justice might be executed and our sins might be forgiven. God is moved toward this self-sacrifice by his infinite compassion.

The term *satisfaction* is not biblical but ecclesiastical, though it is integrally related to expiation and reconciliation. This concept will be dealt with more thoroughly in the section on the theories of the atonement.

Substitution is another extrabiblical term that nevertheless conveys the breadth and scope of the meaning of the cross of Christ. We have already noted the significance of this concept in the beginning of this section. It connotes the truth that Christ died not only on our behalf but also in our place. It is especially apparent in Isaiah 53: "But he was wounded for our transgressions, he was bruised for our iniquities; upon him was the chastisement that made us whole, and with his stripes we are healed. . . . The Lord has laid on him the iniquity of us all" (Isa. 53:5, 6). This vital theme is likewise very much present in Paul: "For our sake he made him to be sin who knew no sin, so that in him we might become the righteousness of God" (2 Cor. 5:21; cf. Rom. 3:23–25; Gal. 3:13). In Paul's theology Jesus Christ is our substitutionary representative: when he died, all died in him (2 Cor. 5:14). The ransom sayings in Mark 10:45 and Matthew 20:28 also carry the implication of substitution.[6]

Justification (dikiaosune) is a biblical term that is primarily forensic: it means to be declared or pronounced just in the context of a law court. To be justified in the Christian sense is to be covered by the righteousness of Christ (cf. Isa. 61:10; Ps. 32:1, 2; Rom. 4:1–8). Because of the sacrifice of Christ God no longer counts our trespasses against us (2 Cor. 5:19). But justification is not mere pardon: it advances man to positive favor with God.

In justifying man God also justifies himself. Sin challenged God's authority, and by taking a position against sin and evil he vindicates himself as Creator. He also reveals himself as a God of mercy as well as of righteousness.

Finally we need to consider the equally authentic biblical concepts of regeneration and sanctification. It is not enough to be pronounced just: we must also be made just in our hearts and in our daily living. The Psalmist declares: "Wash me thoroughly from my iniquity, and cleanse me from my sin!" (Ps. 51:2). In Protestant orthodoxy *regeneration* connotes the initial cleansing by the Holy Spirit and *sanctification* the ongoing process of interior purification which extends throughout life. In the theology of the Reformers regeneration includes both aspects of inner change.

All these terms are associated with the shedding of the blood of Christ on the cross of Calvary. The author of Hebrews maintains that the blood atonement of Christ fulfills and transcends the animal sacrifices of the Old Testament in that this one is wholly efficacious to absolve man from sin and is done once for all times. "Without the shedding of blood," he says, "there is no forgiveness of sins" (Heb. 9:22). Emil Brunner remarks that "blood must actually flow, for man has forfeited his life by his rebellion against his Creator and Lord."[7] Yet the significance of the blood of Christ is not just to be found in the obligation of mankind to pay for sin but in the holy severity of God that can be satisfied only through the supreme sacrifice. Forsyth phrases it very well: "The blood of Christ stands not simply for the sting of sin on God but the scourge of God on sin, not simply for God's sorrow over sin but for God's wrath on sin."[8] One cannot begin to fathom the mystery of the cross unless one perceives both God's anguish over sin and his inviolable holiness that refuses to tolerate sin.

DIFFERING VIEWS ON THE ATONEMENT

Through the ages various theories of the atonement have developed, some of which reflect and others obscure biblical themes. No theory in and of itself exhausts the truth in the mystery of the atonement, but some theories are much closer to this truth than others.

What has come to be known as the classic theory of the atonement depicts the sacrifice of Christ in dramatic terms. Through his cross and resurrection Christ emerges victorious in his struggle with sin, death, and the devil. The idea of ransom is given much prominence. It is said that Christ was given as a ransom to the prince of darkness in exchange for the souls of a lost world, but the devil could not hold on to this ransom for on the third day Christ rose from the dead. Some of these ideas were crudely expressed, but the truth behind them is that there is a cosmic conflict between God and the demonic adversary of God and man, and the cross of Christ signifies the overthrow and demise of this adversary. Surely this idea is solidly rooted in the New Testament. In the Epistle to the Hebrews we read that "he himself likewise partook of the same nature, that through death he might destroy him who has the power of death, that is, the devil" (2:14). 1 John expresses it this way: "The reason the Son of God appeared was to destroy the works of the devil" (1 John 3:8b; cf. Mark 10:45; 1 Tim. 2:6).

In the classic view the atoning work on the cross is seen in organic relationship to the incarnation. The incarnation itself signifies the beginning of reconciliation. God takes the initiative and carries through. God himself performs the sacrifice in the person of his Son. God is both the reconciled and the reconciler.

The classic view is especially prominent in patristic theologians like Athanasius, Origen, and Irenaeus, but it is also very much evident in Martin Luther and Karl Barth.[9] Luther numbers among the tyrants the law of God and His wrath as well as sin, death, and the devil. Barth sees the principal enemy as the chaos or Nothingness, which is the object of God's negation and which is thereby given a provisional or transient reality.[10] For him salvation is primarily from the chaos and only secondarily from sin and death.

Much more prominent in the tradition of Roman Catholic scholasticism and Protestant orthodoxy is the satisfactionist or juridical view of the atonement. This is also known as the Latin view. Some of the ideas associated with this theory were anticipated in Cyprian, Gregory the Great, Ambrose, and Augustine before they were given systematic formulation by Anselm of Canterbury in the eleventh century. In his noted work, *Cur Deus Homo?*, Anselm set forth the thesis that sin against the infinite majesty of God demands an adequate reparation. Man must pay this reparation, but he is unable to do so because being a sinner he cannot offer the perfect sacrifice. Only a perfect man, the God-Man, can make this sacrifice and thereby atone for sin. The principal thrust is on man as the agent of reconciliation, though the atonement is still regarded as in some sense the work of God, since he is the one who planned it.[11] Anselm's stress is on the need for making satisfaction to the wounded honor of God.[12] The payment is primarily the work of Christ's human nature, but the sacrifice is given infinite value because of the union of the human with the divine nature.

Anselm regarded the satisfaction of Christ primarily as a gift or tribute to God and not so much as a punishment for sin, as in later orthodoxy (though this idea is not absent in his thought and indeed looms constantly in the background).[13] The shameful suffering and agonizing death of our Lord were seen as works of supererogation that could be credited to those less worthy, since they went beyond the obedience necessary for maintaining the honor of God.[14]

Thomas Aquinas developed themes already enunciated by Anselm. Thomas was emphatic that the work of satisfaction includes the endurance of punishment, which indeed logically follows from the idea of satisfaction. He also underlined the theme that the merit of Christ's work was not only sufficient but superabundant. Consequently a treasury of merit is presupposed to which the church and its ministers have the keys. Moreover, Christ's merit is seen by Thomas not only in relation to his death but in relation to his whole life. From the beginning of the conception of our Lord he merited eternal salvation for us.

To his credit Thomas sought to do justice to the subjective dimension of the atonement, which was neglected by Anselm. The remission of sins connotes the expulsion of sin in the lives of men as well as the pardon of sin. The application of the merits of Christ to the sinner is not simply an external transaction (as in Anselm) but involves a mystical union of Christ and the believer.

The juridical theory was also very much evident in the theology of the Protestant Reformers as well as in Protestant Orthodoxy, though it assumed new forms. In Calvin satisfaction tends to be subordinated to election. F. Christian Baur declares that for both Calvin and Zwingli the satisfaction of Christ is not the meritorious cause of salvation but only the instrumental cause in carrying out the purpose of redemption.[15] He has admittedly grasped one side of Calvin's theology, but we must also bear in mind that Calvin saw Christ not simply as an instrument of salvation but as its Author and Executor.[16] Calvin can make statements which seem to portray the atoning sacrifice of Christ as the basis of man's reconciliation with God. He can assert: "by this expiation God the Father has been satisfied and duly atoned," "by this intercessor his wrath has been appeased," and "this is the foundation of peace between God and men."[17] Calvin clearly affirmed that God loved us even before the sacrifice of Christ, indeed even before the foundation of the world, but the sacrifice was necessary so that God's love could find a way to us.[18] God's love for his own could not be applied for their personal benefit until the sacrifice on Calvary. The divine decree of election could not take effect except through the obedience of Christ. Perhaps one can say that for Calvin Christ brought to realization and fulfillment a redemption that had already been determined in the eternal counsel of God.

Luther's emphasis was that the satisfaction was made not only to God but by God. It was not simply Jesus as man but God himself who accomplished the work of expiation and satisfaction. Jesus' sacrifice did not create a gracious God, though this sacrifice was necessary for his grace to be revealed to the world and made effectual in it.

A matter of recent dispute among Lutheran scholars is whether Luther is closer to the classic (or patristic) view of the atonement or to the Latin view. Aulén has vigorously maintained that his thinking falls within the framework of the classic view. Many of Luther's statements certainly tend to confirm Aulén's thesis. The following is especially pertinent:

> When we were created and had received all manner of blessings from God the Father, the devil came and led us into disobedience and sin, death and all misery. . . . No counsel, no help or comfort, was there for us until the only and eternal Son of God, in his unfathomable goodness, had pity on our miserable wretchedness and came to help us. Thus all the tyrants and oppressors have been routed, and in their stead is Jesus Christ, the Lord of life, of righteousness, of everything pertaining to our welfare and salvation. . . .[19]

At the same time it can be argued that Luther saw the devil primarily as an instrument of the wrath of God and that the real victory is only achieved when this wrath has been propitiated and appeased.

Paul Althaus follows the Finnish Lutheran scholar Tiilila in support-
ing this position. Althaus expresses what he believes is Luther's dominant view: "The satisfaction which God's righteousness demands constitutes the primary and decisive significance of Christ's work and
particularly of his death. Everything else depends on this satisfaction,
including the destruction of the might and the authority of the demonic
powers."[20] That Luther must definitely be included in the Anselmian
or Latin tradition is evident in this remark of his: "Since He became
a substitute for us all, and took upon himself our sins, that He might
bear God's terrible wrath against sin and expiate our guilt, He necessarily felt the sin of the whole world, together with the entire wrath
of God, and afterwards the agony of death on account of this sin."[21]

Karl Barth takes issue with the Latin tradition in its grounding of
God's forgiveness of sinners in the propitiatory satisfaction of the God-
Man, Jesus Christ. As he sees it Christ does not appease God's anger
but reveals it as the obverse side of his love. God's wrath was not turned
away by Christ but was executed upon Christ. He can therefore speak
of Christ as the "rejected" and the "reprobate," whereas these terms
are applied to unbelievers in historical orthodoxy.

At the same time Barth maintains a certain continuity with the
Anselmian tradition. For example, he continues to make use of the
themes of satisfaction and expiation, though insisting that the Son of
God himself bore this penalty and not the human nature of Christ as
such. The act of reconciliation was already determined in the eternal
counsels of God and was already realized in the preexistent Christ, but
this act was fulfilled and manifested in the cross of Calvary. Juridical
themes are apparent in this remark of Barth's: "He has therefore
suffered for all men what they had to suffer: their end as evil-doers;
their overthrow as the enemies of God; their extirpation in virtue of the
superiority of the divine right over their wrong."[22] Yet for Barth this
must be seen as a conflict that was resolved within the Godhead. The
atonement is only rightly understood when we recognize that God
himself took upon himself the burden of our guilt in the person of his
Son. The cross is therefore to be conceived not so much as a propitiation
directed to eternity but as the incursion of vicarious, triumphant love
into history. The cross signifies the identification of God with man's
guilt and shame, not the satisfaction of the wounded honor of God by
the sacrifice of human innocence.[23]

Still another approach to the atonement is the mystical theory,
which was very much present among many of the early church fathers,
and it continues to exert great influence particularly in the Roman

Catholic and Eastern Orthodox communions. Liberal Protestantism of the type associated with Schleiermacher also reflects this position. In the mystical theory salvation properly speaking does not lie in the cross of Christ but in his person. His divine-human nature is communicable, and salvation lies in this being imparted to us. The purpose of the incarnation is said to be the deification or divinization of man. Christ entered the world as a transforming leaven, and its resulting transformation constitutes his redemption. Among some who have espoused this theory, Jesus Christ is the mirror of divinity who awakens the divine consciousness within all who meet him. He differs from other persons in degree rather than in kind insofar as he is the perfect realization of God-consciousness (Schleiermacher). For Dionysius, the pseudo-Areopagite, Jesus is the chief symbol of the transcendent reality of man's union with God through mystical ascent. According to William Law, by being joined to Christ we allow the seed of divinity within us to burst forth into life. In Law as in Meister Eckhart the birth of the Son in our souls is given more prominence than the objective sacrifice of Christ on the cross.

In the moral influence theory the purpose of Christ's suffering was to subdue the alienation of man by an exhibition of self-sacrificing love. Like the mystical theory it is primarily subjective, since reconciliation is conceived of as a change of attitude that God effects in man, not a change of attitude toward man on the part of God. Jesus is the exemplar of perfected humanity or the model of true piety who saves us by the impact of his love. His death on the cross is exemplary rather than propitiatory or expiatory. Among theologians and philosophers who have held this view in some form or other are Abelard, Socinus, Immanuel Kant, Horace Bushnell, Ritschl,[24] F. D. Maurice, Walter Rauschenbusch, and Martin Luther King. What this theory fails to see is that God is not only love but also light, absolute moral holiness, and this means that sin must be expiated, judged, and punished.

Another position which was more prominent in the past than today is the governmental theory set forth by Hugo Grotius (d. 1645). The atonement is here interpreted as an exhibition of the righteousness of God rather than a satisfaction to the holiness of God. God forgives simply on the basis of his forbearance if we will but acknowledge his righteousness, as manifested in the death of Christ and turn to him in repentance and obedience. Christ's death is not a payment for man's sin but a tribute to the sanctity of divine government. This theory has been adopted by Wardlaw, A. Cave, Creighton, and J. Miley, among others.[25] It is also prominent among the Christadelphians. A principal criticism is that the cross here signifies a relaxation of the Law of God, not the execution of this Law. Christ is pictured as one who died for our sakes but not in our stead. His obedience does not make us righteous but only gives us the opportunity to become so.

Finally we should give attention to the representative theory known also as the theory of vicarious repentance and the moral satisfaction theory. It was anticipated by Rupert of Duytz in the twelfth century and given cogent expression in J. McLeod Campbell, F.D. Maurice, Thomasius of Erlangen, and more recently Vincent Taylor and Malcolm Furness. P. T. Forsyth, Karl Barth, Hans Küng, and Jürgen Moltmann have also incorporated ideas from this tradition. Aspects of it are also to be found in Zinzendorf.

The theory of vicarious repentance is more biblically anchored than either the moral influence or mystical theories in that it preserves the objective dimension of the atonement, though it does not treat the law of God with the seriousness that it deserves. In this theory vicarious identification is stressed over substitutionary expiation and penal redemption. The Son of God identifies himself with the guilt and travail of man and confesses this guilt to the holy Father. This sacrifice satisfies the moral sense of the universe though not the legal claims of God's righteousness. Christ does not suffer the very penalty for sin that men deserve to suffer through their sin, but he does suffer through his moral identification with men. The cross is a demonstration of "the creative sympathy of the holy" (Forsyth), not a propitiation of the wrath of God. It testifies to God's forgiveness but does not effect this forgiveness. The sacrifice of Christ is not a sin offering but a love offering (Vincent Taylor). What Christ gives to God is not an equivalent penalty but "an adequate confession of God's holiness, rising from amid extreme conditions of sin" (Forsyth).[26] The efficacy of the atonement is dependent on our response to God's love shown forth in Jesus Christ.

In all these theories there is some truth, though we contend that the classic and juridical theories are most faithful to the biblical message. The atonement as an objective work of God in Jesus Christ in sacred history is preserved in these theories, whereas the others open the door to subjectivism. The theory of vicarious repentance has much to commend it, but nowhere in Scripture is Christ portrayed as presenting to God a sacrifice of perfect penitence. Yet it contains the truth that God himself participates in man's travail and suffering, an insight that is eclipsed in the Latin theory where identification with man's suffering is said to occur only in the human nature of Christ.

We must not lose sight of the truth that both the deity and humanity of Jesus Christ played a role in the atoning sacrifice for sin on Calvary. His manhood was necessary to satisfy the legal requirements of that sacrifice. The efficacy of that sacrifice lies in the fact that it was initiated and carried through by deity.

THREE ASPECTS OF THE ATONEMENT

A full theory of the atonement will include its triumphal, satisfactionist, and regenerative aspects. Any theory that neglects or obscures any one of these elements does not do justice to the breadth of the atoning sacrifice of Christ.

First of all we should see the atonement as a triumph over the powers of darkness, and this note is definitely underscored in the so-called classic view. Christ is not simply the suffering servant but the reigning king, and his reign is already begun on the cross, but he rules through suffering love, not worldly might. His reign is realized through his passion and crucifixion, but it is consummated in his resurrection. The cross apart from the resurrection would be a catastrophe, for it would mean that death had the final word. But Christ triumphed over death in his resurrection, since death could not hold him. Likewise he was victorious over hell, the devil, and sin. Other tyrants or powers which Christ dispelled were the wrath of God and the law of God (Luther).

To see Jesus as Victor (Johann Christoph Blumhardt) means to see the atonement in terms of a conflict between the power of good and the power of evil. This is not a metaphysical but a moral dualism, since it presupposes not two co-eternal powers at variance with one another but the rebellion of the creature against his Creator who alone is Almighty and Eternal. It also attests that this battle is a spiritual one that is waged for the souls of men. The devil is a supernatural adversary of God and man, a fallen angel, who has become through man's sin the "prince" and "god" of this world (John 12:31; 14:30; Eph. 2:2; 2 Cor. 4:4). He goes under various names in Scripture including the serpent, the dragon, Lucifer, Leviathan, and Satan. Through his sacrificial death and glorious resurrection Christ brought down the principalities and powers of darkness. They have suffered an irrevocable and crushing defeat, but they continue to fight on. This great victory of Christ over the adversary of God and man was already prophesied in Genesis 3:15 where God says to the serpent: "He shall bruise your head, and you shall bruise his heel." The deliverance of the children of Israel from the fiery serpents in Numbers 21:4 (and following) is a type of the redemption of the world through Christ. The bronze serpent on the pole which redeems the stricken people from their afflictions is a figure of the Messiah who will redeem all people from their sins.

The danger in the triumphal theory of the atonement is that it sometimes overlooks the truth that the devil, death, and sin are simply agents of the wrath of God and that no final redemption can come until the wrath and holiness of God have been satisfied. We must also refrain from saying with some of the early fathers that the devil acquires certain rights over man or that his defeat was brought about by deception. The devil has acquired power over man, and he indeed was deceived concerning the scope of his power, but it is clear from Scripture that he recognized that his antagonist was the Son of God himself and not simply the man Jesus.

A full theory of the atonement must also include the ideas of satisfaction, expiation, and propitiation. God's love has brought about our redemption, but the redemption is from the wrath of God against sin.[27] God's holiness must be placated, his righteous law must be satisfied, before man can be released from the condemnation which invariably follows from sin. The merely ethical Christian asks, "I am sick. How can I be made well?" The biblical Christian asks: "How can God's violated right be restored?" This is the deeper spiritual issue behind the ethical question.

Atonement means more than mere forgiveness (as in Ritschl). It is an act of God to satisfy his holiness before it is a declaration of forgiveness to sinful man. In the person of Jesus God takes upon himself our sin and guilt so that we may be released from the penalty of sin. Karl Barth has put it this way: Jesus Christ "has not only borne man's enmity against God's grace, revealing it in all its depth. He has borne the far greater burden, the righteous wrath of God against those who are enemies of His grace, the wrath which must fall on us."[28] And again: "In His own Word made flesh, God hears that satisfaction has been done to His righteousness, that the consequences of human sin have been borne and expiated, and therefore that they have been taken away from man—the man for whose sake Jesus Christ intervened."[29]

It can be said that Christ made satisfaction for us in a twofold way. By his life of perfect obedience he fulfilled the law for us. By his death on the cross he satisfied the law for us.[30] The cross of Christ is "the actual execution in strict rigour of justice of the unrelaxed penalty of the law. . . ."[31] This means that Christ suffered not just *like* a sinner but *as* a sinner.

The satisfactionist theory of the atonement is also capable of distortion. If it is seen as the only valid interpretation of the atonement, the triumphal and regenerative aspects are subverted. The whole idea of a cosmic conflict with the demonic adversary of God is either neglected or denied. A. A. Hodge dismisses the view that Christ was provided by God to ransom his people out of the hands of Satan as "grotesque," despite the fact that biblical references to the conflict with the devil abound. The idea of ransom is interpreted by him as being bought "from the claims of that law by which we were held."[32]

Still another danger in the satisfactionist theory is that satisfaction is said to be offered to a distributive justice rather than to personal holiness, to a legal claim rather than to a person. To be sure Christ satisfied the demands of the law, but even more he satisfied the Author of the law, the holy God himself. Moreover, his sacrifice goes beyond the claims of the law; it transcends and abrogates as well as fulfills the divine law of retribution. God's love is deeper and broader than the rational ideal of justice.

Finally, we must repudiate that version of the satisfactionist theory which sees the atoning sacrifice as made exclusively or primarily by Jesus Christ as man and as intending to appease the wrath of a vengeful God who otherwise would not or could not love sinful mankind. This smacks of the pagan idea of trying to force the hand of the gods or alter their disposition through ritual offerings. This also leads to tritheism, since it separates the Son, who is pure love, from the Father, who is depicted as holiness and wrath. Our contention is that the atoning sacrifice was made by the Son of God in the form of the human Jesus to the Father and that his wrath is the counterpart of his love. God's attitude toward man *does change* in the light of the sacrifice of Christ, but this change was already apparent in his own eternal decision to identify himself with the sins of man and to bear the penalty of these sins. The cross in human history is a consequence and not the precondition of the cross in the heart of God (cf. 1 Pet. 1:20; 2 Tim. 1:9; Rev. 13:8). God was already forgiving and loving before the sacrifice on Calvary, but his forgiveness had to be realized and manifested on the plane of history in the momentous event of the crucifixion. His love could not be made available to his children until his holiness had been satisfied concretely in history. The cross, therefore, signifies both the judgment of God on sin and the love of God for the sinner. The holy God makes himself the object of his own wrath in the person of his Son Jesus Christ. The sacrifice must be made from the side of man and by a representative of mankind, but this role can only be fulfilled by the Son of God incarnate in human flesh. Luther declared that God's wrath "is so great that no creature can carry it nor effect atonement except the Son of God alone through His own sacrifice and death."[33] The Son Jesus Christ had to die so that God could treat us as sons and no longer as transgressors. But the deeper meaning is that God in the person of his Son experiences the death and hell which humankind deserves, and in this identification his holy love is both demonstrated and satisfied.

Forsyth is absolutely right when he says: "The sinner's reconciliation to a God of holy love could not take place if guilt were not destroyed, if judgment did not take place on due scale, if the wrath of God did not somehow take real effect."[34] Yet Forsyth and Barth as well are also right in reminding us that the deepest meaning of the cross is not that God's wrath was poured out on a perfect or innocent man, a scapegoat for human sin, but that God turned his wrath upon himself in the person of his Son. The offering was not made to a God who stood apart waiting to receive it. Rather it was an offering that fully expressed God's love and righteousness. It was an offering made not simply by man to God but by God to God, "the self-sacrifice of the perfectly holy Son to the perfect holiness of the Father."[35]

Lastly, we should consider the regenerative aspect of the atonement. The atonement entails not only the propitiation of God and the expiation of guilt but also inward cleansing, regeneration, sanctification. God must not only be reconciled to man, but man must be reconciled to God. J. N. D. Anderson declares:

> Man does, indeed, need a radical change of heart; he needs to begin to hate his sin instead of loving it, and to love God instead of hating him; he needs, in a word, to be reconciled to God. And the place, above all others, where this change takes place is at the foot of the cross, when he apprehends something of the hatred of God for sin and his indescribable love for the sinner.[36]

The atonement is not only the source of pardon but also the wellspring of new life in Christ. It consists not only in forensic justification but also in mystical regeneration. It not only liberates us objectively from the powers of sin and darkness but also frees us inwardly from the compulsion to sin. Holiness is not only accounted to us but imparted to us as we confront the cross of Christ in faith. Through the cross man makes contact with liberating love and is thereby enabled to enter creatively into the sufferings of others (Moltmann).

OBJECTIVE AND SUBJECTIVE ATONEMENT

Another facet of soteriology that has given rise to much discussion is the exact relationship between the objective and subjective dimensions of the atonement. While the focus of Anselm, A. A. Hodge, Barth, and Aulén was on the objective pole of the atonement, other theologians including Abelard, Eckhart, Schleiermacher, and Bultmann were much more concerned with the subjective pole. It is our position that both poles must be held together in dialectical relation and balance.

First it must be said that the atonement does have an objective basis in the life and death of Jesus Christ. Something happened for our salvation in the death and resurrection of Christ independent of our belief or response. Reconciliation and redemption are an accomplished fact (Rom. 5:10; 2 Tim. 1:10; Heb. 7:27; 9:12), an objective reality that is not affected by the subjective attitude of man (Rom. 3:3; 2 Tim. 1:9; 2:13). "His death on the Cross," Emil Brunner declares, "is not only a parabolic suggestion of the divine reconciliation, *it is* this reconciliation, its completion, its reality."[37] The atonement of Jesus Christ signifies a transformation of the human situation, and not simply the possibility of a future salvation. Through the propitiatory sacrifice of Christ God took upon himself the severity of his judgment and now accepts the world in self-giving love. In Christ we become reconciled to God as God has become reconciled to us. Luther put it this way: "Christ took our sins and the sins of the whole world as well as the Father's wrath on his shoulders, and he has drowned them both in himself so that we are thereby reconciled to God and become completely righteous."[38]

P. T. Forsyth reminds us of the cosmic dimensions of the atonement:

It is a reconciliation of *the world as a cosmic whole.* The world as one whole; not a person here and another there, snatched as brands from the burning; not a group here and a group there; but the reconciliation of the whole world.[39]

His victory is the basis of every man's reconciliation, not an invitation only (Forsyth). He brings to us not simply the possibility of salvation (as in Bultmann and Ebeling) but the very reality of salvation. We have been liberated, justified, and redeemed in that the demonic forces have been objectively dethroned and defeated, God's wrath has been dispelled, the curse of the law has been lifted, and this is true for everyone, both believers and unbelievers.

The sacrifice of Christ on the cross cannot be repeated or extended. As the author of Hebrews says: "He has no need, like those high priests, to offer sacrifices daily, first for his own sins and then for those of the people; he did this once for all when he offered up himself" (7:27). The atonement of Christ cannot be recreated or duplicated in the mass or in religious experience. Walter Kreck declares: "In the message of the cross the unique event of reconciliation is proclaimed as valid for all time, so that the possibility is excluded that it would ever be repeated, supplemented, or surpassed."[40]

Yet though the work of Christ is finished *for* the sinner, it is not yet finished *in* the sinner. Our salvation has been completed and fulfilled objectively, but it is not yet completed subjectively, in the lives and experiences of people. The first stage of redemption is completed, but redemption in its second stage, which has to do with the activity of the Holy Spirit, is only now being unfolded. The atoning work of Christ on the cross is consummated, but it must be followed by the revealing and regenerating work of the Spirit if man is to be saved de facto (in fact) as well as de jure (in principle). Salvation includes not only deliverance from the guilt and penalty of sin secured by the mediatorial work of Christ; it also consists in deliverance from the power and presence of sin effected by the operation of the Holy Spirit.

In giving due recognition to the interior work of the Holy Spirit, we must always seek to keep the external work of Christ in prominent view. We must not say, as is Bultmann's inclination, that salvation is real only for faith. But we can and must say that salvation is real *for me* only through faith. The situation of man has been objectively and radically changed, and this is Barth's emphasis. Yet the new reality of Christ's redemption must penetrate and transform the inner being of man if he is to be included in the body of Christ. Christ suffered and atoned for all vicariously, but man remains bound to the powers of sin and corruption until he is brought by the Spirit into personal contact with the saving work of Christ.

Martin Luther perhaps better than any other theologian grasped the integral relation between the objective and subjective aspects of our salvation. He saw that salvation is not simply an objective event in the past but an objective-subjective event which must affect the very being of man in the present. He declared: "This is the mystery of the riches of divine grace for sinners; for by a wonderful exchange our sins are now not ours but Christ's, and Christ's righteousness is not Christ's but ours."[41] Yet for Luther this exchange takes place not only in Christ but also in faith. Faith is therefore a part of reconciliation itself.

The redemption of Christ on the cross is correlative with the decision of faith. The word of reconciliation does not achieve its validity through our acceptance, but it does become efficacious in this way. All people have been redeemed objectively and de jure, but only the believer is redeemed in toto and de facto, since only he has personally appropriated the reality of Christ's salvation. Only he is *in Christ* actually and not simply virtually or symbolically. Only he truly benefits from the salvation wrought by Christ on the cross, in the sense that only he begins to live in the full dispensation of the freedom that is now available to the whole world.

Hanson has made this perceptive remark: "The atonement is not the prelude to our forgiveness but the enactment and focus of it."[42] And yet we go astray if we assume that we are forgiven no matter what we believe or what we do. God's forgiveness does not become an efficacious reality in our lives apart from faith and repentance. His forgiveness to be sure is more than an offer, but this is only true for those who respond in faith. In faith we discover that we have already been forgiven; at the same time we are moved to appropriate this forgiveness so that it becomes a present saving experience in the here and now.[43]

The doctrine of the substitutionary atonement signalizes that we are saved through and by Christ alone *(solus Christus)*. Yet we must have in mind not only Christ on the cross but also Christ in our hearts. He saves us not only by dying for us but also by being reborn within us by his Spirit. We need to do justice to both the forensic and mystical dimensions of the work of Christ if we are to have a comprehensive theory of the atonement.

PARTICULAR AND UNIVERSAL ATONEMENT

A controversy that has raged in evangelical Protestantism and that continues in conservative circles is whether the atonement of Christ is particular or universal. While Calvinists have stressed limited or particular atonement, Arminians and Lutherans have emphasized the universality of the atonement. Some Arminians have distinguished between impetration, the purchase of salvation, which is general, and application which is personal and definite. There are many passages in Calvin that attest the universal outreach of the atonement, but he maintained that though the cross of Christ is sufficient for the salvation of the world, it is efficient or effectual only for some. For Calvin it might be said that all is of grace, but grace is not for all. Wesley and Luther on the other hand held that all is of grace and grace is for all, but not all are for grace. Karl Barth, who unites the Calvinist emphasis on irresistible or triumphant grace and the Arminian stress on the universality of the atonement, maintains that grace encompasses all but every person is set against grace; at the same time every one is caught up in the movement of grace even where there is continued opposition to it.

In general it can be said that Reformed Christianity has emphasized the particularity of the atonement while Pietism and revivalism, including some revival movements within the Reformed churches, have placed the emphasis on universal atonement. Zinzendorf echoes the views of many within German Pietism:

> For all at once all sin is atoned for on the Cross, the entire Fall is erased, and the whole obligation to Satan and the entire sentence passed upon the fall of Adam is torn up, cancelled, and annulled by the nails of Jesus. . . . On the wood of the Cross the world was saved all at once, and whoever is lost loses himself, because he will not receive the Saviour, because he falls again and repeats the fall of Adam. . . .[44]

A. A. Hodge is one who adamantly holds to limited atonement.[45] "We believe," he says, "that as far as the heathen are concerned, to whom Christ is never offered, salvation is no more objectively available than subjectively possible."[46] Following the older Reformed theology he subordinates redemption to election. Christ dies only for those who have been predestined into the kingdom of God from all eternity. Does this mean that God loved only the elect? This seems to be the case for Hodge: "God, eternally anterior to their creation and irrespective of their character, loved the elect, and hated the non-elect, predestinating the first to holiness and happiness, and the other to *sin* and misery forever."[47]

Needless to say there is truth on both sides of this controversy, but in our opinion those who emphasize the universal atonement of Christ are more faithful to the witness of Scripture, since we are told that God loved the whole world (John 3:16) and that Christ gave his life as a ransom for all (1 Tim. 2:6; cf. 1 John 2:2; Titus 2:11). Yet the Calvinists are right that the atonement not only makes salvation possible but also secures it, and in this sense it encompasses only those who respond in faith. Every human being is a blood-bought soul, as Wesley affirmed, but not all take advantage of their God-given opportunity. The truth in the doctrine of limited or definite atonement is that its efficacy does not extend to all persons. It is universal in its outreach and intention but particular in its efficacy.[48]

Perhaps we can say that all mankind is reconciled and justified in principle (de jure) but not in fact (de facto) insofar as not all have apprehended and appropriated their justification and redemption. Barth declares that ontologically all people are redeemed but existentially most people are still unredeemed in that their eyes have not been opened to the fact of their redemption, which Christ has objectively wrought on their behalf in his obedience unto death.

The question remains, however, whether Scripture expressly teaches that all mankind is already in the state of redemption, that the whole human race is redeemed in actuality, a motif which is implicit if not explicit in the Barthian theology. Scripture tells us that the grace of Christ has appeared for the salvation of all (Titus 2:11), but nowhere is it explicitly affirmed that the salvation of the whole human race is actually and effectively completed in the work of Christ. Paul declares that God has consigned all men to disobedience that he may have mercy upon all (Rom. 11:32), but he is here speaking not about the work on the cross but about the final revelation of God's grace, which was to be sure anticipated by the cross. There is also some basis for believing that he is referring to the corporate unities of Gentiles and Jews rather than to every single person. Even if it were granted that God's mercy was poured out on all at the cross—and with this we have no problem, it must not be assumed that this means universal salvation, since God's mercy is realized in the lives of people in different ways. Paul makes very clear that effectual salvation is contingent on the decision of faith: "If, because of one man's trespass, death reigned through that one man, much more will those who receive the abundance of grace and the free gift of righteousness reign in life through the one man Jesus Christ" (Rom. 5:17; cf. 8:9, 10; 10:9–13).

Barth has argued on the basis of 2 Corinthians 5:14 and 15 that in Christ the whole of sinful mankind has died, and therefore all are necessarily included in the new humanity created by Christ.[49] Barth sees this inclusion in a realistic and not merely a symbolic sense. Our position is that the immediate reference of this text is to all believers rather than to all humankind. Christ dies on behalf of all, the benefits of his death extend to all, but only those who are "in Christ" are a new creation (cf. 2 Cor. 5:17). Floyd Filson contends that Paul's statement "therefore all have died" (v. 14) refers to all "who as members of his body, the church, are vitally linked with him in all things."[50] Paul, he says, "thinks of Christ as the new Adam, the representative and head of the new humanity" which includes only those who respond to Christ's offer in faith and baptism. At the same time we must not deny that Christ is also the Representative of fallen mankind (see v. 21), and in a wider and deeper sense it *can be affirmed* that the whole human race was crucified on the cross.[51] Christ is the surrogate or substitute for all people, pagans and Jews as well as Christians, but his death is efficacious only for believers. His atoning sacrifice is applicable to all and even reckoned to all in principle, but its benefits are realized only in some. Though Christ died for all, only those who have been engrafted into his body in faith can be said to have died in and with him in the full sense.

Another relevant and equally controversial verse is 1 Corinthians 15:22: "For as in Adam all die, so also in Christ shall all be made alive." Barth's view is that "all" in both cases signifies the totality of human-ity.[52] Clarence Tucker Craig on the other hand contends that "the *all* are to be qualified by *in Christ.*"[53] Here again we are faced with the paradox that though Christ claims all, not all receive the blessing of eternal life, since only some believe. This is not to deny that even unbelievers are affected by Christ's sacrifice which is universal in its scope and intention, and that even they will participate in the resurrec-tion of the dead because of his sacrifice.[54] Yet theirs will be a resurrec-tion unto judgment rather than a resurrection unto glory (John 5:29).

When we relate the atonement of Christ to its implications and consequences in the world we are at once confronted with a paradox, which must be respected rather than explained away. One is compelled to make this double affirmation: only those who believe have been effectively redeemed by Christ, and only those who are effectively re-deemed come to believe. This is not necessarily a commitment to lim-ited atonement, however, since the ultimate number of those who be-lieve is hidden with God. It must also be affirmed that even those who do not believe are benefited by the cross and resurrection of Christ, since the devil and his hosts were objectively overthrown and defeated irrespective of man's response to the cross. Moreover, God's forgiveness is offered to all regardless of their obedience or disobedience, though we must insist that his forgiveness is realized only in the decision of re-pentance and faith. In contrast to both Calvinistic and Arminian ratio-nalism we recognize that we are dealing with a rationally insurmount-able mystery wherein the universality of God's electing love is held together with the particularity of realized salvation.

The illustration of the liberation of a prison by an outside invading force may shed some light on this mystery. The prison has been stormed, and the gates of the prison have been opened, but unless we leave our prison cells and go forward into the light of freedom, we are still unredeemed in actuality. Yet if we do respond to the word of our liberators and believe the news that the gates are now open, the glory and credit must go to our liberators and not to ourselves. In one sense all are redeemed by the invading force of freedom, but in another sense only some are redeemed, since only some respond in faith. The others prefer to live in the darkness of fearfulness and unfreedom. Or they are beguiled by the voices of their former captors who loudly boast that they are in full control of the situation, though their power has been taken from them (Col. 2:15); yet they still wield a modicum of power through their deception.

All are under the sign of divine predestination, all are called to liberation and salvation, but this predestination takes effect in different ways depending on whether there is a response in faith. Those who believe become the sons and daughters of God, whereas those who reject their election in Christ become servants of God even against their wills.[55] We affirm a single predestination but a twofold way in which this is implemented.[56] All are foreordained to be signs and witnesses of Christ, but some through their stubbornness and negligence become signs of contradiction. All are elected to be theaters of his glory, but his glory is reflected in condemnation as well as salvation. All are appointed in some way to share in the benefits of Christ's salvation, but those who taste of these benefits without repentance and faith will invariably bring judgment upon themselves (1 Cor. 11:28–30; 2 Cor. 2:15, 16).

As can be seen I am remarkably close to Karl Barth in his affirmation of the universality of calling and election, but the difference is that I emphasize the particularity of how these are realized in humanity. My position is in accord with one strand in Barth—his acknowledgement that not all respond to the divine calling and become children of God in actual life and practice—though he sees all as children of God de jure, by virtue of the election of all humankind in Jesus Christ.[57] All are ordained for fellowship with Christ, but only some are "set in this fellowship," only some realize their destiny to be sons and daughters of God.[58] At the same time there is another strand in Barth in which predestination virtually rules out the possibility of any being excluded from the family of God. Barth propounds a universalism of hope which sees man's sinful resistance being overcome by the invincible and sovereign love of Jesus Christ. In his view one cannot posit a final universal restoration *(apokatastasis)* as a rational conclusion of faith, since this is not explicitly asserted in the Bible. Yet one can be permitted to harbor the joyous expectation that non-Christians too will be moved to acclaim Jesus Christ as Lord and King, an expectation borne of the realization that God's grace is more powerful than man's sin. We also uphold a universalism of hope in which no person is given up as lost, in which even the most depraved can be reclaimed by sovereign grace;

yet at the same time we cannot close our eyes to the biblical testimony that only some will persevere to the end, that some will finally be cut off from the promises of the kingdom.

THE OBLIGATION OF THE CHRISTIAN

Another lingering controversy in the church concerns the obligation of the Christian in the light of Christ's all-sufficient atonement. The question is often asked whether we do not have to do something for our salvation, whether we do not have to suffer too. Here we must reply that the atoning work of Christ on the cross is completed and needs no supplementation or fulfillment by man. Christ suffered the condemnation of sin in our place, and this means not only the eternal consequences of sin but also its temporal consequences. It is incumbent on us to acknowledge and receive the gift of Christ's salvation, but we no longer have to work out our debts, since these have been paid by Christ. We no longer have to carry the curse of the law, though we now suffer the trials of faith as we follow Christ in costly discipleship. We need to work out the consequences and implications of our salvation (Phil. 2:12), but we do not procure our salvation through our works. This would be a form of works-righteousness, which is solidly refuted in Paul's Epistles as well as in the Protestant Reformation.

In medieval theology it was said that the work of Christ assures forgiveness only for original sin, but we need further forgiveness from God because of our subsequent sins. Therefore the sacrament of Penance was considered as vital to our salvation as the sacrament of Baptism. It was also propounded that only the eternal consequences of sin have been removed by Christ's sacrifice and that man must still suffer the temporal consequences in this life and in a purgatory beyond death. Against this view we contend that God's forgiveness is radical and total. We read: " 'For I will be merciful toward their iniquities, and I will remember their sins no more' " (Heb. 8:12). To be sure man needs purification before he can see the face of God (Heb. 12:14), but this, just as much as reconciliation and justification, is assured to him through his faith in Christ. Man needs to be purified of his sins by the work of the Spirit within him, but he does not need to earn either this purification or salvation by works of love. Purification by the Spirit is a gift of grace even as is salvation itself.

In the late middle ages a kind of semi-Pelagianism arose in which man's works were seen as necessary to the fulfillment of Christ's salvation. Gabriel Biel declared: "Though the passion of Christ is the principal merit on account of which grace is infused, the kingdom opened and glory granted, yet it is never the sole and complete meritorious cause."[59] And again: "If we do not add our merits to those of Christ, the merits of Christ will not only be insufficient, but non-existent." It was also said that the faithful on earth could by their good works render atonement for one another and thereby effectively bring about the remission of the temporal punishment for sin.[60]

Against this type of theology Luther and Calvin emphasized *solus Christus* and *sola gratia,* that our salvation is a work of Christ alone and a work of grace alone. These themes of the Reformation were reaffirmed in Puritanism and Pietism. "We are reconciled to God," declared Zinzendorf, "not by our own works, not by our own righteousness, but wholly and solely by the blood of Christ."[61]

Here also we see the decisive difference between evangelical religion and the mystical religion of the Orient, especially Hinduism and Buddhism, in which it is said that people must work out the damnable consequences of their sin and folly in successive reincarnations.[62] In this perspective one's works, thoughts, and deeds in this life irrevocably fix one's lot in future existences.[63] In evangelical Christianity on the other hand the burden of sin or karma is borne by Christ himself (cf. Ps. 55:22). He frees us from the curse of the law, from the deleterious effects of our sin (Rom. 8:2). The bond which stood against us with its legal demands has been cancelled having been nailed to the cross (Col. 2:14).[64] To be sure, if we do not abide in Christ the law of sin and consequences reemerges in our lives, a situation that is tolerated by God only as a reminder of the sin and guilt that have been banished from our lives once for all by the cross of Christ. Insofar as we are in Christ we are freed from this law, but insofar as we remain outside of Christ we still suffer pangs of guilt and remorse.[65] But even this suffering is borne by Christ within us and converted into another kind of suffering—the suffering for the sake of our neighbor and the kingdom. Paul says that there are two kinds of sorrow, the sorrow that comes to us because of sin and the godly sorrow that leads to repentance (2 Cor. 7:9, 10); the first is transformed into the second when the Spirit works within us convicting us of our sin.

The law of sowing and reaping still holds true for the Christian (Gal. 6:7, 8), but in a new way. The Christian reaps both good and evil on the basis of his works, but the good is a superabundant good, the gift of eternal life, which is merited only by the saving work of Jesus Christ. In this sense the Christian reaps beyond what he sows (cf. Ps. 126:5, 6;

Matt. 20:1–16; Matt. 25:23, 28; John 4:36–38; 2 Cor. 9:10). When he sins he reaps the pangs of guilt and death, but he does not reap eternal death which he deserves to suffer because of sin for the burden of his sin has already been borne by Christ. Moreover, in his resurrection Christ forever broke the power of death, sin, and hell. As Paul says: "For the law of the Spirit of life in Christ Jesus has set me free from the law of sin and death" (Rom. 8:2). And again: "Now to one who works, his wages are not reckoned as a gift but as his due. And to one who does not work but trusts him who justifies the ungodly, his faith is reckoned as righteousness" (Rom. 4:4, 5). The Christian is no longer under the iron law of retribution, but he is now under the law of Christ (1 Cor. 9:21). This means that he is granted the permission and privilege of following Christ amid suffering and death, but he is no longer obligated to make reparations for his sins because this has been taken care of by Christ. While Christ bore our guilt which is heavy, it is laid upon us to bear his yoke which is light (Matt. 11:29, 30).

The superseding and redirecting of the law of retributive justice by divine grace is also abundantly attested in the Old Testament. After telling the children of Israel that their pain and guilt are incurable and irremediable, Jeremiah assures them that God will heal their wounds because their enemies revile them as outcasts (Jer. 30:12–17). Hosea proclaimed God's love to a stubborn and disobedient people: " 'I will heal their faithlessness; I will love them freely, for my anger has turned from them' " (14:4). And in the words of Micah (7:18, 19):

Who is a God like thee, pardoning iniquity, and passing over transgression for the remnant of his inheritance? . . .

He will again have compassion upon us, he will tread our iniquities under foot. Thou wilt cast all our sins into the depths of the sea.

One incident in the Old Testament merits special attention. David had sinned grievously in the sight of God by plotting the murder of Uriah, but the prophet Nathan reproved the king, who then repented of his sin. Nathan said to David: " 'The Lord also has put away your sin; you shall not die. Nevertheless, because by this deed you have utterly scorned the Lord, the child that is born to you shall die' " (2 Sam. 12:13, 14). The New English version reads: " 'The Lord has laid on another the consequences of your sin. . . .' " (v. 13). As Christians we see that the full impact of this prophecy is fulfilled in Jesus Christ, for only he has suffered the consequences of everyman's sin. God "did not spare his own Son" in giving himself "up for us all" (Rom. 8:32). The death of David's child is a type of the death of Christ on the cross, the death of the child in Bethlehem, who is also of the lineage of David. There on the cross Jesus Christ, the Son of God, reaped the consequences of what a fallen mankind has sown, namely, sin, death, and hell. All mankind is now set free, though our freedom is aborted unless we lay hold of it in a life of repentance, faith, and obedience.

We acknowledge that the substitutionary atonement has been so interpreted in the past that it has become a form of cheap grace practically exempting the Christian from the divine imperative to do good works (cf. 1 Tim. 6:18). Yet rightly understood it can be a tremendous source of spiritual power and motivation in living a Christian life. James Denney has declared: "Whoever says 'He bore our sins' says substitution; and to say substitution is to say something which involves an immeasurable obligation to Christ, and has therefore in it an incalculable motive power."[66] The Christian is impelled to do good works out of gratefulness for what Jesus Christ has done on his behalf. He is inwardly motivated to give glory to God by upholding Jesus Christ in his words and actions. He is obliged to take up his cross and follow Jesus Christ in costly discipleship in order to demonstrate his love and gratefulness for the supreme sacrifice of his Savior.

MISUNDERSTANDINGS IN MODERN THEOLOGY

In modern theology, with a few exceptions, the traditional meaning of the sacrifice of Christ on the cross has been drastically altered. In some cases to be sure the misunderstanding is only slight, but once the door is opened to cultural or philosophical intrusions into biblical faith, grave consequences usually follow.

It is customary in modern theology to deprecate the concept of propitiation on the grounds that God's holiness does not need to be propitiated but only revealed and that consequently the sacrifice of Christ is the mediation of God's forgiveness to the world and not its condition. It is commonly said that only man needs to be reconciled to God but that God, being pure love, is already reconciled to his creation. These ideas in various forms can be detected in Ritschl, Pannenberg, Barth, Tillich, Nygren, Vincent Taylor, and Jürgen Moltmann. Penal redemption has been supplanted by vicarious identification whereby God in Christ participates in the estrangement of the human condition in order to draw us into fellowship with him. It is said that Christ is the representative of God rather than the substitute for man (Dorothy Sölle). He is the New Being (Tillich), the mediator of God-consciousness

(Schleiermacher), the symbol of divine-human unity (Hegel) rather than a divine Savior who takes upon himself the curse of sin in our stead so that we might appear guiltless before the throne of God.

The mystical and moral influence theories of the atonement have made a dramatic comeback on the modern scene. Christ saves us by contagious love (J. A. T. Robinson) or by the shock effect which his death has upon us, resulting in repentance and conversion (Herman Wiersinga). Teilhard de Chardin seeks to supplant the cross of expiation with the "cross of evolution" whereby Christ is depicted as the apex of man's moral and spiritual progress.[67] It is said that Jesus inspires us to give of ourselves through his sacrificial life and death (Thomas O'Meara). Many of these ideas contain an element of truth. We particularly need to note that the atonement, in order to be effective in the lives of people, must take root within them. It involves not only the objective imputation of righteousness but the subjective participation in this righteousness.

It must be acknowledged that the theory of penal redemption can itself give rise to profound misinterpretations. We must indeed say that God is wrathful outside of Christ, but at the same time we should insist that God is loving toward all, since all are elected to be in Christ. The deepest meaning of substitutionary atonement is that God takes upon himself his own wrath out of his boundless love. This has already been accomplished in the preexistent Jesus Christ, but it needs to be demonstrated, revealed, and fulfilled in an atonement within history. Already before the shedding of the blood of Christ on the cross God determined to unite himself with humanity in order both to satisfy the demands of his holiness and to reveal the depth of his love. The cross of Jesus Christ can therefore be regarded as the condition as well as the revelation and mediation of divine forgiveness.

Some in our time have said that the atonement is effected only by God and made necessary only by his love. Others on the conservative side of the theological spectrum maintain that the atonement is effected from the side of man. It is seen as a sacrifice made by Jesus as man and offered to God. We hold that the atonement is made by Jesus Christ as the God-Man who turns away God's wrath because he embodies God's righteousness and love. It is both a royal victory and a priestly sacrifice. It signifies vicarious identification with the sin of man as well as an expiation of the guilt of man. The sacrifice is both eternal and historical. What is sacrificed is both human innocence and divine majesty. God's mercy goes beyond justice, but it does not negate the law of justice. The merits of Christ are not only sufficient but superabundant (Thomas Aquinas); they not only pay the price of sin but assure an eternal reward in heaven.

The forgiveness of God is unconditional, in that it goes out to the undeserving, but it is also demanding. It demands that God's law be satisfied. Salvation is more than accepting the fact that one is accepted (as in Tillich). It entails heartfelt repentance for sin and total commitment to Jesus Christ as the divine Savior from sin. Jesus Christ alone has satisfied the requirements of God's law, but it is incumbent upon us to live according to the spirit of this law as a sign of our infinite debt to a God of boundless compassion.

We maintain that reconciliation involves a change not only in man but also in God—in both his feeling toward man and his treatment of man. Both God's attitude toward us and his practical relation to us had to be changed for him to treat us as sons and daughters and not as transgressors. Yet this reconciliation took place in eternity before it took place on the cross of Calvary. This is why we can affirm that God loved the whole world even prior to the incarnation, and why the incarnation and the atonement as well must be seen as a movement of divine love toward man. We agree with Luther that the work of Christ does not create a gracious God but presupposes it. As the prophet declared: "In all their affliction he was afflicted . . . , in his love and in his pity he redeemed them. . . . (Isa. 63:9).

Yet in our emphasis on God's love we must remember that reconciliation could not take place unless the holiness of God were mollified. Christ was not only obedient unto death but obedient unto radical judgment, the judgment of holiness. Yet we must see in this obedience and suffering the presence of God himself. Indeed God not only demands but makes the offering, but in the garb of humanity and for the sake of humanity. As Forsyth averred: "It is God in Christ reconciling. It was not human nature offering its very best to God. It was God offering his very best to man."[68] At the same time we must not forget that the offering must be made from the side of man, since it is man who has sinned, and it is man who must make restitution (cf. 1 Tim. 2:5, 6). The Gospel is that the Son of God in union with humanity makes the one sacrifice that absolves mankind from all guilt, the substitutionary sacrifice on Calvary. God's wrath has been assuaged, his holiness has been satisfied, but only because God in his love chose to identify himself with sinful man and in the person of Jesus suffer what we deserve to suffer because of our sin.

God loved us before the foundation of the world, but he could not establish a fellowship of love and reconciliation with fallen humankind until the incarnation and vicarious atonement of his Son. In Jesus Christ his love and wrath are both revealed, his holiness is satisfied, and his grace is demonstrated. The cross signifies the incursion of triumphant divine love and grace into human history but for the purpose of reconciling fallen man to Eternity.

NOTES

1. Leon Morris rightly reminds us that we can speak of God being reconciled only in a qualified sense, since God's love is ever-present. See Leon Morris, *The Apostolic Preaching of the Cross* (Grand Rapids: Eerdmans, 1965), pp. 220–221.

2. J. I. Packer, *Knowing God* (Downers Grove, Ill.: InterVarsity Press, 1973), pp. 170–172.

3. Arthur Crabtree contends that the world *hilasterion* in Romans 3:25 "signifies both the expiation or covering over of sin and the propitiation or placation of God." In his *The Restored Relationship* (Valley Forge, Pa.: Judson Press, 1963), p. 63. Leon Morris gives an excellent treatment of "propitiation" in *The Apostolic Preaching of the Cross,* pp. 125–185. He persuasively argues that *hilaskomai* and its cognates include as an integral part of their meaning the turning away of the wrath of God. Also cf. William Sanday and Arthur C. Headlam, *A Critical and Exegetical Commentary on the Epistle to the Romans* reprint of 5th ed. (Edinburgh: T. & T. Clark, 1955), pp. 92, 130; and C. E. B. Cranfield, *A Critical and Exegetical Commentary on the Epistle to the Romans,* vol. 1 (Edinburgh: T. & T. Clark, 1975), pp. 214–218.

4. A. A. Hodge, *The Atonement* reprint (Grand Rapids: Baker Book House, 1974), p. 184.

5. D. Martyn Lloyd-Jones, *Romans: An Exposition of Chapters 3:20–4:25* (Grand Rapids: Zondervan, 1971), p. 77.

6. See Gerhard Kittel, ed., *Theological Dictionary of the New Testament,* vol. 4, trans. G. W. Bromiley (Grand Rapids: Eerdmans, 1967), p. 343.

7. Emil Brunner, *The Christian Doctrine of Creation and Redemption,* trans. Olive Wyon (Philadelphia: Westminster Press, 1952), p. 284.

8. P. T. Forsyth, *The Cruciality of the Cross* (London: Independent Press Ltd., 1948), p. 99.

9. Charles A. M. Hall presents a cogent case that the *Christus Victor* motif is also widely pervasive in John Calvin, though it is united with the juridical view. See Hall, *With the Spirit's Sword* (Richmond, Va.: John Knox Press, 1968).

10. For a further discussion of this concept see Donald G. Bloesch, *Jesus is Victor! Karl Barth's Doctrine of Salvation* (Nashville: Abingdon Press, 1976), pp. 41–42, 124–126.

11. Anselm's doctrine, therefore, does not require that there be any change of attitude on the part of God, though this is often supposed. The satisfaction is offered to the abstract retributive justice of God rather than to his personal wrath.

12. Anselm seeks to unite the motifs of justice and honor. Compensation is due to the injured honor of God, but his offended justice requires satisfaction. One critic comments that these are two incompatible ideas which account for some of the inconsistencies in Anselm. See George Cadwalader Foley, *Anselm's Theory of the Atonement* (London: Longmans, Green & Co., 1907), pp. 148–153.

13. Aulén convincingly argues that the idea of vicarious punishment is definitely present in Anselm, even though he may try to minimize it. Gustaf Aulén, *Christus Victor,* trans. A. G. Hebert (New York: Macmillan, 1960), pp. 93, 94. Aulén also reminds us that this idea was very much evident in Anselm's predecessors on whom he depended. The motif of vicarious punishment is certainly evident in this statement of Ambrose: "He also took up death that the sentence might be fulfilled and satisfaction might be given for the judgment, the curse placed on sinful flesh even to death." In *Saint Ambrose: Seven Exegetical Works,* trans. Michael P. McHugh (Washington, D.C.: Catholic University of America Press, 1972), pp. 314, 315.

14. Foley notes the inconsistency in Anselm whereby on the one hand he asserts that Christ's death is the only adequate satisfaction, and on the other he contends that this death went beyond his required obedience. *Ibid.,* pp. 123,139.

15. Note that Alexander Hodge concurs in the judgment of Christian Baur on Calvin. See Hodge, *The Atonement,* p. 389. Calvin did affirm that Christ merited our salvation by his obedience, but his merits did not originate with himself but had their source in the decree and ordinance of God.

16. This indeed is the position of Wendel, who depicts Calvin as very much a Christocentric theologian. See François Wendel, *Calvin,* trans. Philip Mairet (London: Collins, 1963), pp. 227, 228.

17. John Calvin, *Institutes of the Christian Religion,* trans. John Allen, II, 16, 2, p. 553. Cf.: "And there is much contained in the word 'propitiation'; for God, in a certain ineffable manner, at the same time that he loved us, was nevertheless angry with us, till he was reconciled in Christ." *Ibid.,* II, 17, 2, p. 580.

18. Robert Paul argues convincingly that the theory of penal redemption was to some extent qualified in Calvin, since he saw God's love as the ground of Christ's sacrifice and held that all believers should be sharers in this sacrifice. Robert S. Paul, *The Atonement and the Sacraments* (New York: Abingdon Press, 1960), p. 97 f.

19. *Dr. Martin Luther's Large Catechism* (Minneapolis: Augsburg Publishing House, 1935), p. 118. Cf.: "For just as Christ was at once a mortal and an immortal Person, He was indeed subject to death by reason of His humanity; but because His whole Person could not be slain, it happened that death failed, and the devil succumbed in slaying Him; and thus death was swallowed up and devoured in life. In this way the curse was swallowed up and conquered in the blessing, sorrow in joy, and the other evils in the highest good." *Luther's Works,* vol. 29, p. 136.

20. Paul Althaus, *The Theology of Martin Luther,* 2d print. trans. Robert C. Schultz (Philadelphia: Fortress Press, 1970), p. 220.

21. Martin Luther, *Sermons On the Passion of Christ,* trans. E. Smid and J. T. Isensee (Rock Island, Ill.: Augustana Press, 1956), p. 25.

22. Karl Barth, *Church Dogmatics* IV, 1, pp. 552, 553.

23. It is clear that Barth does not wholly discard the themes of penal substitution and satisfaction: "What took place is that the Son of God fulfilled the righteous judgment on us men by Himself taking our place as man and in our place undergoing the judgment under which we had passed." *Ibid.*, p. 222. Yet for Barth this judgment was already pronounced on Christ in eternity, and it was already realized in the incarnation of Christ. The eternal decision of the Son of God to assume human flesh is the basis of our salvation, and the cross simply reveals and confirms what has already taken place.

24. Though Ritschl basically belongs to the moral influence school, his depiction of justification as God's forgiveness to sinful man tends to reflect the Reformation conception. At the same time he believes that this justification becomes effective only in reconciliation, which signifies an alteration in the subjective disposition of man. Jesus' sacrifice is a sacrifice of obedience by which he makes justification accessible to men by revealing it. God forgives so that man can be free to pursue the values of the kingdom of God personified and revealed in Jesus. One interpreter comments that Ritschl's "reconstruction of the work of Christ is a creative restatement of the Abelardian view." David L. Mueller, *An Introduction to the Theology of Albrecht Ritschl* (Philadelphia: Westminster Press, 1969), p. 174.

25. John Miley, an American Arminian theologian, states the case for the Governmental theory in his *The Atonement in Christ* (New York: Hunt & Eaton, 1889).

26. P. T. Forsyth, *The Work of Christ* (London: Hodder and Stoughton, 1910), p. 169.

27. In his discussion of the New Testament idea of ransom *(lutron)* F. Büchsel presents a persuasive case that the ransom is offered to God to satisfy the demands of his holiness. In Gerhard Kittel, *Theological Dictionary of the New Testament,* vol. 4 trans. Geoffrey W. Bromiley (Grand Rapids: Eerdmans, 1967), p. 341 f.

28. Karl Barth, *Church Dogmatics* II, 1, p. 152.

29. *Ibid.,* p. 403.

30. In Reformed and Lutheran orthodoxy the distinction is often made between Christ's active obedience by which he fulfills the law in his life and his passive obedience by which he endures the suffering for sin on the cross. The difficulty with this distinction is that it tends to overlook the fact that Christ was active as well as passive in both his obedience in life and suffering in death.

31. A. A. Hodge, *The Atonement,* p. 31 The chasm between Hodge and Barth is apparent in this statement by the latter: "Righteousness *by the blood of Jesus* is always *righteousness apart from the works of the law;* apart, that is, from everything human which may, before God and man, be declared righteous." Karl Barth, *The Epistle to the Romans,* trans. from 6th ed. by Edwyn C. Hoskyns (New York: Oxford University Press, 1968), paperback, p. 112. In his *Church Dogmatics* Barth relates Christ's salvation more integrally to the law, but he nevertheless maintains that the righteousness of Christ radically transcends legal or rational justice.

32. A. A. Hodge, *The Atonement,* p. 194.

33. Cited in K. Barth, *Church Dogmatics* II, 1, p. 363.

34. P. T. Forsyth, *The Work of Christ*, p. 132.

35. P. T. Forsyth, *The Christian Ethic of War* (London: Longmans, Green & Co., 1916), p. 94.

36. J. N. D. Anderson, *Christianity: The Witness of History* (London: Tyndale Press, 1969), p. 81.

37. Emil Brunner, *The Christian Doctrine of Creation and Redemption*, p. 337.

38. Martin Luther, W. A. 10 III, 137.

39. P. T. Forsyth, *The Work of Christ*, p. 77.

40. "Walter Kreck, 'The Word of the Cross' " in *Interpretation* 24:2, (April 1970), [pp. 220–242], p. 232.

41. Martin Luther, W. A. 5, 608.

42. R. P. C. Hanson, *The Attractiveness of God*, p. 149.

43. One can say that God's forgiveness is both unilateral and mutual in that it goes out to all, but it is not really completed until it is accepted.

44. Nicholaus Ludwig Count von Zinzendorf, *Nine Public Lectures on Important Subjects in Religion*, trans. and ed. George W. Forell (Iowa City: University of Iowa Press, 1973), p. 68.

45. Other modern theologians who hold to limited atonement in the strict sense are Charles Hodge, Arthur Pink, Benjamin Warfield, and Cornelius Van Til.

46. A. A. Hodge, *The Atonement*, p. 360.

47. *Ibid.*, p. 390.

48. Roger Nicole prefers "particular redemption" to "limited atonement" in expressing the basic intention of Calvinism. We are not averse to this term so long as it is maintained that Christ desires all to enter his fold. See Roger R. Nicole, "A Call to Great Preaching" in *Presbyterian Communique* 8:4 (August 1975), pp. 1–3.

49. Karl Barth, *Church Dogmatics* IV, 1, pp. 295 f.

50. Floyd V. Filson, "The Second Epistle to the Corinthians: Introduction and Exegesis" in *The Interpreter's Bible*, vol. 10 (Nashville: Abingdon Press, 1953) [pp. 265–425], p. 335.

51. Tasker says: "Christ's death was the death of all, in the sense that He died the death they should have died; the penalty of their sins was borne by Him." Quoted in Philip E. Hughes, *Paul's Second Epistle to the Corinthians* (Grand Rapids: Eerdmans, 1962), p. 194.

52. Karl Barth, *Christ and Adam*, trans. T. A. Smail (Edinburgh: Oliver & Boyd, 1956), p. 8.

53. Clarence Tucker Craig, "The First Epistle to the Corinthians: Introduction and Exegesis" in *The Interpreter's Bible*, vol. 10 [pp. 3–262], p. 235.

54. One expositor remarks: "The meaning may be that all will be raised, will be quickened, which is not the same as saying that all will be saved." Archibald Robertson and Alfred Plummer, *A Critical and Exegetical Commentary on the First Epistle of St. Paul to the Corinthians* (New York: Scribner's, 1911), p. 353.

55. Against the older Calvinist orthodoxy we affirm that reprobation is not the antithesis of election but resistance to election.

56. If we must speak of double predestination we would do so in Barth's

sense, namely, that Christ takes the decree of condemnation upon himself. At the same time we do not go along with Barth that there is no longer a condemnation and judgment that will befall those outside of Christ. Barth is ambiguous on this question, since occasionally he alludes to a future judgment, though it seems that this will only be the revelation of what has already taken place on Calvary.

57. Barth generally uses the term *adoption* for the incorporation of people into the body of Christ by the work of the Spirit. At the same time in the logic of his theology, all are adopted or at least "elected to be adopted" into the family of God by virtue of their being included in the personal saving history of Jesus Christ.

58. Karl Barth, *Church Dogmatics* IV, 3 b, pp. 534, 535.

59. In Heiko Oberman, *The Harvest of Medieval Theology*, p. 268.

60. That this is still a part of official Catholic dogma is attested by Ludwig Ott: "The Faithful on earth can, by their good works performed in the state of grace, render atonement for one another." In his *Fundamentals of Catholic Dogma*, ed. James Canon Bastible and trans. Patrick Lynch (St. Louis: B. Herder Book Co., 1954), p. 315.

In defense of their position Catholic exegetes often cite Colossians 1:24 where Paul says: "Now I rejoice in my sufferings for your sake, and in my flesh I complete what is lacking in Christ's afflictions for the sake of his body, that is, the church. . . ." We understand Paul to be referring not to the atoning work of Christ, which is completed, but to his present suffering through the members of his body, the Church, for it is here that his victory on the cross is realized in the lives of his people in the world. Because of the mystical union of all believers with Christ what Paul suffers for the sake of the church can properly be called "Christ's afflictions" (cf. 2 Cor. 1:5; 4:10). The lack or imperfection is not in Christ's suffering on the cross but in the Christian's fellowship or communion with this suffering and in the present suffering of Christ in his role as Intercessor. For the very helpful comments of F. F. Bruce, see F. F. Bruce and E. K. Simpson, *Commentary on the Epistles to the Ephesians and the Colossians* (Grand Rapids: Eerdmans, 1957), pp. 214–217.

61. Quoted in Iain Murray, *The Puritan Hope* (London: Banner of Truth Trust, 1971), p. 133.

62. Christian theologians who have held to some form of the doctrine of reincarnation are Origen in the patristic period, and Leslie Weatherhead, Nels Ferré, Quincy Howe, Jr., Hannah Hurnard, and Geddes MacGregor in our own day. Quincy Howe, Jr. states the case for reincarnation in his *Reincarnation for the Christian* (Philadelphia: Westminster Press, 1974). Howe's opposition to the doctrine of vicarious atonement is evident in this remark: "The cross is not so much an act of atonement for man's sin as the price Christ was willing to pay in order to assure men of God's love" (p. 107). John Hick gives a discriminating though not wholly satisfactory critique of reincarnation in his *Death and Eternal Life* (New York: Harper & Row 1976), pp. 363–394. Hick proposes ascending levels of spiritual existence beyond death as an alternative to reincarnation.

63. James Sire perceptively points out that since a person can choose his future acts, the law of karma (whereby one reaps what he sows) does not

necessarily entail determinism or fatalism. See his *The Universe Next Door* (Downers Grove, Ill.: InterVarsity Press, 1976), p. 141.

64. Compare Ambrose: "When that old man of ours was fastened to the cross, the sin was destroyed, the sting blunted, the guilt annihilated." *Saint Ambrose: Seven Exegetical Works,* p. 323.

65. Cf. Luther: "Insofar as Christ is made alive in us, we are without the law, sin, and death. But insofar as he is not yet made alive in us, we are to that extent still under the law, sin, and death." W. A. 39 I, 356.

66. James Denney, *The Death of Christ* (New York: A. C. Armstrong & Son, 1904), p. 100.

67. Teilhard de Chardin, *Christianity and Evolution,* pp. 216 f. The meaning is that Christ bears the weight of a world in evolution (p. 219).

68. P. T. Forsyth, *The Work of Christ,* p. 24.

VIII.
SALVATION BY GRACE

No one can come to me unless the Father who sent me draws him; and
I will raise him up at the last day.

John 6:44

For all alike have sinned . . . and all are justified by God's free grace
alone, through his act of liberation in the person of Christ Jesus.

Romans 3:23, 24 NEB

Let human merits, which perished through Adam, here keep silence,
and let God's grace reign through Jesus Christ.

Augustine

We . . . maintain, that man is not only justified freely once for all,
without any merit of works, but that on this gratuitous justification the
salvation of man perpetually depends.

John Calvin

Men will never believe with a saving and real faith, unless God inclines
the heart; and they will believe as soon as He inclines it.

Blaise Pascal

THE GIFT OF GRACE IN BIBLICAL PERSPECTIVE

The Scriptures are very emphatic that salvation is a free gift of God,
that it cannot be earned or merited by our good behavior. The reason
is that our good works are not good enough to satisfy the stringent
requirements of God's law. If man is to be saved he must be pardoned
on the basis of the perfect righteousness of the Son of God who conde-
scended to stand in man's place. As Paul put it: "There is no distinction;
since all have sinned and fall short of the glory of God, they are justified
by his grace as a gift, through the redemption which is in Christ Jesus.
. . ." (Rom. 3:22–24).

Contrary to what some dispensationalists allege, the theme of salvation by grace alone (sola gratia) is very much evident in the Old Testament as well as in the New. The words of Yahweh to Moses are quite
explicit on this question: "I will be gracious to whom I will be gracious,
and will show mercy on whom I will show mercy" (Ex. 33:19). One of

the perennial temptations of the children of Israel in their conquest of the land of Canaan was to attribute their good fortune to their own righteousness rather than to God's unmerited generosity. It is no wonder that they are given this admonition: "Do not say in your heart, after the Lord your God has thrust them out before you, 'It is because of my righteousness that the Lord has brought me in to possess this land'; whereas it is because of the wickedness of these nations that the Lord is driving them out before you" (Deut. 9:4). Jacob's humble confession to Jehovah is paradigmatic of the truly righteous man: "I am not worthy of the least of all the steadfast love and all the faithfulness which thou hast shown to thy servant. . . ." (Gen. 32:10). This same attitude is reflected in Daniel; "We do not present our supplications before thee on the ground of our righteousness, but on the ground of thy great mercy" (9:18).

The total dependence of man on the grace of God is especially evident in the Book of Isaiah. The prophet confesses: "Yet, O Lord, thou art our Father; we are the clay, and thou art our potter; we are all the work of thy hand" (Isa. 64:8). Salvation is portrayed not as an achievement of the man of righteousness but as an act of God upon the man of sin. Even though Israel continued its backsliding it was given the promise of healing and salvation (Isa. 57:17, 18). Though the prophet was conscious of his sin he could nevertheless exclaim: "I will greatly rejoice in the Lord, my soul shall exult in my God; for he has clothed me with the garments of salvation, he has covered me with the robe of righteousness. . . ." (Isa. 61:10; cf. Zech. 3:4). That salvation is not the culmination of man's quest for God but resides in the initiative of God toward man is also given strong attestation: " 'I was ready to be sought by those who did not ask for me; I was ready to be found by those who did not seek me' " (Isa. 65:1).

The great theologian of grace in the Scriptures is, of course, St. Paul. It was he who inveighed against the Judaizers who were trying to preserve Jewish ceremonial practices, including the rite of circumcision, as a condition for salvation. The Christian is no longer under the law but under grace (Gal. 3:25, 26; 4:5, 6). "But if it is by grace," he says, "it is no longer on the basis of works; otherwise grace would no longer be grace" (Rom. 11:6). Paul is adamant that even faith is a gift of God, that the very ability of man to respond to God "depends not upon man's will or exertion, but upon God's mercy" (Rom. 9:16). It is the Holy Spirit who empowers man to lay hold of God's grace; such a transforming event cannot be attributed to the natural free will of man. Paul declares: "No one can say 'Jesus is Lord' except by the Holy Spirit" (1 Cor.

12:3; cf. John 16:13). Not only faith but everything worthwhile in man's life is to be seen as a gift of God's mercy. "What have you that you did not receive? If then you received it, why do you boast as if it were not a gift?" (1 Cor. 4:7; cf. James 1:17).

This Pauline emphasis is also very much present in the pastoral Epistles. It is said that God "saved us and called us with a holy calling, not in virtue of our works but in virtue of his own purpose and the grace which he gave us in Christ Jesus ages ago. . . ." (2 Tim. 1:9). Our salvation is assured "not because of deeds done by us in righteousness, but in virtue of his own mercy, by the washing of regeneration and renewal in the Holy Spirit. . . ." (Titus 3:5).

The sovereignty of grace is definitely underscored in the Gospel of John. John the Baptist declares: "No one can receive anything except what is given him from heaven" (John 3:27). The words of Jesus are thus recorded: "For as the Father raises the dead and gives them life, so also the Son gives life to whom he will. . . . No one can come to me unless the Father who sent me draws him; and I will raise him up at the last day" (John 5:21; 6:44). It is the Spirit who "will convince the world of sin and of righteousness and of judgment. . . ." (16:8).

People, moreover, are not only saved by grace but also kept by grace (cf. John 17:11; Phil. 1:6; 1 Pet. 1:5). Jesus is not only the author of our faith but also the finisher of our faith (Heb. 12:2 KJ). F. F. Bruce comments on Hebrews 12:15: "If it is the grace of God that sets a man's feet at the entrance of the pathway of faith, it is equally the grace of God that enables him to continue and complete that pathway."[1] The company of the faithful shall never perish, and no one can snatch them from the hands of Christ (John 10:28).

When we move to the Synoptic Gospels and Acts we are compelled to recognize that more weight is given to the role of man in coming to salvation. Yet a careful examination of these texts reveals that they too uphold salvation as a free gift of God. Luke declares: "And when the Gentiles heard this, they were glad and glorified the word of God; and as many as were ordained to eternal life believed" (Acts 13:48). Human responsibility is underlined in the parables of Jesus, but we nevertheless have passages such as this: "So you also, when you have done all that is commanded you, say, 'We are unworthy servants; we have only done what was our duty'" (Luke 17:10). The kingdom of God is consistently depicted as a gift, a treasure, a pearl of great price, though it is up to man to lay hold of this. When grace comes upon him, man cannot remain passive but is compelled to respond to God's gracious invitation.

A passage that is commonly appealed to in liberal and Pelagian

circles in defense of justification by works is Luke 7:36 f. which records
the story of the woman of sin who anoints the feet of Jesus with perfume. Jesus remarks: " 'Therefore I tell you, her sins, which are many,
are forgiven, for she loved much; but he who is forgiven little, loves
little' " (v. 47). It might appear that this woman was forgiven because
she loved much, but this is a gross misunderstanding. Luke wishes to
tell us that her love was the result, the outcome, of the fact that she
had been forgiven. In gratefulness for the fact that Jesus had accepted
her even in her sins, she demonstrated her love by bathing his feet in
perfume. Geldenhuys remarks that it is clear that the woman had
already accepted him as Redeemer and had gained assurance of pardon.[2] In light of the indignation of the Pharisee in whose home this took
place, one can conclude that those who lack forgiveness have little love
to give.

A passage used even more frequently in support of salvation by
works is the parable of the Last Judgment (Matt. 25:31 f.). It appears
that people are to be judged on their response to the poor and needy,
the naked and the hungry. At the same time we must recognize that
the "brethren" who are referred to are the messengers of Christ, and
it is very difficult to separate the message from the person. It seems
indisputable that we are to be judged on how we respond to the message
and the Savior, who is the content of the message, as well as to those
who bring this message to us.[3] Moreover, it is well to bear in mind that
both parties, the "sheep" as well as the "goats" are surprised at the
verdict of the Judge. The elect are not aware that they have done such
wonderful things for Christ, while the rejected are under the misappre-
hension that they did do such things. The intent of the parable is to
show us that we will be judged on the basis of the fruits that our faith
brings, though when we relate this passage to its wider context we see
that the fruits of faith are at the same time the work of grace within
us. They are the evidence and consequence of a grace already poured
out on us. We are to be judged according to our works, but we are saved
despite our works. Both affirmations must be made if we are to do
justice to the mystery of the free gift of salvation. The final judgment
is the confirmation of the validity of a justification already accomplished in Jesus Christ.

Often cited in the Old Testament by liberals and Unitarians as
exemplifying the essence of true religion is Micah 6:8: "What does the
Lord require of you but to do justice, and to love kindness, and to walk
humbly with your God?" Do we see here a definite gulf between Judaism with its ethical thrust and Pauline Christianity with its emphasis

on free grace (as some have claimed)? When this passage is examined in its context, however, we see that the call to ethical action is preceded by the proclamation of grace in verse 4: "For I brought you up from the land of Egypt, and redeemed you from the house of bondage." The people have been set free for works of loving-kindness and justice because they have been recipients of redeeming grace. That faith and trust in the living God are regarded as the foundation or rationale for ethical action is made apparent in Micah 7:7: "But as for me, I will look to the Lord, I will wait for the God of my salvation; my God will hear me." The fruits of faith are works of self-giving love, but the soul of faith is prayer.

One further and even more formidable passage that on first reading seems to imply justification by works is Acts 10:34, 35: "And Peter opened his mouth and said: 'Truly I perceive that God shows no partiality, but in every nation any one who fears him and does what is right is acceptable to him.'" This passage together with Acts 10:4 was frequently appealed to in the later medieval period by Roman Catholic theologians who sought to show that conversion is preceded by a prior obedience made possible by grace but nevertheless dependent on man's cooperation and merit. It has also been used by neo-Protestant and neo-Catholic theologians in the modern period in support of the view that those without conscious faith in Christ may still be saved by a righteous or moral life.

First it is necessary to understand that Peter is addressing Cornelius, a God-fearer among the Gentiles, that is, one who frequented the Jewish synagogue; we are told that his almsgiving and prayers were acknowledged by God (Acts 10:2–4). Yet this must not be taken to suppose that God gives his grace as a reward for natural moral goodness. Cornelius was able to pray and to seek for the true God because he had been exposed to the Hebrew Scriptures which testify to Jesus Christ. There is also reason to believe that he was acquainted with the story of salvation concerning Jesus which was circulating throughout Judea at that time. Grace was already at work in his life thereby enabling him to seek for God, and yet he was not accounted righteous apart from his faith, since Peter makes clear that only those who believe in Christ receive the remission of sins through his name (Acts 10:43). Cornelius did not receive the Spirit until he was confronted by the Gospel preached to him by Peter and led into faith and repentance (Acts 10:44; 11:17, 18). Only then, in the moment of decision, did the righteousness of Christ become his own and cleanse him of his sins.

Verse 35 of ch. 10, which speaks of God accepting all who fear him and who do what is right, must be taken to mean all who are enabled to fear him through the prior grace that is given through the knowledge of Jesus Christ and faith in his atonement. Otherwise Peter would not make the remission of sins contingent on man's faith and repentance (Acts 10:43; 11:17). It is well to note also that this is the same Peter who had previously declared: " 'And there is salvation in no one else, for there is no other name under heaven given among men by which we must be saved' " (Acts 4:12).

In Calvin's view Cornelius is to be placed in the category of the Old Testament fathers who hoped for the salvation of the Redeemer before it was revealed. He was accounted righteous by virtue of his faith in Christ which was yet to be completed or placed on a firm foundation. Calvin interprets the outpouring of the Spirit in verse 44 as referring to the gifts or graces of the Spirit and not to the gift of regeneration; here we would take issue with him. Yet we agree with him that even in the case of Cornelius works are the result and not the precondition of grace. It is well to pay heed to his astute comments on Acts 10:

> Good works do indeed purchase for us the increase of grace, but not by their own desert. For they cannot be acceptable to God without pardon, which they obtain by the benefit of faith. Wherefore it is faith alone which maketh them acceptable. Thus did Cornelius obtain more perfect knowledge of Christ by his prayers and alms, but in that he had God to be favourable and merciful to his prayers and alms, that did depend upon faith. . . . . . .
>
> And we do not deny that God accepteth the good works of the saints; but this is another question, whether man prevent [anticipate] the grace of God with his merits or no, and insinuate himself into His love, or whether he be beloved at the beginning, freely and without respect of works, forasmuch as he is worthy of nothing else but of hatred. Furthermore, forasmuch as man, left to his own nature, can bring nothing but matter of hatred, he must needs confess that he is truly beloved; whereupon, it followeth that God is to Himself the cause that He loveth us, and that He is provoked [actuated] with His own mercy, and not with our merits.[4]

Commenting specifically on verse 35 Joseph Addison Alexander gives this illuminating appraisal, which we readily endorse:

> This verse has sometimes been abused, to prove that the knowledge of the Gospel is not necessary to the salvation of the heathen; whereas it merely teaches that this knowledge is attainable by them, as well as others. The essential meaning is that whatever is acceptable to God in one race is acceptable in any other. *Feareth God and worketh righteousness* are not meritorious conditions or prerequisites to the experience of divine grace, but its fruits and

evidences. He who possesses and exhibits these may know that God accepts him, whatever his descent or country.[5]

Whether the grace of God is particular or universal in its intention and outreach is a question already broached in the preceding chapter. God's mercy encompasses all mankind (Rom. 11:32), though whether his mercy is effectual in the lives of people cannot be separated from their response of faith. The apostle declares that "the grace of God has appeared for the salvation of all men" (Titus 2:11), though it is also clear that we can receive the grace of God in vain (2 Cor. 6:1) and that we can fall away from grace (Gal. 5:4, 7; Heb. 6:4–6). We shall have more to say about this in the third section of this chapter, but we here affirm that when man does apprehend and receive the grace of God this is to be attributed to the power and impact of grace itself, and when he resists and rejects the grace of God this is to be attributed to the hardness of his heart.

Reformed theology has traditionally approached the problem of universal and particular grace by drawing a distinction between common and saving grace. The former is given to all peoples enabling them to survive in a world broken and ravaged by sin. Saving grace on the other hand is given only to the elect, to those who are received into the body of Christ. While disputing the limitation placed on saving grace in the plan of salvation, we concur that there is scriptural basis for affirming a common grace that pertains to the order of preservation rather than redemption. Paul declares to the Athenians: "In past generations he allowed all the nations to walk in their own ways; yet he did not leave himself without witness, for he did good and gave you from heaven rains and fruitful seasons, satisfying your hearts with food and gladness" (Acts 14:16, 17; cf. Ps. 145:8, 9). Jesus proclaimed that the Father in heaven "makes his sun rise on the evil and on the good, and sends rain on the just and on the unjust" (Matt. 5:45). As an evangelical theologian I hold that the history of salvation encompasses only the community of faith, though this history is open for all to enter. God's providential care on the other hand is present and effective in all human history and among all peoples no matter how depraved.

We must pay heed to the biblical witness that grace is revealed definitively and fully in Jesus Christ. In the words of the Fourth Gospel "The law was given through Moses; grace and truth came through Jesus Christ" (John 1:17). Against neo-Lutheran theology we contend that this must not be taken to mean that the law is annulled or superseded by grace. The law of God is itself a gift of grace, and it is fulfilled in the Gospel. The ceremonial law was indeed negated by the coming of Christ, but the moral law was epitomized and radicalized in Jesus Christ. Reformed theology has historically affirmed that the second face of the Law is the Gospel, and the second face of the Gospel is the Law. We concur with Calvin that the Gospel ratifies and confirms what had been promised in the Law.

The New Testament especially makes it clear that grace comes to man while he is yet in his sins (Rom. 5:6–8). Grace also inwardly renews and transforms, but this renewal is based on the prior remission of sins accomplished through the death of Jesus Christ. Even the sanctifying work of the Spirit is enacted in those who do not merit or deserve this. Benjamin Warfield aptly describes the biblical concept of grace as "free sovereign favor to the ill-deserving."[6]

AN AGE-OLD CONTROVERSY

The relation between grace and man's natural free will has been a subject of continual controversy in the church from the very beginning. The early church fathers for the most part adhered to a synergistic orientation in which the role and activity of man were deemed highly significant in the process of salvation. Among the apologists grace came to be seen as "nothing else than the stimulation of the powers of reason existent in man", and revelation was viewed as "supernatural only in respect of its form. . . ."[7] Salvation was conceived by some of the fathers as "ultimately the highest grade of paedagogy. . . . with the Logos as the Teacher."[8]

Cyprian prepared the way for the later biblical-classical synthesis in the area of salvation by his marked emphasis on merit. In his view

it is possible by special sanctity to acquire an accumulation of merit over and above what is needed for the highest grade of the heavenly reward. This surplus of merit may pass over to the benefit of others, through the intercession of those to whose credit it stands; though the benefit can only be obtained by an act of God's grace, conditioned by the relative worthiness of those for whom intercession is made by the saints. He can grant indulgence and He can refuse it: and the bishops and priests of the Catholic Church may be used as the means through which He gives it.[9]

In the late fourth and early fifth centuries Pelagius, a British monk, enunciated a position that was later condemned by the Catholic church as heresy. He denied original sin and salvation by infused grace and affirmed the very real possibility for man to live without sin. The function of Christ is to provide the forgiveness of sins in baptism and to give an example of a sinless life.

Pelagius' views were roundly attacked by St. Augustine, Bishop of Hippo. He declared in opposition to Pelagius that Adam's sin injured not himself alone but the whole human race. Man still possesses a free will, but it is a will that is unable by itself to do good or come to the good. He has free will in the psychological sense, a capacity to make a choice, but the right use of free will is wholly dependent on grace. "Free will is a sufficient cause of evil, but for good it can do nothing unless aided by the Almighty Good."[10] Good works are not the condition of grace but its fruit: "Grace . . . is bestowed on us, not because we have done good works, but that we may be able to do them,—in other words, not because we have fulfilled the law, but in order that we may be able to fulfill the law."[11]

The later Augustine teaches that it is God in his mercy who inspires the response of faith in the helpless sinner. This is not his position in his *De libero arbitrio (On Free Will)* which assumes that the initiative to accept God's offer of grace still belongs to fallen man. Augustine in his maturity speaks of the *servum arbitrium,* the bondage of the will, and he here anticipates Luther and also Calvin. In his view man retains natural freedom but has lost the freedom to do the good.[12] Man's will must be transformed by an infusion of grace before it can seek the good and do the good. And this divine grace is irresistible, since it overpowers and converts man's will. Augustine at one point likened the work of grace upon man to a rider who guides the blind instincts of the horse. The horse is acted upon, and consequently there is no positive cooperation in the procuring of salvation but only submission.

Pelagius' views were condemned at the Synod of Carthage in 418, but semi-Pelagianism then reared its head and became a perennial temptation throughout Catholic history. Jerome ascribed to the human will a share in conversion. For him grace is an aid to the human will but does not actually impel the will to do the good. In his treatise on *Grace* (474) Faustus, abbot of Lérins, contended that grace inclines or assists man's weakened free will to do the right; yet man's will is by no means enslaved to sin and still has the capacity to choose the good. John Cassian held that "the will always remains free in man, and it can either neglect or delight in the grace of God." In his view man on his own can take the initiative in coming to God.[13]

At the Second Council of Orange (529) semi-Pelagianism was likewise condemned. It was asserted that it is grace which causes us to ask for grace. In the third canon we read: "If anyone says that the grace of God can be conferred in answer to man's petition, but that the petition itself is not due to the action of grace, he contradicts the Prophet Isaias and the Apostle, who both say: 'I was found by them that did not seek me, I appeared only to them that asked not after me. . . .' " Yet the Council left some questions unanswered. It did not acknowledge that grace is irresistible and clearly affirmed the capacity of man to cooperate with grace after baptism to accomplish what is pleasing to God.[14]

Despite the staunch affirmation of the Second Council of Orange on the priority and all-sufficiency of grace, semi-Pelagianism reappeared ever again in the Roman church. It was reflected in Abelard who contended that "our free choice is by itself capable of some good."[15] It was particularly conspicuous in late medieval theology and in the theology of the Counter-Reformation. At the same time the Pauline and Augustinian strands within the Catholic church constantly reasserted themselves, and presently, as we shall see, this strand is making a partial comeback.

The evangelical emphasis on free grace resurfaced in Bernard of Clairvaux whose writings were frequently quoted by Calvin and Luther. Bernard made this trenchant observation:

> First of all, it is necessary to believe that you cannot have forgiveness of sins apart from God's mercy. Second, you can have no good work at all unless he gives it. Finally, you cannot merit eternal life by any works unless that is also given free.[16]

Thomas Aquinas reflected biblical and evangelical motifs in his emphasis on the free gift of salvation, but he still sought to give man a role in the accomplishment of justification. For him Christian freedom is a gift wholly beyond the power of fallen man. Yet man's natural will healed and aided by grace contributes to the act of justification.[17] Man is a beneficiary of God's unmerited loving-kindness while still in his sins, but after conversion he is able, by a godly life, to contribute to the increase of his justification.

Thomas differed from the Franciscan spirituality (running from Bonaventure and Alexander of Hales to Duns Scotus, Occam, and Biel)[18] in holding that grace has absolute priority over all human merit. There is no preparation for justification except that which is worked in man by God. It is an "error" to claim "that faith is given by God to us on the merit of our preceding actions."[19] When "anyone is justified without preceding merits, he can be said to have been created as though made from nothing."[20] The Franciscans and Biel on the other hand held that before the infusion of grace man can do works of "equitable or congruous merit" *(meritum de congruo)* which God accepts without any obligation to do so. After conversion he can do works of deserved merit *(meritum de condigno)* and thereby earn for himself an eternal reward. Thomas also referred to the *meritum de condigno*, but for him even this merit is not a matter of strict justice, since justice in the strict sense exists only between equals.[21] He clearly rejected the notion that godly acts are meritorious because of the inner value they possess apart from God's grace. Following Augustine he maintained that in rewarding our merits God is but crowning his own gifts.

Thomas's concern was to make a real place for human responsibility while at the same time affirming salvation as a free gift of God. Although he recognized the role of merit in the realizing of one's salvation, he also emphasized that there is no merit without grace. He was insistent that we must never place our trust and hope in our merits, however much God in his mercy deigns to regard them. We hope for eternal glory "not by reason of our merits, but purely from grace."[22]

At the same time Thomas opened the door to Pelagianism and semi-Pelagianism when he remarked: "To him who does what in him lies, God does not deny grace."[23] He went on to say that God would not only not deny grace to such a person but possibly give him a special direct revelation. The consensus of Catholic scholarship is that Thomas was not referring to the man unaided by grace but to the man already under the influence of grace. To the man who does what is in him with the aid of prevenient grace, the way is prepared for the gift of justifying grace. Nonetheless, such ideas served to promote the semi-Pelagian tendencies that seem endemic in the Roman Catholic tradition.

While acknowledging that Thomas for the most part steers clear of Pelagianism and semi-Pelagianism, some of his Protestant critics have nevertheless argued that his system is still legalistic because he holds that final salvation is contingent on meritorious works of love. Thomas follows Augustine in speaking of merits of grace which God duly rewards. As has been indicated Thomas does not believe that man of himself can make any claim upon the justice of God, nor does he suggest that our trust and hope should be in our merits; nonetheless the principle of merit remains, which radically distinguishes Thomas' position from that of the Reformation. Brian Gerrish offers these astute comments:

> If . . . the Thomistic starting-point is, not merits *de congruo*, but grace, this does not mean that the notion of merit is excluded. There is, to be sure, no

possibility of man's claiming the grace of justification by doing the best that native powers allow. Grace anticipates merit. But, nevertheless, merits must follow grace. Thomas's scheme clearly cannot be considered "legalistic" in the sense that *grace* can be earned, but it is legalistic in the sense that *salvation* is earned. He never imagines that grace is granted in recognition of "natural" works, but he does claim that grace is given to make possible "supernatural" works. Grace is not the prize for merit, but the principle of merit. And eternal life is still a matter of reward.[24]

Medieval theology after Thomas veered sharply in the direction of Pelagianism and semi-Pelagianism. This can be seen in the writings of the late medieval mystics as well as the nominalists. According to the author of *The Cloud of Unknowing,* "All men were lost through Adam's sin but all those who by their good will manifest a desire to be saved shall be saved by Christ's redeeming death."[25] Meister Eckhart maintained that through prayer we can obtain "remission of sins, decrease of temptations, closer contact with spiritual things, and eternal salvation."[26] Moreover, he made clear that real prayer includes charitable works, fasting, and almsgiving.

John Duns Scotus despite his emphasis on divine predestination nevertheless held that man can prepare himself for the gift of grace by acts of penitence and prayer. Such acts or dispositions have the character of congruous merits, though he was often inclined to regard even these dispositions as manifestations of grace.[27] While Thomas tended to affirm the Augustinian doctrine of irresistible grace according to which revelation determines irresistibly the intellect and with it the will of man, Duns Scotus appeared to favor the synergistic view in which the reception of divine revelation is conditional on the cooperation of man's free will.[28]

The Occam-Biel school representing late scholastic nominalism taught that fallen man by his own natural powers and free will could prepare or dispose himself for the grace of justification. By living up to the highest within him, he could merit the grace of justification *(meritum de congruo).* For William of Occam, Gabriel Biel, and other Nominalists God is committed to give his grace to all who do what is in them. In Oberman's interpretation of this school of thought, *"grace is not the root but the fruit of the preparatory good works"* that lead to justification.[29]

For Gabriel Biel the fruits of the works of Christ "are only applicable to those who participate in the moral order meritoriously. . . ."[30] In his view it is not good will but reason or knowledge which is the source of all virtue. The primary task of the church consequently is to provide information about God which necessarily leads to moral improvement, not to announce the event of redeeming grace which converts man's will. The preached Word is not the redemptive Word of God (as in the Reformation) but an "exhortation that prods the sinner onto the path of righteousness."[31]

The view of the Reformation sharply contradicted the mind-set of late medieval theology and signalized a renewal of Augustinianism. Yet even with Augustine there were some major differences. While Augustine understood justification as a life-long process, the Reformers perceived it as a once-for-all act of God by which he declares the sinner righteous. Regeneration or sanctification represents the inward process of purification that endures throughout life. Again Augustine made a place for merit, though only on the basis of grace, while the Reformers maintained that even man's good works, the works that proceed from faith, are not deserving of God's grace because they are always mixed with evil motivations.

Luther did not deny that people do on occasion seek and ask for the grace of God. Yet in his view "this very wishing and asking, seeking or knocking, is the gift of prevenient grace, not of our eliciting will."[32] Man on his own cannot prepare himself in the slightest for the reception of the gift of God. The natural man is not in quest of God but in flight from God. "God's Word," he says, "comes to me without any preparation or help on my part."[33] The root of our trouble "lies not in our works but in our nature; our person, nature, and entire being are corrupted through Adam's fall."[34] Because of sin within man his works will always fall short of the righteousness that God demands. Even our works after conversion cannot merit God's forgiveness; they can only attest and proclaim it. "No one should doubt that all our good works are mortal sins, if they are judged according to God's judgment and severity and not accepted as good by grace alone."[35] Therefore the mercy of God revealed in Jesus Christ "alone is our righteousness, not our own works."[36]

In the prevailing Catholic view later enunciated at the Council of Trent man is accepted by God because of the righteousness implanted within him by the Holy Spirit. In the Reformation view it is man as a sinner who is justified, though justification definitely has concrete effects in the life of man. Calvin declared: "God does not graciously accept us because He sees our change for the better, as if conversion were the basis of forgiveness; He comes into our lives, taking us just as we are out of pure mercy."[37] The Lutheran theologian Osiander returned to the Catholic view that justification is based on internal sanctifying grace, but he was roundly condemned by both Luther and Calvin.

Both Reformers were very insistent that grace is not simply an offer to be accepted or rejected by man at will but an invasion of the inner being of man so that he is impelled to accept and believe. Following Augustine Calvin declared: "Grace is by no means offered by God to be rejected or accepted as it may seem good to one: it is that same grace alone which inclines our heart to follow its movement, and produces in it the choice as much as the will; so that all the good works that follow after are the fruits of the same."[38]

While Martin Bucer affirmed free will, he stood with the mainline Reformers in maintaining that it can do nothing to procure salvation: "When we inquire into the range of this faculty, how far our free will extends, we must in the end confess that of itself our free will is of no avail for the appropriation of things that belong to true godliness, but only for their refusal and rejection."[39] This resembles Luther's contention that man is free in the things below, in the purely horizontal relationships of everyday living, but in the things above, in the relationship to God, he is bound by sin. Bucer quoted St. Ambrose with approval: "We are saved by mercy alone, not by our will or effort."[40]

The Reformers intended not to denigrate good works but to give them a new motivation and purpose. We cannot make ourselves acceptable to God by our works, but we can show forth our gratefulness for what God has done for us in his great work of salvation accomplished in Jesus Christ. Our works do not make us righteous, but they spring from the righteousness of Christ who now dwells within us. Luther put it this way: "Not that the righteous person does nothing, but that his works do not make him righteous, rather that his righteousness creates works. For grace and faith are infused without our works. After they have been imparted the works follow."[41]

The left-wing Reformation gave more emphasis to the practice of the Christian life than did the mainline Reformers, but for the most part it too upheld salvation as a free gift of God. Menno Simons was quite insistent on the priority of grace over works in attaining the remission of sins. Elizabeth, Dutch Anabaptist martyr in the sixteenth century, declared: "We can merit nothing, but must through grace inherit salvation."[42] In the words of George Fox, founder of the Quakers: "So it is not good works, nor good life, that brings salvation but . . . grace."[43]

The Council of Trent (1545–1563) was the answer of the Catholic church to the Reformation, but it left unclear the precise relationship between faith and works. While it forthrightly condemned an emphasis on faith alone that excluded good works, it is uncertain whether an implicit semi-Pelagianism was present in the Council. The contemporary Catholic theologian Schillebeeckx maintains that Trent "leaves open the *possibility* that man can prepare himself for grace in some way . . . by his own strength and without grace."[44] This view is strongly disputed by such scholars as Küng and McSorley, but it cannot be doubted that Trent sees justification as contingent on a preparatory action on the human side. Niesel comments: "Clearly the act of justification itself is also conditioned by a man's preparatory action and cooperation. Human preparation is not just a prerequisite for receiving justification but affects justification itself."[45] In Reformed thinking such a view connotes synergism which means that man on his own can contribute to his justification. In the Catholic perspective this is not necessarily synergism, since the human will in this case is aided or empowered by grace. In the Reformed view our free will does not need to be assisted so much as converted or transformed.

It cannot be gainsaid that after Trent semi-Pelagianism made a partial comeback. The Jesuit Louis Molina (1536–1600) contended that justification depends on the union of the creaturely will with prevenient grace. He perceived a cooperation between free will and grace, which made salvation partly dependent on the efforts of man.[46] For Molina grace is at the free disposal of all and whether it takes effect depends on the free will of the subject. Francisco Suarez (d. 1617) developed and modified Molina's views, but the role of the human will was still considered highly important in the salvific process.[47]

The Jansenist movement within Roman Catholicism sought to reaffirm the Augustinian principles of original sin, salvation by grace alone, and divine predestination. Pascal, one of the ablest defenders of this evangelical movement, declared: "Men will never believe with a saving and real faith, unless God inclines their heart; and they will believe as soon as He inclines it."[48] At the instigation of the Jesuits Jansenism was condemned by Pope Clement XI in 1713. Among the theses that were censured were the following: "The grace of Jesus Christ is necessary for every good work"; "Without the grace of the Liberator, the sinner is not free except to do evil"; "Faith is a gift of the pure liberality of God." A Lutheran scholar makes this caustic comment: "The urge to repudiate everything that smacked of the Reformation has here gone to such an extreme that the Church has abandoned the greatest of its fathers, St. Augustine himself. . . . The condemnation of Jansenism is a clear proof that post-Tridentine Catholicism, so far from mitigating its opposition to the Reformation, accentuated it."[49]

Both Barth and Berkouwer contend that the semi-Pelagian cast of modern Catholicism is especially evident in its developing Mariology in which Mary is seen as the outstanding example of the cooperation of the creature with divine grace in the accomplishment of salvation. It is sometimes said that Mary was chosen to be the Mother of God as a reward for her piety and humility. In such theologians as Bonaventura and Thomas Aquinas, Mary's merits could only be *de congruo,* though for Gabriel Biel Mary could have earned her status as Mother of God *de condigno.*[50] The general view in later Catholicism was that Mary cooperated with the prevenient grace of God in preparing the way for the gift of justification for all mankind. She is sometimes depicted as the co-redemptress *(coredemptrix)* who prepares the way for Christ (but on the basis of prior grace) and who brings souls to Christ through her intercession in heaven.[51] In Bernard of Clairvaux Mary is the staircase of Christ, and in Gabriel Biel she is in addition the staircase of salvation. Pope Benedict XV declared: "Thus she suffered with her suffering and dying Son and virtually died with Him. Thus for the salvation of men she renounced her motherly privileges in relation to her Son, and to appease the divine justice offered her Son . . . so that one can justly say that with Christ, *she herself redeemed* mankind."[52] And in the words of Pope Pius IX: "Our salvation is based upon the holy Virgin . . . so that if there is any hope and spiritual healing for us we *receive it solely and uniquely from her.*"[53] She is said to cause the stream of grace to flow not directly but indirectly by means of her intercession. A contemporary Catholic theologian contends that Mary "co-merited" our salvation "alongside her Son."[54] She shows us "how anyone can deserve a reward before God" by making use of the grace by which we cooperate in laying hold of salvation.

Evangelical Protestantism does not denigrate the role of Mary, though an anti-Marian bias can be detected in some of the perverse forms of this tradition. Luther himself hailed Mary as a supreme example of fidelity and piety in his *Magnificat.* Both Luther and Zwingli perceived the significance and value of the *theotokos* (Mary as Mother of God), though with their Catholic brethren they rightly understood Mary as chosen for this role by God and therefore as basically subordinate and inferior to her Creator. More recently Karl Barth has affirmed the *theotokos* partly in order to stem the tide of Nestorianism within modern Protestantism. On the question of Mary's role in the plan of salvation, however, the leading lights of Evangelicalism are united in seeing this as an instrumental role. The birth of the Savior was conditional not on a cooperation between the divine and the human but on the unilateral decree of God which was announced to Mary. Berkouwer observes: "The angel's words do not bear the character of a divine proposal, but of a *sovereign* act of grace *made known* to Mary."[55] She voluntarily assented, to be sure, but on the basis of grace and through the power of grace.

Semi-Pelagianism has continued into modern day Catholicism. J. Pohle, for example, holds "contrary to the opinion of a few theologians . . . that even a man in mortal sin, provided he cooperate with the first grace of conversion, is able to merit *de congruo* by his supernatural acts not only a series of graces which will lead to conversion, but finally justification itself."[56] A semi-Pelagian if not a Pelagian cast is evident in this remark of Martial Lekeux's: "Now at last you can see that to be a saint only one thing is necessary, as far as we are concerned: good will."[57] The Dutch theologian J. C. Groot speaks of a "positive point of contact," a "positive possibility on the part of nature" to acknowledge and respond to grace.[58]

Despite his incontestable adherence to the doctrine of salvation by grace, Karl Rahner maintains that man is free to say yes or no to himself and to God. Yet he recognizes that man is in slavery as well as in freedom and that his will therefore needs to be assisted or aided by grace. At the same time he rejects the notion of synergism, "the idea that the God of grace and free man collaborate in the process of salvation in the manner of partial causes, almost as if each did half the work."[59] He affirms a cooperation with grace but only on the basis of grace. Nevertheless his insistence that grace is available to all men, that all are "surrounded by grace," gives rise to the idea that the salvation that comes to man is in some measure conditional upon man's free cooperation with a prevenient universal grace. Everyone, he says, experiences grace "in the depths of his being," and the special revelation is simply a confirmation and fulfillment of man's universal religious experience.[60]

Rahner also opens the door to semi-Pelagianism when he propounds that there is within man a *potentia obedientalis,* a capability of hearing the word of revelation. He seems to understand this not as a mere negative possibility but as a positive disposition for grace.[61] In his view there is, at the foundation of man's nature, "a reaching out of finite love towards God."[62] He also avers that man can freely decide to be a "listener" and to stand attentively before the free and personal God who may choose to speak or remain silent.[63] Rahner definitely gives the impression that historical or existential man has some positive role in the realization of his justification and salvation.[64]

Despite the ever-recurring shadow of semi-Pelagianism, the evangelical strand has indeed persisted within Roman Catholicism, and this is why there is still hope of an ecumenical rapprochement. St. Thérèse of Lisieux declared: "When I am charitable, it is Jesus alone who is acting in me. . . . Any glory that I shall have will be a gratuitous gift from God."[65] She was convinced that the eloquence of the greatest saints could not inspire her to loving action were it not for grace which touches the heart. Instead of the mystic ladder to heaven, by which man ascends to the pinnacle of perfection through works of love, she preferred to speak of a lift to heaven, the lift of free grace.[66] Hans Küng also strongly affirms the tradition of *sola gratia:* "Thus man is justified through God's grace alone; man achieves nothing. . . . Rather man simply submits to the justification of God; he does not do works; he believes."[67] Such scholars as Louis Bouyer, Ida Frederike Goerres, Stephen Pfürtner, and Harry McSorley all concur that salvation is by the grace of God alone and that human merit plays absolutely no role in the initial gift of grace, though some would make a place for merit after grace. Even Karl Rahner, who prefers to speak of grace as assisting man's "injured freedom" rather than bringing man a radically new kind of freedom, maintains that man's "free 'yes' to God's liberating grace is itself once more a gift of God's grace. . . . Of ourselves *alone* we cannot do anything at all which could make God direct his grace towards us. . . ."[68] Rahner has indeed advocated that both the church and the individual Christian must hold fast to the one thing needful: "trust in the grace of God alone."[69]

In our criticisms of modern Catholicism we must not lose sight of the fact that post-Reformation Protestantism has also lapsed time and again into a kind of semi-Pelagianism. The early Pietists and Puritans for the most part remained true to the Reformation doctrine of salvation by grace alone, but in their emphasis on the need to prepare the heart to receive the gift of salvation they created a climate in which the focal point of attention shifted from God's gracious initiative to the inner conflicts of man's soul.[70] To be sure they generally recognized that man's seeking for salvation prior to justification was itself a work of the Holy Spirit within him, but they nonetheless opened the door to the peril of synergism by which man collaborates with the Spirit of God in finding his way to salvation. It was suggested in some of the latter-day Pietistic circles that one must make atonement by one's own sorrow over sin before receiving the grace of forgiveness.[71]

A Pelagian or semi-Pelagian outlook also reappeared in Arminian and Wesleyan religion. In Methodism repentance came to be seen as a precondition of faith rather than a result of faith (as in Calvin).[72] The revivalist Charles Finney went so far as to say that "sinners are not converted by direct contact of the Holy Ghost" but "by the influence of truth, argument, and persuasion."[73] In this view "a change of heart is the sinner's *own* act", though he is urged on by the Spirit of God. The Holiness preacher John Morgan considered the attainment of a certain degree of holiness a necessary condition for justification. A synergistic orientation is again reflected in J. Sidlow Baxter, a critic of Holiness theology from within the movement: "The unconverted have utterly no power to regenerate themselves, but they do have the moral capacity to appreciate and *receive* what God graciously offers."[74]

In the theosophic mysticism of Swedenborg it is said that sinful man retains the moral capacity to come to God by his own free will: "God cannot spiritually regenerate man, except so far as man according to his laws regenerates himself naturally."[75] For Swedenborg the work of salvation is entirely subjective: justification is pardon granted on repentance. He repudiated the vicarious, substitutionary atonement of Christ as a "mere human invention."

Schleiermacher, in whom Pietism and rationalism come together, spoke of a receptivity in human nature which enables it to take in the potency of God-consciousness. While acknowledging that man through sin has no capacity to originate good, he was adamant that man is certainly capable of responding to the goodness of God in His redeeming activity for "were we to affirm that the capacity for redemption has been lost, we should come into conflict with our very belief in redemption."[76] Faith for Schleiermacher therefore becomes a human possibility, and this is the rationale for his apologetics to the cultured despisers of religion.

At the same time the more authentic evangelical strand within Protestantism was by no means muted, and it quickly came to the fore particularly in those periods when the Reformation was rediscovered. Against the revivalist emphasis on making oneself acceptable to God by righteous acts, Abraham Kuyper averred: "All our running and racing, toiling and slaving, can not create in us a holy disposition. God alone can do that. As He has the power by regeneration to change the *root* of life, so can He also by sanctification change the *disposition* of the affections."[77] In the view of James Denney: "An absolute justification is needed to give the sinner a start. He must have the certainty of 'no condemnation,' of being, without reserve or drawback, right with

God through God's gracious act in Christ, before he can begin to live the new life."[78] According to Charles Spurgeon "the work of the Holy Spirit . . . must be done in and on the spirit of a man before that man can be saved."[79] Augustinian and Calvinist motifs are particularly evident in this statement of Peter Forsyth's: "He does more than justify faith, He creates it. It is His more than ours. We believe because He makes us believe—with a moral compulsion, an invasion and capture of us."[80] In the theology of crisis associated with such names as Barth, Brunner, and Kraemer the biblical and Augustinian doctrine of the sovereignty of grace again became prominent, though this doctrine was compromised in the left wing of this movement by the search for a "point of contact" with secular man in the interest of apologetics.

The synergistic outlook has made at least a partial comeback in the movements of secular and liberation theology where it is assumed that man can build the kingdom of God on earth through social engineering. As in the old Social Gospel movement a neo-Enlightenment utopianism has supplanted the realism of the Reformation which took seriously the lust for power embedded in the very being of man that so easily corrupts every human dream and achievement and whose most virulent manifestation is the collective pride of races and nations.

Not much has been said thus far about the position of the Eastern Orthodox church on grace and works, but it should be recognized that the synergistic orientation prevails over an evangelical one, despite the fact that evangelical voices have been heard in that Communion, for example, Archibishop Lucaris in the sixteenth and seventeenth centuries. In the large Russian Catechism of Philaret it is asserted that one is saved by faith and good works together and that the imitation of Christ's life is tantamount to salvation.[81] The modern Russian Orthodox treatise on spirituality *The Way of a Pilgrim,* which has already become somewhat of a spiritual classic, illustrates the prominent role given to man's free will in the procuring of salvation. When the pilgrim inquires of the Abbot how one can save his soul, the Abbot replies: " 'Save your soul? Well, live according to the commandments, say your prayers, and you will be saved' ".[82] It is said that man cannot acquire faith without prayer, though prayer is not purely within his own power. At the same time the frequency of prayer as over against the quality is "within the province of his will," and by the ceaseless repetition of the Jesus prayer one can enter into a living communion with God and thereby assure his salvation.

THE PARADOX OF SALVATION

In our historical analysis of the controversy over grace and free will we did not intend to suggest that the truth lies exclusively on one side. Synergism is of course a real danger, but we must also recognize the complementary danger of monergism in which God is portrayed as the sole actor in our salvation.[83] God is the sole source and mainspring of all redemptive action, but he is not the sole actor. He is the sole efficient cause of salvation but not the only causal factor in salvation. There are also secondary or instrumental causes that have to be taken into account.

One must be careful not to convert man into an automaton or robot. He must be recognized as a free agent, though the power and motivation by which he exercises his freedom come wholly from God. To give all the glory to God in the accomplishing of our salvation is not to reduce man to nothing. Yet we must also not say that man gets some of the credit for his salvation, that man can help in the procuring of his salvation. On the one hand is the peril of a divine determinism or fatalism which makes a mockery of human freedom; this is more Stoic than Christian. On the other hand is an egalitarian voluntarism that makes salvation wholly conditional on man's free response. Christ then becomes only half a Savior, and it is no longer possible to speak of the sovereignty of grace.

What is necessary to understand is that the act of salvation is a paradox or mystery which defies and eludes rational comprehension. The lapses into synergism and monergism can be accounted for by the ever-recurring attempts to resolve the paradox of salvation into a rationally understandable formula. When faith is no longer a human decision but solely a work of God in the human soul (as in the early Barth) then we are no longer doing justice to an important dimension of the gift of salvation. On the other hand when salvation is depicted purely as a human action by which man lays hold of the grace of God which is ever at his disposal, then salvation becomes a human achievement.

Our position is that we must affirm both the sovereignty of grace and the responsibility of believers. The two errors to be avoided are the following: that one is saved exclusively by the work of grace upon him thereby not including or allowing for personal faith and decision in the salvific process; and that one is saved by grace and free will together so that salvation depends partly on grace and partly on free will. The first error tends to make salvation something extrinsic to man even when it is admitted that faith is implanted within man by the Spirit. The second error gives man a determinative role in his justification so that he virtually becomes a co-redeemer with Christ. One is not saved irrespective of one's personal response, but at the same time one's own response to grace is itself a product of grace.

The paradox of salvation might be expressed in this way: only the person who is transformed by divine grace can make a positive re-sponse to God's gracious invitation, but only the one who does make such a response is indeed transformed by grace. God's grace does not cancel out creaturely freedom but places it on a wholly new foundation. Man is impelled to respond voluntarily when his will is converted by the grace of God. He will inevitably say yes when his inward eyes have been opened to the meaning of Christ's death on his behalf. Far from violating man's personality, God's grace appeals to his deepest yearn-ings, and therefore when exposed to grace man is intrinsically drawn toward it.

In the act of salvation man is both passive and active. He is passive in that he can only submit when he is grasped by the grace of God, when the Holy Spirit invades his life, but he is made active by the Spirit in surrendering and clinging to Christ as his only hope and salvation. He is helpless, totally helpless to save himself, but he becomes an overcomer and conqueror (Rom. 8:37) when the Holy Spirit indwells him and fills him with power from on high.

It is sometimes said that man on his own can seek for God but cannot come to faith apart from the grace of God. Yet this contradicts the biblical testimony that no man can seek for God, that man in his natural state is in flight from God (Ps. 14:1–3; 53:1–3; Rom. 3:11, 12). All people yearn for God, but seeking implies moving in the direction of faith and of God. The one who begins seeking in this authentic sense cannot claim merit before God, since this very seeking reveals that prevenient grace is at work in his life.[84] Bernard of Clairvaux with much wisdom affirmed: "No one can seek you unless he has already found you."[85] This insight was reiterated by Luther, Calvin, John of the Cross, Pascal, and many other theologians of grace. We cannot seek God unless our wills have already been turned around by God. To seek for God in the genuine sense of this word means that we have already been made beneficiaries of grace, that our conversion has already begun (cf. Isa. 55:6). Salvation is being led to the city of God by his light and truth (Ps. 43:3); it is not a process by which we discover the truth on our own.

For Pelagius the divine assistance remains outside the human will whereas for Augustine divine grace works in and through the human will thereby converting the will. Augustine saw as did Calvin much later that "without the grace of God" the human will "cannot be called free," since "it is subject to the assaults and enslavement of the passions".[86] The Reformed tradition following Augustine and Calvin emphasizes the total inability of man to come to God. Man is not only unwilling but unable to make a free response to the offer of salvation. Yet the doctrine of inability does not mean "that we cannot believe, but only that we cannot believe in our own strength."[87] When we believe and respond we do so through the new power that has come into our lives, the power of the Holy Spirit. This is why it is more proper to speak of a liberated will than of free will in the work of salvation.

St. Paul cogently expressed the paradox and mystery of salvation: "Therefore, my beloved, ... work out your own salvation with fear and trembling; for God is at work in you, both to will and to work for his good pleasure" (Phil. 2:12, 13). And again: "But by the grace of God I am what I am, and his grace toward me was not in vain. On the contrary, I worked harder than any of them, though it was not I, but the grace of God which is with me" (1 Cor. 15:10). Paul was not willing to disregard the indispensable role of human decision: "You have received the grace of God; do not let it go for nothing" (2 Cor. 6:1 NEB). He perceived the impossible possibility of spurning the free offer of salvation, and yet he saw that it is only by grace that we can accept and believe. It is also only by grace that we can go forward in the life of faith: "It is for this I struggle wearily on, helped only by his power driving me irresistibly" (Col. 1:29 JB).

The Book of Revelation too relates the gift of grace and the decision of the believer in an organic and integral fashion. The children of God are able to break free from the powers of darkness only because "the salvation and the power and the kingdom of our God" have burst into their lives (Rev. 12:10). They conquer not through their own power but through the power of the blood of the Lamb and the Word of God (Rev. 12:11). Man is set free to drink of the water of life because he has first been addressed by the Spirit of God as He speaks to and through the church: "And the Spirit and the bride say, Come. And let him that heareth say, Come. And let him that is athirst come. And whosoever will, let him take the water of life freely" (Rev. 22:17 KJ).

In their firm emphasis on the sovereignty of grace, theologians like Augustine, Calvin, and Luther sometimes gave the impression that man is only a puppet in the hands of an all-powerful and capricious God who elects some and hardens others. In Luther's *Bondage of the Will* the stress on the passivity and helplessness of man tends to rob the encounter with Christ of its decision-character. The concept of faith as decision and surrender to Christ is definitely present in some of his sermons and commentaries, but it is scarcely evident in his *De Servo Arbitrio*.[88]

The stress on the helplessness and passivity of man in the praise of grace is even more prominent in the Lutheran theologian Matthias Flacius Illyricus, who was an avowed opponent of liberalizing tendencies in Melanchthon and sixteenth century Lutheranism. Flacius defined man as a lump of clay who was simply acted upon and molded by God. Regeneration signified the creation of a new self completely unrelated to the old self. He defined total depravity as the complete loss of everything that makes man a genuine person. Man can only be passive in respect to the action of grace.

It is an open question whether Abraham Kuyper too did justice to the role of human decision in salvation. "In regeneration," he wrote, "man is neither *worker* nor *co-worker;* but is merely wrought upon."[89] Yet he held that in conversion, the second stage in regeneration, man becomes active and cooperates with the Holy Spirit. He is right that in the initial work of grace man is a receiver and not an actor, but we maintain that even in this first stage man becomes active, and regeneration is not realized in his life apart from his response and decision. As soon as man receives he is impelled to vigorous action. We here concur with Thomas Aquinas that "the movement of faith towards God coincides with the infusion of grace."[90]

The paradox of salvation was astutely expressed by Jonathan Edwards: "In efficacious grace we are not merely passive, nor yet does God do some, and we do the rest. But God does all, and we do all. God produces all, and we act all. . . . God is the only proper author and fountain; we only are the proper actors."[91] Edwards perceived that grace does not override the will but releases the will for creative action.[92]

In our time A. W. Tozer of the Christian and Missionary Alliance has at least on occasion succeeded in grasping the mystery and paradox of divine election and human freedom. While acknowledging the blessedness or terror that may hang on human choice, he recognizes that behind this choice is the sovereign right of God to call those whom he chooses.

Salvation is from our side a choice, from the divine side it is a seizing upon, an apprehending, a conquest by the Most High God. Our "accepting" and "will-

ing" are reactions rather than actions. The right of determination must always remain with God.[93]

This brings us to the question of whether grace is irresistible. This can and must be affirmed but in a somewhat qualified sense. Grace is irresistible in the sense that it is efficacious, that once it enters into the life of man it will penetrate his inner being and alter his will. When man is awakened by grace to the wretchedness of his sins and the infinite love of his Savior he will be inwardly impelled to confess his sins and grasp the hand of his Savior. Jonathan Edwards believed that we can resist and reject the convictions of wrongdoing brought about by the action of the Spirit upon our conscience, but we cannot impede the gift of regeneration which turns our will in a completely new direction. When we are granted illumination to behold the excellency and goodness of Christ, we are infallibly drawn to him. Augustine, Thomas, Calvin, and Barth have expressed this mystery in a similar way.

Yet we must not blind our eyes to certain scriptural passages that seem to contravene the doctrine of irresistible grace. For example, we must consider this lament of our Lord: " 'O Jerusalem, Jerusalem, killing the prophets and stoning those who are sent to you! How often would I have gathered your children together as a hen gathers her brood under her wings, and you would not!' " (Mat. 23:37). Or these words of the apostle: "See to it that no one fail to obtain the grace of God; that no 'root of bitterness' spring up and cause trouble. . . ." (Heb. 12:15). We should also give attention to the parable of the ten virgins or the talents which reveals that even the sons of the kingdom will be cast into the outer darkness. To contend that those who are finally lost were not really the objects of God's grace in the first place does not do justice to the texts in question.

We find Karl Barth very helpful here. He maintains with Augustine that man is set free by grace only to believe and obey, not to believe or reject the Gospel. True freedom is the freedom which results in genuine liberation from sin, death, and the devil. The will of man is most properly free when it is in accord with the law of man's own being, the law which is written on the conscience of every man. Irresistible grace releases man for the freedom of obedience, the freedom that attests both the sovereignty of grace and the integrity and genuine desire of the man reborn by grace. Man now follows Christ in costly obedience because this is his inward desire. Before the invasion of grace into his life his desires were toward evil, but now he desires to do the good.

Yet we must still ask: why do some after being enlightened by grace still resist and reject grace? Karl Barth calls this an "ontological impossibility," since the man in grace can only believe and respond. Yet Barth acknowledges that this impossibility nevertheless occurs. The reborn man is no longer able to sin because he is united with Christ, and yet in his insane folly he may try to sin, and God in his judgment allows the sin to take place. The man who has once been enlightened by the Holy Spirit and who then deliberately denies his Savior and persists in his denial is committing the unforgivable sin, the sin against the Holy Spirit, because this means rejecting forgiveness. The redemptive freedom which is given in revelation contains within itself the abysmal possibility of unfreedom, though this mystery defies rational explanation.

It is still possible, however, to speak of irresistible grace even in the case of the one who falls away from grace. Grace still triumphs but now in the form of wrath and judgment. The love of God necessarily becomes destructive to the one who rejects this love, but it is never withdrawn from the sinner, even from the apostate. He meets his deserved retribution not despite the grace of God but in the face of grace and at the hands of grace.

When we say that grace is irresistible we mean not only the first entry of grace into our lives but also the fact that grace cannot ultimately be defeated. Grace is irresistible in the sense that we cannot act either for, with, or against it until it is showered upon us. We are dead apart from grace (Eph. 2:5). We can swim against the stream of grace but only on the basis of grace and then only for a time. It is true that God may withhold his grace from us, but this too is only for a time. God's grace cannot be permanently thwarted; it will finally have its way in the life of man, though this may mean man's condemnation and not his salvation. Perhaps it is more proper to speak of efficacious or effectual grace than irresistible grace since man, even after having been exposed to grace ever and again, inexplicably but incontestably descends into the depths of absurdity and tries to defy the grace of God.[94] But when in his folly he denies his salvation, grace is still triumphant though in a different way, and when he gladly acknowledges the blessing assured to him, he does so because he is irresistibly drawn to the love and light of Jesus Christ.

Against the older Calvinists we maintain that grace will eventually be given to all, that it is not reserved for a select group of the elect.[95]

Against the Arminians we contend that grace cannot be permanently thwarted or resisted, that grace is inescapable and unrelenting. Against them too we hold that grace does not simply dispose the corrupt will toward the good but actually transforms man's will so that he seeks to do the good. Our position is that grace is both universal and sovereign even where people defy it.

In the reaction against Roman Catholic synergism the churches of the Reformation often fell into the heresy of cheap grace whereby salvation became a passport to heaven that was assured to one simply through baptism or a public affirmation of faith or by birth in the covenant community. The inseparable relationship of grace and a life of costly discipleship was broken by an overemphasis on the all-sufficiency of the grace of God revealed in Christ. There was widespread acceptance of the idea of instant salvation, that salvation is realized in toto in baptism or the act of faith. Salvation came to be equated exclusively with forensic justification, and there was a failure to recognize that justification itself is not fulfilled except in and through sanctification, which is a lifelong process.

The fact that the free gift of salvation demands not simply an outward intellectual assent or a voluntary submission to the Gospel but total commitment and lifelong discipleship under the cross was lost sight of in the mainstream of Protestantism. The parables of the kingdom in which the gift of salvation is likened to a treasure in the field or a pearl of great price that one must sell all to possess were practically ignored. Calvin was right that the kingdom of God is not the servants' wages but the sons' inheritance,[96] but what some of his followers failed to see is that such an inheritance must be acknowledged and appropriated in a life of total surrender and discipleship. Calvin himself understood this, and his life is a poignant testimony to the validity of his theological insights, but it remained for the Pietists and Puritans to make crystal clear that there is no salvation through the cross of Christ apart from a life of bearing the cross. The Christian life is not simply a by-product or fruit of faith but the field or arena in which faith is worked out amid much tribulation and opposition.

Dietrich Bonhoeffer perhaps more than any other theologian of our time has reminded us that we must be on guard against the twin perils of works-righteousness and cheap grace. The Reformers were much more alert to the danger of works-righteousness, since this was the chief heresy of their time. The Pietists and Puritans as well as many of the Catholic mystics were especially sensitive about cheap grace and the need to live a holy life. For Bonhoeffer salvation entails both grace and good works; while the first has ontological priority over the second, the second may have chronological priority though our feeble efforts remain a dead work of the law until the intervention of grace. "The only man," he says, "who has the right to say that he is justified by grace alone is the man who has left all to follow Christ."[97] The work of "grace and active obedience are complementary. There is no faith without good works, and no good works apart from faith."[98] In Bonhoeffer's view it is not good works but evil works that hinder and destroy faith.

Luther was absolutely correct that good works are not the basis of grace, but grace is the source of good works. "For works do not drive out sin," he said, "but the driving out of sin leads to good works."[99] Yet we must also maintain that the driving out of sin by grace has its purpose and goal in good works. Good works are not only the evidence but the culmination of the work of grace in our lives. To lose sight of this truth is to cheapen grace and to take away the seriousness of the call to the Christian life.

We should remember with Karl Barth that grace wills not only to be received and known but also to rule. "There is no grace," he says, "without the lordship and claim of grace."[100] It is not enough to accept Jesus Christ as Savior. We must also acknowledge him as Lord and follow him as our Example and Pattern for living. Such discipleship does not earn or procure salvation, for this would be works-righteousness. But it is a poignant reminder that we must walk in the light as well as believe in the light lest the darkness overtake us (John 12:35). It bids us consider that grace that does not become the ruling factor in our lives may be withdrawn, and our final status may be worse than our first (2 Pet. 2:20–22). We are summoned not only to accept the cross of Christ for our salvation but also to carry the cross that he places upon us for the realization of our vocation; if we reject or ignore this divine command our vocation will be aborted, and our salvation will thereby be emptied of meaning (cf. 2 Pet. 1:9, 10).

THE MEANS OF GRACE

An evangelical catholic theology speaks not only of the gift of grace but also of the means of grace. God does not work directly or immediately upon the soul but through certain external channels including the Gospel, the Bible, and the sacraments. It is these means of grace that comprise the church.

In the Roman Catholic view the sacraments are the primary means of grace, and they are seven in number: baptism, the Lord's Supper, penance, holy orders, extreme unction, holy matrimony, and confirmation. The sacraments are said to impart supernatural power (infused grace) to the faithful. They were instituted by Christ either directly or indirectly as effectual signs of his presence. All the sacraments are not necessary for every individual, but baptism and penance in particular are so crucial that salvation cannot ordinarily be attained without them.[101] The sacraments are believed to work *ex opere operato* (by the work worked). Since the Church is a sacramental institution, it too can be regarded as a unique and indispensable means of grace.

The Reformers perceived the means of grace as the means by which we appropriate the fruits of our salvation.[102] Grace was conceived of in personal rather than substantial terms (as in Roman Catholic scholasticism). The sacraments, it was said, do not contain grace but testify to grace. By the action of the Spirit they also communicate God's favor and power to those who believe. They become channels of God's gracious condescension by which people are strengthened and confirmed in the faith. Calvin generally used the terms *sign, seal,* and *instrument* to describe them. The Word alone is the original or foundational means of grace, and the sacraments are signs of the Word.

For both Calvin and Luther the sermon—the preaching of the Gospel—was the primary means of grace, not the Mass. Preaching itself came to be seen as sacramental. Baptism and Holy Communion were regarded as ordinarily necessary for salvation but not indispensable. The Christian life was also seen as a means of grace but subordinate to the Gospel. In post-Reformation orthodoxy the emphasis shifted from the spoken to the written Word.

The Left-Wing Reformation, especially the Spiritualists, called into question the whole concept of the means of grace and stressed a direct contact with Christ by means of the Holy Spirit. Caspar Schwenkfeld in the sixteenth century denied both the Word and the sacraments as means of grace. They were signs of the inward work of the Holy Spirit which alone should be regarded as the means of grace.

In the tradition of evangelical Pietism the life of grace tended to overshadow the means of grace. The external rites of the church were considered of less consequence than the Christian life, prayer, and fellowship *(koinonia)*. For Zinzendorf fellowship virtually became a third mark of the true church.

Schleiermacher, who saw himself as "a Pietist of a higher order," understood the means of grace as anything that serves to awaken and cultivate God-consciousness which is universal. Preaching was deemed important, but the emphasis was on sharing one's own experience.

In the neo-orthodox movement the doctrine of the means of grace was sharply called into question. Karl Barth in effect abolished the concept of the means of grace. For him only Jesus Christ is the means of grace, the sacrament of the presence of God. The preaching of the Gospel and the sacramental rites of the church simply attest and point to what God has already done for us in Jesus Christ. The sermon is a servant or sign of the Word of God rather than a means by which grace is dispensed. God's Word may well accompany the preacher's words, but the latter are not the necessary vehicle of the Word. "God's action," he says, occurs "with" but never "in and under," always over and opposite to human activity.[103]

Joseph Haroutunian universalizes the concept of the means of grace.[104] Every Christian is a means of grace to every other. Every person can be a means of grace to his neighbor. The divine-human encounter is virtually identified with the human-human encounter. The lines between the sacred and secular are practically erased in his later theology.

More recently Arthur Cochrane has attacked the traditional understanding of the sacraments as "means of grace."[105] For him the work of the Spirit must always be "immediate," individualized, and miraculous. Instead of interpreting the Lord's Supper as a rite by which we receive grace, he sees it as an agape meal or love feast which commemorates the poured-out love of God in Jesus Christ. Moreover, he recommends that we rediscover the ethical dimensions of this rite and invite to the supper the outsiders, the despised, and the oppressed.

It is our view that there are certain designated means of grace by which God encounters us and also infuses his energy into us. This energy is not an impersonal force but the Spirit of power. The Holy Spirit is not tied to these means of grace, but we are so bound to them, since they were commanded by Jesus Christ. God ordinarily works through the means of grace, but in extraordinary circumstances he may well pour out his Spirit upon people apart from the external means of grace, though no one will come to a saving faith in Christ apart from a knowledge of the Gospel.

We shall say much more on the role of preaching in Volume II but for our purposes here we maintain that only Baptism and the Lord's Supper may properly be understood as sacraments, since only they entail outward symbols as well as being expressly commanded by Christ. This is not the place to make an exhaustive examination of these rites,[106] but we contend that they are not only signs of grace but means in that through the rite itself Jesus Christ reveals himself by his Spirit. The integral relation of baptism to salvation is underlined in Titus 3:5 which affirms that he saved us "in virtue of his own mercy, by the washing of regeneration and renewal in the Holy Spirit. . . ." Most biblical scholars of an ecumenical orientation maintain that the washing of regeneration refers to baptism (cf. 1 Pet. 3:21). It was through the breaking of the bread that the inward eyes of the two disciples on the road to Emmaus were opened to the identity of Jesus as the risen Christ (Luke 24:30, 31). The real presence of Christ in the Lord's Supper is attested by Paul: "The cup of blessing which we bless, is it not a participation in the blood of Christ? The bread which we break, is it not a participation in the body of Christ?" (1 Cor. 10:16).

We affirm that while the Word and sacraments are objective means of grace, there are also subjective means—prayer and the Christian life. These subjective means were deemphasized by Roman Catholicism and the Reformation. Roman Catholics stressed that the Christian life is a means of accumulating and retaining grace rather than bringing grace to our neighbor. For the Reformers the Christian life is more a fruit of grace than a means of grace.

In our view the Christian life can also be an objective means of grace if it is correlated with a knowledge of the Word of God. It cannot stand by itself, but neither can the preaching of the Word stand by itself. The preaching of the Word apart from love becomes a "clanging cymbal" (1 Cor. 13:1). Life and Word go together. We must not only hear the Word from someone whose life testifies to the Word,[107] but also preach the Word as well as follow the Word.

As catholic evangelicals we wish to retain the sacraments but avoid sacramentalism. We desire to uphold the preaching of the Word as the primary means of grace, but to eschew the vice of verbalism. With the Pietists we desire to make a real place for the Christian life as a means of grace, but to avoid slipping into the heresy of moralism.

In relating the doctrine of *sola gratia* to the means of grace, we must beware of any doctrine that sees the church or the sacraments as sources of grace. They are but instruments of grace and then only by the free condescension of a personal God.[108] It is a mistake to speak of the church as dispensing grace, since this tends to make the church a co-redeemer with Jesus Christ. Nor should we see the priest as a second Christ who makes salvation available to people through the sacrifice on the altar. The church and its ministers are not masters but only servants and heralds of the Word. Through the witness they make and the rites they perform Christ deigns to reveal himself to his children. But this is a gift that we cannot take for granted, a gift for which we must hope and pray. Christ alone is the Savior even when he wills to unite his Word with the words and acts of his ministers. Calvin rightly warned against a sacramentalism which sees grace automatically conferred through external rites or ceremonies.[109] Jonathan Edwards reflects this same attitude in his contention that the means of grace are forever to be subordinated to the Giver of grace: "And though means are made use of in conferring grace on men's souls, yet it is of God that we have these means of grace, and it is he that makes them effectual."[110]

CURRENT QUESTIONS

The classical debate on the relation of grace and nature has been revived with the advent of philosophies and theologies of a vitalistic and naturalistic bent. In this perspective grace is a spiritual dimension or creative force within nature.[111] Grace does not build on nature but transfigures it from within so that man is not so much elevated above the world as united with the ground and depth of the world. Process and neo-naturalist theologians affirm the potential in man to actualize the spiritual dimension of the self. For Teilhard de Chardin grace is the ascending force of evolution by which people become personalized and the race becomes hominized. Langdon Gilkey, who has moved in the direction of a naturalistic theology, sees grace as a fulfillment of "man's natural life in the world" and is thereby accused by a Catholic critic of minimizing the depth of the transformation that God brings about in his creatures.[112]

Against naturalistic theology and philosophy evangelical theology understands grace not as a universal life-force but rather as the personal favor of God that results in salvation. Grace, moreover, does not simply enable man to choose the good (as in modern neo-Catholicism) but so transforms the being of man that he can do nothing but follow the course opened to him by God.

In our view grace does not simply add on to nature nor is it a creative energy within nature; instead it radically alters nature so that man indeed becomes a new creature (2 Cor. 5:17). Forsyth expresses this very tersely: "The gospel of grace is superhuman as well as supernatural; it is as much above natural affection as above natural law. The central act of grace is as much beyond the natural heart to do as it is beyond the natural reason to explain."[113] We concur wholeheartedly in the judgment of James Packer: "Evangelical theology is at war with all views which graft salvation on to natural goodness or revelation on to natural knowledge, on the grounds that such views fail to grasp both the sinfulness of sin and the graciousness of grace."[114] We affirm that grace is something wholly supernatural, that it does not simply fulfill nature but overthrows it, turns it in an entirely new direction. In the event of conversion grace invades nature and thereby transfigures it.

It is fashionable in some circles today to hold that nature prepares the way for grace (K. Rahner) or that there is an inherent receptivity to grace in nature (Tillich). Our contention is that grace creates its own point of contact within nature, that man is placed in a new situation which was inaccessible to him before the incursion of grace. Karl Barth well expresses our own position on this question: "There is *no* way which leads to this event; there is *no* faculty in man for apprehending it; for the way and the faculty are themselves new, being the revelation and faith, the knowing and being known enjoyed by the new man."[115]

In the current dialogue with the world religions we are compelled to wrestle again with the problem of the relation of grace and merit. One interpreter of Buddhism comments: "The 'acquisition of merit' has much to do with the extent to which a man becomes . . . a channel" of "the cosmic energies."[116] In religions such as Buddhism, Hinduism, and Jainism one's sin (karma) is expiated by oneself through a series of existences that finally lead to separation from the world of illusion. Gerald Heard, who was very much influenced by Eastern mysticism, believes that "there will be no Kingdom unless and until we do so climb to that station. For only those who have attained may safely be given the powers, the spiritual powers whereby, and only whereby, God's Kingdom may come on earth."[117] I. C. Sharma, an Indian philosopher who seeks to mediate between Christianity and Hinduism, claims that the "Grace of God is the result of the constant effort of the Entity to love God at all times, through loving all human beings, and to attain the knowledge of at-onement with God through meditation."[118] He further explains:

Karma is the means for the development of the soul and Grace is the goal. Karma is the effort, Grace is the prize. . . . The shackles of Karma cannot be broken without Grace and Grace is not a free gift. If negative past Karma has caused bondage of the soul and ignorance of man's potential divinity, virtuous Karma with the will to love, can set the soul free.[119]

Against the preceding views we maintain that grace is not the reward for good works but instead their basis and source. We are here completely in accord with the Anglican scholar R. P. C. Hanson: "Grace means the free, unmerited, unexpected love of God, and all the benefits, delights, and comforts which flow from it. It means that while we were sinners and enemies we have been treated as sons and heirs."[120]

Kierkegaard, who stressed the indispensable role of the Christian life, nevertheless pointed to the priority and efficacy of grace: "It is by no means man's effort which brings atonement, but it is the joy over the reconciliation, over the fact that atonement has been made, it is the joy which produces an honest striving."[121] The tension between the divine command to live a righteous life and the biblical message of justification by grace alone is poignantly brought out in this statement of Kierkegaard's: "Christianity's demand is this: your life, exerted to the limit, should express works. One thing more is demanded, that you humble yourself and confess: 'But for all that I am saved by grace.' "[122]

It is not only mysticism and occultism but also much popular revivalism that obscures the gracious prerogative of God and subverts the doctrine of the sovereignty of grace. God's forgiveness is too often made to appear conditional on man's repentance and decision of faith. Our position is that God's forgiveness, far from being contingent on man's repentance, actually makes possible genuine repentance. Through repentance we discover God's forgiveness and also gain assurance of his favor. Forgiveness is both an attitude and action. God's forgiveness is for all, but the way in which it is carried out, the way it becomes effective, differs according to the response of the hearer. Yet the response of the hearer by no means creates the divine forgiveness but instead bears witness to it. God's forgiveness does not bear fruit except in and through man's decision and repentance, but on the other hand the latter come into being by virtue of the prior act of forgiveness.

Finally we come to the question of the meaning of justification. Justification is seen in a wider perspective today than in the period of the Reformation, and much of this is to the good. Tillich has reminded us that justification pertains not only to man's moral life but also to his intellectual life. Our theologies need to be justified just as much as our inner being.

It is also coming more and more to be seen that justification by grace alone excludes every form of self-justification. Evangelicals often appeal to the experience of justification as the guarantee of their salvation. Hanson reminds us that this is the last illusion of Evangelicalism and also the subtlest form of justification by works.[123] We are not even justified by faith if faith is understood as a work or achievement of man and not as a gift of God. Faith-moralism is as much an enemy of the kingdom of God as cheap grace. To be sure, man is not only an object of grace but a participant in grace, and this entails an experience of salvation and heartfelt repentance for sin. At the same time we must insist that man is a participant in grace only on the basis of grace. We are justified not by grace plus experience or by grace plus obedience but by grace alone.

NOTES

1. F. F. Bruce, *Commentary on the Epistle to the Hebrews* (Grand Rapids: Eerdmans, 1964), p. 365.

2. Norval Geldenhuys, *Commentary on the Gospel of Luke* reprint (Grand Rapids: Eerdmans, 1966), p. 232 f.

3. This point is made with great clarity by Duane H. Thebeau, "On Separating Sheep From Goats" in *Christianity Today* 16:22 (Aug. 11, 1972), pp. 4, 5.

4. John Calvin, *Commentary upon the Acts of the Apostles,* vol. 1 trans. Henry Beveridge (Edinburgh: T. & T. Clark, 1859), pp. 322, 344, 345.

5. Joseph Addison Alexander, *The Acts of the Apostles* (New York: Scribner, 1857), vol. 1, p. 409. A slightly different interpretation but one which still affirms the necessity of faith in Christ for salvation is given by G. T. Stokes: "St. Peter's meaning is quite clear when we consider the circumstances amid which he stood. He had hitherto thought that the privilege of accepting the salvation offered was limited to the Jews. Now he had learned from Heaven itself that the offer of God's grace and mercy was free to all, and that wherever man was responding to the dictates of conscience and yielding assent to the guidance of the inner light with which every man was blessed, there God's supreme revelation was to be proclaimed and for them the doors of God's Church were to be opened wide." G. T. Stokes, *The Acts of the Apostles (The Expositor's Bible)* (New York: Funk & Wagnalls, 1900), vol. 2, pp. 131, 132. Our position is that Cornelius was not yielding assent to the dictates of conscience so much as to the prevenient grace that had been communicated to him through the Scriptures. Although he was not yet born again through faith he had experienced a rudimentary fear of God and was moving toward the righteousness that is acceptable to God. The ultimate basis for his acceptance by God was his election in Christ realized in his seeking for salvation and his eventual faith; his good works were a sign and witness of his election.

6. Benjamin Warfield, *Selected Shorter Writings of Benjamin B. Warfield,* vol. 2, ed. John E. Meeter (Nutley, N.J.: Presbyterian & Reformed, 1973), p. 427.

7. Adolf Harnack, *History of Dogma,* vol. 2 (Boston: Roberts Brothers, 1897), p. 225.

8. Ben Drewery, "Deification" in Peter Brooks, ed. *Christian Spirituality* (London: SCM Press, 1975) [pp. 35–62], p. 55.

9. J. F. Bethune-Baker, *An Introduction to the Early History of Christian Doctrine* (London: Methuen & Co. Ltd., 1934), p. 355.

10. Augustine, *De Correptione et Gratia* cap. XI, 31. For another rendering see *The Fathers of the Church,* vol. 2, trans. John Courtney Murray (New York: Fathers of the Church, 1947), p. 283.

11. Augustine, *de Spiritu et Littera* XVI. *Saint Augustin: Anti-Pelagian*

Writings, in *A Select Library of the Nicene and Post-Nicene Fathers,* ed. Philip Schaff (New York: Scribner's, 1908), vol. 5 p. 89.

12. He can even say: "When by free will sin was committed, sin being the conqueror, free will was lost; *for by whom a man is overcome, to the same also is he bound as a slave."* St. Augustine: Faith, Hope, and Charity, 4th ed., trans. Louis A. Arand (Westminster, Md.: Newman Press, 1963), p. 38. Also cf. "Since the Fall the mercy of God is even greater, because free will itself needs to be freed from the bondage of which the masters are sin and death." *Ibid.,* p. 101.

13. Cassian declared: "When He [God] sees in us any beginning of good will, straightway He enlightens it and strengthens it and stimulates it to salvation, giving increase to that good will which He planted Himself, or sees has sprung up by our own effort." In Bethune-Baker, *op. cit.,* p. 322.

14. Berkouwer contends that the Council of Orange falls short of affirming the absolute sovereignty of grace. In his view synergism is still possible even if one allows for the priority of grace. See G. C. Berkouwer, *The Conflict with Rome,* p. 316.

15. Abelard's position was condemned by a provincial Council of Sens in the twelfth century. See Piet Schoonenberg, *Man and Sin,* p. 73.

16. From Bernard of Clairvaux, *On the Feast of the Annunciation of the Blessed Virgin* 1, 1, 3. Cited by John Calvin, *Institutes* ed. McNeill, III, II, 41, p. 589. Cf.: "Yet it is difficult, impossible for a man, by his own power of free will to turn wholly to the will of God"; instead he follows "his own will." *On Loving God* II, 5 in *The Works of Bernard of Clairvaux,* vol. 5, trans. Jean Leclercq and Henri Rochais. *Treatises* II (Washington, D.C.: Consortium Press, 1974), p. 98.

17. See McSorley, *Luther: Right or Wrong?,* p. 181.

18. Although Gabriel Biel was not a Franciscan (he belonged to the Brethren of the Common Life), the spirituality he upholds stands in the Franciscan tradition. On the Franciscan spirituality see Arthur Crabtree, *The Restored Relationship,* pp. 124, 125.

19. Thomas Aquinas, *Commentary on Saint Paul's Epistle to the Ephesians* Trans. Matthew L. Lamb (Albany, N.Y.: Magi Books, 1966), p. 96.

20. *Ibid.,* p. 97.

21. See McSorley, *op. cit.,* pp. 170, 171.

22. *Summa Theologica* II-II, 17, 1 ad 2. Quoted in S. Pfürtner, *Luther and Aquinas on Salvation,* p. 89.

23. See McSorley, *op. cit.,* p. 168. It should be noted that Thomas in his Commentary on the *Sentences* defended a positive disposition for grace on a purely naturalistic basis, though Thomists are quick to remind us that this is not his mature position as expressed in his *Summa Theologica* and *Summa Contra Gentiles.* For the discussion see Heiko Oberman, *The Harvest of Medieval Theology,* pp. 142, 143.

24. Brian A. Gerrish, *Grace and Reason* (London: Oxford University Press, 1962), p. 125. McSorley criticizes Gerrish on the grounds that he does not consider that for Thomas "man's merit before God is essentially different from man's merit before men. . . ." McSorley, *op. cit.,* p. 171.

25. William Johnston, ed., *The Cloud of Unknowing and the Book of Privy Counselling* (Garden City, N.Y.: Doubleday, 1973), ch. 25, p. 82. Cf.: "Moreover,

God is always eager to work in the heart of one who has done all he can to prepare the way for his grace," ch. 26, p. 83.

26. Meister Eckhart, *Meister Eckhart Speaks,* trans. Elizabeth Strakosch (New York: Philosophical Library, 1957), p. 58. We acknowledge that there are many other passages in Eckhart where the accent is on the initiative of grace and the necessity for faith; yet it seems clear that the synergistic orientation overshadows the evangelical one. Eckhart's stress was on inward humility more than on outward works as the precondition for grace.

27. McSorley, *op. cit.,* p. 169.

28. Wilhelm Windelband, *A History of Philosophy,* vol. 1 (New York: Harper Torchbooks, 1958), p. 334.

29. In Oberman, *The Harvest of Medieval Theology,* p. 141.

30. *Ibid.,* p. 43.

31. *Ibid.,* p. 22.

32. *Luther's Works,* vol. 29, p. 125.

33. Martin Luther, W.A. 12, 497. Cf.: "There is nothing else that leads to the grace of God, or eternal salvation, but the word and work of God—grace, or the Spirit, being that very life to which the word and work of God lead us." Martin Luther, *The Bondage of the Will,* trans. J. I. Packer and O. R. Johnston (Westwood, N.J.: Fleming H. Revell Co., 1957), p. 139.

34. Luther, W.A. 10, 1, 1, p. 508. Cf. *Luther's Works,* vol. 32, p. 224 f.

35. *Luther's Works,* vol. 32, p. 91. Cf. Calvin: "He therefore excludes from man's justification not only works which are morally good, as they are commonly termed, and which are performed by the natural instinct, but also all those which even believers can possess." John Calvin, *The Epistles of Paul the Apostle to the Romans and to the Thessalonians,* eds. David W. Torrance and Thomas F. Torrance, trans. Ross Mackenzie (Grand Rapids: Eerdmans, 1961), ch. 3:21, p. 71.

36. *Luther's Works,* vol. 34, p. 113.

37. *Corpus Reformatorum* Calv. 39, p. 120.

38. *Institutes* II, 3, 13. Cited in Francois Wendel, *Calvin,* pp. 273, 274.

39. D. F. Wright, trans. and ed., *Common Places of Martin Bucer* (Appleford, Abingdon, Berkshire: Sutton Courtenay Press, 1972), p. 148.

40. *Ibid.,* p. 154.

41. *Luther's Works,* vol. 31., ed. Harold J. Grimm (Philadelphia: Muhlenberg Press, 1957), pp. 55, 56.

42. Hans Joachim Hillerbrand, ed., *The Protestant Reformation* (New York: Walker & Co., 1968), p. 151.

43. In Jessamyn West, ed., *The Quaker Reader* (New York: Viking Press, 1962), p. 95.

44. E. Schillebeeckx, "The Tridentine Decree on Justification: A New View" in *Concilium* 5 (1965), pp. 177, 178.

45. Wilhelm Niesel, *The Gospel and the Churches,* trans. David Lewis (Philadelphia: Westminster Press, 1962), p. 62. Heiko A. Oberman goes further in his "Tridentine Decree on Justification in the Light of Late Medieval Theology" in *Journal For Theology and the Church* vol. 3, ed. Robert W. Funk (New York: Harper & Row, 1967), pp. 28–54. Oberman concludes that "notwithstanding the Thomistic efforts," it was "the decision of the Tridentine fathers to

safeguard the merit *de congruo* as a merit based on God's goodness and liberality rather than on God's justice" (p. 54).

46. For Barth's criticism of Molina see Karl Barth, *Church Dogmatics* II, 1, p. 569 f. The chief leader of the Thomistic opposition to Molina was Dominicus Banez (1528–1604).

47. For a cogent Thomistic criticism of Suarez's teaching on divine grace and human freedom see Thomas U. Mullaney, *Suarez on Human Freedom* (Baltimore: Carroll Press, 1950).

48. Blaise Pascal, *Pensées and the Provincial Letters* (New York: Modern Library, Random House, 1941), trans. W. F. Trotter and Thomas M'Crie, p. 97.

49. Walter von Loewenich, *Modern Catholicism,* trans. Reginald Fuller. (New York: St. Martin's Press, 1959), p. 27.

50. Oberman, *The Harvest of Medieval Theology,* pp. 299, 300.

51. Note that Mary as Co-Redeemer is not a dogma of the Catholic church but a pious opinion that conceivably could someday be elevated to the status of dogma.

52. In the Encyclical *Intersodalicia* (1918). Quoted in Niesel, *The Gospel and the Churches,* p. 116.

53. Encyclical of Feb. 2, 1849. Niesel, *The Gospel and the Churches,* p. 117.

54. John A. Hardon, *The Catholic Catechism* (Garden City, N.Y.: Doubleday, 1975), p. 169.

55. Berkouwer, *The Conflict with Rome,* p. 167.

56. J. Pohle, "Merit" in *The Catholic Encyclopedia,* ed. Charles Herbermann, et al. vol. 10, (New York: Gilmary Society, 1911), [pp. 202–208], p. 208.

57. Martial Lekeux, *Holiness Is For Everyone,* trans. Paul J. Oligny (Westminster: Newman Press, 1953), p. 22.

58. In Berkouwer, *The Conflict with Rome,* p. 99.

59. Karl Rahner and Herbert Vorgimler, *Theological Dictionary,* 3d ed., ed. Cornelius Ernst, trans. Richard Strachan (New York: Herder & Herder, 1968), p. 452.

60. Karl Rahner, *Theological Investigations,* vol. 6, trans. Karl-H and Boniface Kruger (Baltimore: Helicon Press, 1969), p. 394.

61. He here appears to differ from Thomas Aquinas who saw this more as a negative possibility within man. Yet for Rahner this capacity or possibility for obedience is not in the essence of man but in the historical existential situation of man which God has ordered. This is why he can speak of a "supernatural existential," a dimension of transcedence within man that makes it possible for him to apprehend and receive grace. This "supernatural existential" is the point of contact with the special revelation of Jesus Christ.

62. Karl Rahner, *Hearers of the Word,* trans. Michael Richards (New York: Herder & Herder, 1969), p. 101

63. Our objection to Rahner is similar to that raised by Karl Barth against Emil Brunner in their debate on "the point of contact" between God and man. Brunner was adamant that man possesses a "capacity for revelation," but Barth correctly saw that this took away from the sovereignty of divine grace. See Peter Fraenkel, ed. and trans., *Natural Theology* (London: Centenary Press, 1946).

64. An associate of Rahner's intimates that there is within man a "radical

capacity for accepting freely the gift of God in himself." Juan Alfaro, "Nature and Grace" in Karl Rahner, ed., *Encyclopedia of Theology: The Concise Sacramentum Mundi* (New York: Seabury Press, 1975) [pp. 1033–1038], p. 1033. Yet Rahner himself declares: "The self-communication as such also effects its acceptance; the actual and proximate ability to accept is itself a supremely free grace." *Ibid.,* p. 589.

65. Thérèse of Lisieux, *The Autobiography of St. Thérèse of Lisieux,* trans. John Clarke (Washington, D.C.: Institute of Carmelite Studies, 1975), pp. 221, 267.

66. One of her biographers comments: "Thérèse learned by experience that all human efforts toward self-sanctification are highly questionable and in themselves impotent, given even the 'strongest' of wills and the best of intentions; that all our running takes us nowhere, that nothing avails us but the grace of God." Ida Friederike Görres, *The Hidden Face,* p. 103.

67. Hans Küng, *Justification,* p. 252.

68. Karl Rahner, *Theological Investigations* VI, p. 228.

69. In Karl Rahner, *"Kirche und Parusie"* in *Catholica,* 1963, p. 113 ff. Quoted in Berkouwer, *The Second Vatican Council and the New Catholicism* (Grand Rapids: Eerdmans, 1965), p. 208.

70. See Norman Pettit, *The Heart Prepared: Grace and Conversion in Puritan Spiritual Life* (New Haven: Yale University Press, 1966).

71. For a powerful indictment of this kind of Pietism as it existed in Sweden see the scintillating novel by Bo Giertz, *The Hammer of God* (Minneapolis: Augsburg Publishing House, 1960).

72. It is a matter of debate whether Wesley's position was synergistic, since in his view man's cooperation with saving grace is only possible on the basis of prevenient grace. David Shipley and Robert Chiles are unwilling to label this cooperative element "synergism," while Colin Williams and Robert Monk are of the opinion that it can be considered a qualified synergism. According to Williams Wesley's position is not a semi-Pelagian synergism, since it rests on the assumption that salvation is a matter of personal dependence on Christ, not of moral achievement. Colin W. Williams, *John Wesley's Theology Today* (Nashville: Abingdon Press, 1960), p. 72.

73. Charles Finney, *Lectures on Revivals of Religion,* reprint ed., William C. McLoughlin, Jr. (Cambridge, Mass., 1960), pp. 53, 175 f., 280.

74. J. Sidlow Baxter, *A New Call to Holiness,* 4th printing (Grand Rapids: Zondervan, 1975), p. 155.

75. Emanuel Swedenborg, *The True Christian Religion,* vol. 1, p. 111.

76. Friedrich Schleiermacher, *The Christian Faith,* vol. 2, ed. H. R. Mackintosh and J.S. Stewart (New York: Harper Torchbooks, 1963), par. 70, p. 283.

77. Abraham Kuyper, *The Work of the Holy Spirit,* p. 467.

78. James Denney, *The Death of Christ,* 2d ed. (New York: A. C. Armstrong, 1903), p. 290.

79. Cf.: "Who was it that opened your blind eyes to see a dying Savior? Who was it opened your deaf ear to hear the voice of pardoning love? . . . Who was it that broke your hard heart and made a way for the Savior to enter and dwell therein? It was that precious Holy Spirit." In Ernest W. Bacon, *Spurgeon Heir of the Puritans* (Grand Rapids: Eerdmans, 1968), p. 115.

80. P. T. Forsyth, *The Justification of God* (London: Independent Press Ltd., 1948), p. 47.

81. "The Longer Catechism of the Eastern Church" in Philip Schaff, ed., *The Creeds of Christendom* II (New York: Harper & Row, 1905), [pp. 445–542], pp. 474, 520.

82. *The Way of a Pilgrim*, trans. R. M. French (London: S.P.C.K., 1954), p. 3.

83. Adolf Köberle perceptively observes that an absolute monergism "with its hard and fast formulas. . . . overrides the personal character of the human spirit and makes God a tyrannical, mechanically operative force." *The Quest for Holiness*, trans. John C. Mattes (Minneapolis: Augsburg Publishing House, 1938), p. 142. Köberle rightly holds that monergism makes God the author of damnation as well as of salvation whereas synergism makes man a coauthor of salvation (p. 138f.).

84. Cf. Calvin: "Men indeed ought to be taught that God's loving-kindness is set forth to all who seek it, without exception. But since it is those on whom heavenly grace has breathed who at length begin to seek after it, they should not claim for themselves the slightest part of his praise." *Institutes of the Christian Religion,* ed. McNeill II, III, 10, p. 304.

85. Bernard of Clairvaux, *On Loving God* VII, 23 in *The Works of Bernard of Clairvaux,* vol. 5, p. 115.

86. Augustine, *Letters* cxlv. 2. In *Fathers of the Church* Vol. III, p. 163. See Calvin, *Institutes,* Ed. McNeill. II, II, 8, p. 265.

87. John E. Meeter, ed., *Selected Shorter Writings of Benjamin B. Warfield,* vol. 2, p. 726.

88. In this work Luther maintains that man not only can do nothing to prepare himself to enter the kingdom but also "does and endeavors nothing towards his perseverance in that kingdom." Martin Luther, *The Bondage of the Will,* p. 268. But this palpably conflicts with such texts as Phil. 2:12; Eph. 6:18; Heb. 4:11; and Heb. 12:14. We concur with the main thesis in Luther's work that the man in sin is in dire bondage and is helpless to help himself until acted upon by grace. But once under grace man can act in faith toward God as well as act in love toward his neighbor. Though not clearly evident in *The Bondage of the Will,* this idea is certainly apparent in Luther's *On the Freedom of the Christian.*

89. Abraham Kuyper, *The Work of the Holy Spirit,* p. 306.

90. Thomas Aquinas, *Commentary on Saint Paul's Epistle to the Ephesians,* p. 95.

91. Jonathan Edwards, "Miscellaneous Remarks" in *The Works of Jonathan Edwards,* ed. Edward Hickman (London, 1879), II, p. 557.

92. For an illuminating analysis of Edwards' doctrine of grace see Carl W. Bogue, *Jonathan Edwards and the Covenant of Grace* (Cherry Hill, N.J.: Mack Publishing, 1975).

93. A. W. Tozer, *The Divine Conquest* (Harrisburg, Pa.: Christian Publications, 1950), p. 49. Copyright with Fleming H. Revell Co.

94. We can also legitimately speak of conquering grace and conquering love. Love conquers even where love is denied, and is not this the state of hell?

95. Also we do not affirm reprobation as equivalent to election, since the

former is something temporary. There is real reprobation, exclusion from the benefits of grace and salvation, but it should be seen as a means to election.

96. John Calvin, *Institutes of the Christian Religion,* ed. McNeill, III, 18, 2, p. 822.

97. Dietrich Bonhoeffer, *The Cost of Discipleship,* p. 43.

98. *Ibid.,* p. 266.

99. *Luther's Works,* vol. 35, p. 10.

100. Karl Barth, *Church Dogmatics* II, 2, p. 12.

101. Ludwig Ott says that three of the sacraments "are in the ordinary way of salvation so necessary, that without their use salvation cannot be attained. Thus, for the individual person, Baptism is necessary in this way and after the commission of a grievous sin, Penance is equally necessary; while for the Church in general, the Sacrament of Holy Orders is necessary. The other Sacraments are necessary in so far as salvation cannot be so easily gained without them." In his *Fundamentals of Catholic Dogma,* pp. 338, 339.

102. Zwingli in contrast to Calvin and Luther downplayed the concept of means of grace. He declared that "a channel or vehicle is not necessary to the Spirit." One interpreter remarks: "Strictly speaking, the spoken or material Word is no means of grace at all, let alone the sacraments." In Otto H. Heick, *A History of Christian Thought,* vol. 1 (Philadelphia: Fortress Press, 1965), p. 357. Karl Barth in this respect stands closer to Zwingli than to Luther or Calvin.

103. Barth, *Church Dogmatics* III, 4, p. 521.

104. See Joseph Haroutunian, *God With Us: A Theology of Transpersonal Life* (Philadelphia: Westminster Press, 1965).

105. See Arthur C. Cochrane, *Eating and Drinking with Jesus: An Ethical and Biblical Inquiry* (Philadelphia: Westminster Press, 1974), pp. 128, 147.

106. For a more extended discussion see Donald G. Bloesch, *The Reform of the Church* (Grand Rapids: Eerdmans, 1970), pp. 35–95.

107. This does not mean that the Holy Spirit may not and does not speak through preachers whose lives do not testify to the Gospel. The Spirit is free to act as he will and so long as this objective Gospel message is being proclaimed, the possibility is there that the Spirit may also be at work (cf. Phil. 1:15–18). Yet we contend that the Spirit is much more likely to work where the Gospel is attested by life as well as by words.

It should be noted that Luther in his correspondence with the Ultraquists advised them to seek ministers who were "worthy." He even went so far as to say that it is better to abstain from sacraments other than baptism when these are offered by "impious and sacrilegious men." The sacrifices of the church should be offered "only by one who is spiritual, that is, by a Christian who has the Spirit of Christ." *Luther's Works* 40, 29. For a discussion of Luther's position on this matter see Jaroslav Pelikan, *Spirit versus Structure* (London: Collins, 1968), p. 43 f.

108. The sacraments are effective not *ex opere operato* (by the mere fact of being performed) nor *ex opere operantis* (by the work of the priest) but by the work of Christ *(ex opere Christi).*

109. He declared: "Wherefore, the common opinion, by which baptism is supposed to be necessary to salvation, ought to be so moderated, that it should

not bind the grace of God, or the power of the Spirit, to external symbols, and bring against God a charge of falsehood." John Calvin, *Genesis,* vol. 1 trans. and ed. John King (Edinburgh: Banner of Truth Trust, 1975), p. 458.

110. *The Works of Jonathan Edwards,* vol. 2, ed. Edward Hickman, p. 4.

111. See Bernard Meland, "Grace: A Dimension within Nature?" in *The Journal of Religion* 54:2 (April 1974) pp. 119–137.

112. See Avery Dulles' devastating critique of Langdon Gilkey's *Catholicism Confronts Modernity* (New York: Seabury Press, 1975) in *The Review of Books and Religion* 4:9 (Mid-June 1975), pp. 1, 16.

113. P. T. Forsyth, *The Gospel and Authority,* ed. Marvin Anderson, p. 153.

114. James Packer, "Taking Stock in Theology" in *Evangelicals Today,* ed. John C. King (London: Lutterworth, 1973) [pp. 15–30], pp. 22, 23.

115. Karl Barth, *The Word of God and the Word of Man,* p. 197. Cf. Thielicke: "There can be no reaching him [Christ] by human initiative, whether it be intellectual apprehension, religious receptivity or affinity, or the activism of imitation of Christ." *Evangelical Faith* II, p. 453.

116. Jacob Needleman, *The New Religions* (Garden City, N.Y.: Doubleday, 1970), p. 192.

117. Gerald Heard, *The Creed of Christ* (New York: Harper & Row, 1940), p. 83.

118. I. C. Sharma, *Cayce, Karma, and Reincarnation* (New York: Harper & Row, 1975), p. 106.

119. *Ibid.,* pp. 95, 96.

120. R. P. C. Hanson, *The Attractiveness of God,* p. 138.

121. Soren Kierkegaard, *Soren Kierkegaard's Journals and Papers,* vol. I, A–E, eds. and trans. Howard V. Hong and Edna H. Hong (Bloomington, Ind.: Indiana University Press, 1967), p. 428.

122. Soren Kierkegaard, *For Self-Examination,* trans. Edna H. Hong and Howard V. Hong (Minneapolis: Augsburg Publishing House, 1959), p. 11.

123. Hanson, *op. cit.,* p. 145.

IX.
FAITH ALONE

And he believed the Lord; and he reckoned it to him as righteousness.

Genesis 15:6

We hold that faith in Christ rather than fidelity to the law is what justifies us.

Galatians 2:16 JB

It is ordained of God that whoever believes in Christ shall be saved, and he shall have forgiveness of sins, not through works but through faith alone, without merit.

Ambrosiaster

Now the article of justification, which is our sole defense, not only against all the force and craft of men, but also against the gates of hell, is this: that by faith only in Christ, and without works, we are pronounced righteous and saved.

Martin Luther

Paul declareth nothing on behalf of man concerning his justification but only a true and lively faith, which [itself] is a gift of God.

John Wesley

THE MEANING OF FAITH

The Scriptures make clear that faith is the means by which we receive and appropriate the salvation purchased for us by Jesus Christ on the cross. Paul declares that we receive the Spirit not "by works of the law" but "by hearing with faith" (Gal. 3:2). Faith moreover is not an achievement of man but a gift of God. It is an inner awakening given to man by the Holy Spirit by which he is moved to give of himself in trust and surrender to Jesus Christ. Man believes but not on the basis of his own free will but on the basis of the free grace of God. According to Thomas Aquinas, "Free will is inadequate for the act of faith since the contents of faith are above human reason."[1] Paul expressed it this way: "For by grace you have been saved through faith; and this is not your own doing, it is the gift of God—not because of works, lest any man should boast" (Eph. 2:8, 9).

Faith might be defined as a radical commitment of the whole man to the living Christ, a commitment that entails knowledge, trust, and obedience. While Protestant Orthodoxy was inclined to stress the elements of knowledge (notitia) and intellectual assent (assensus), the Pietists put the emphasis on trust and venture (fiducia). For William à Brakel, the Dutch Pietist, faith is not the act of the mind assenting to divine truth but the trusting of the heart in the salvation offered by Christ. In his view faith has its seat not in the understanding but in the will. It is more proper to affirm that faith has its ground in the Holy Spirit who simultaneously illumines the mind and empowers the will of man. Faith is a divine work within us whereby the will is liberated and the mind illumined so that we are now enabled and moved to believe and obey Jesus Christ as Lord and Savior.

Faith is not mere intellectual assent but an inward spiritual change in man. It is not simply a new comprehension but a new creation. It entails knowledge of the Gospel as well as commitment to the Gospel. But this knowledge is not a mere intellectual understanding but an existential understanding, one that imparts certainty and confidence to the subject. These two aspects of faith can be seen in Calvin's definition: "Faith . . . is a steady and certain knowledge of the Divine benevolence towards us, which, being founded on the truth of the gratuitous promise in Christ, is both revealed to our minds, and confirmed to our hearts, by the Holy Spirit."[2] Calvin leaves no doubt that this is not an ordinary kind of knowledge: "When we call it knowledge, we intend not such a comprehension as men commonly have of those things which fall under the notice of their senses. For it is so superior that the human mind must exceed and rise above itself in order to attain to it."[3] Calvin would indubitably concur with Bernard of Clairvaux: "I believe though I do not comprehend, and I hold by faith what I cannot grasp with the mind."[4]

Luther distinguished between the "faith which believes what is said of God is true" and the "faith which throws itself on God." It is the latter which is the true saving faith, though such faith will certainly entail a right understanding of the meaning of the cross. While Calvin's stress was on knowledge, Luther's was on trust (fiducia), but both elements must always be present in an authentic act of faith.

John Wesley too underlined the need for personal trust as well as intellectual conviction in faith: "Justifying faith implies, not only a divine evidence or conviction that 'God was in Christ, reconciling the world unto Himself,' but a sure trust and confidence that Christ died for *my* sins, that He loved *me* and gave Himself for *me.*"[5]

Just as we must qualify our understanding of the noetic element in faith so we must make a similar qualification of the voluntaristic element. Faith is not simply commitment but consecration. It is not a mere decision but a full surrender. Forsyth put it this way: "Faith is not simply surrender, but *adoring* surrender, not a mere sense of dependence, but an act of intelligent committal, and the confession of a holiness which is able to save, keep, and bless for ever."[6] It is not so much an outward profession as an inward conversion.

In the act of faith both God and man are active. Man is passive in the reception of the knowledge of salvation, but he is made active by the Holy Spirit in his response and obedience. Adolf Schlatter perceived two characteristics inherent in faith: it is worked by God and willed by man.[7] According to Karl Barth, "Faith is altogether the work of God, and it is altogether the work of man. It is a complete enslavement, and it is a complete liberation."[8] What is necessary to maintain is that man's activity is grounded in and made possible by God's prior activity, the action of free grace.

Faith in its essence is receiving, but it becomes giving in practice, the giving or surrender of oneself to God. Faith is both receiving and giving, the receiving from God of his mercy and the giving of oneself in dedication to God. Faith is an empty vessel as far as man's justification is concerned, but it is creative endeavor in regard to the fulfillment of man's vocation.

Having established that faith involves knowledge, assent, and trust, we must go on to affirm that it is an experience as well. Calvin contended that "no one can well perceive the power of faith unless he feels it by experience in his heart."[9] Luther too was very adamant that faith is an inner experience by which we feel and enjoy the presence of Christ: "You yourself in your own conscience must feel Christ himself. You must experience unshakably that it is God's Word, even though the whole world should dispute it. As long as you do not have this feeling, you have certainly not yet tasted of God's Word."[10] Pietism accentuated the experiential dimension of faith, and in later Romanticism this was emphasized almost to the exclusion of the other elements in faith. Schleiermacher, for example, declared: "Faith is nothing but the incipient experience of the satisfaction of our spiritual need by Christ."[11] Such a definition betrays a subjectivizing of faith whereby Christ becomes the means to the satisfying of man's spiritual needs rather than the object and goal of man's faith.

It is important to note that although the Reformers made a definite place for the experiential side of faith, they were explicit that this is an experience qualitatively different from sense experience. It is indeed an experience that transcends the senses, since its object is inaccessible to empirical investigation or verification. Luther described faith as "being rapt and translated from all things of sense, within and without, into those things beyond sense within and without, namely into the invisible, most high and incomprehensible God."[12] Faith entails feeling, but it also goes beyond feeling, even religious feeling, and sometimes it contradicts our feelings. Luther warned: "You should not believe your conscience and your feelings more than the word which the Lord who receives sinners preaches to you."[13] And again: "This is real strength, to trust in God when to all our senses and reason He appears to be angry; and to have greater confidence in Him than we feel."[14]

Hannah Whitall Smith, one of the luminaries of the Holiness movement, was noted for her admonitions against placing too much trust in one's own religious experience. In this respect she was true to Reformation and Pauline theology which emphasized the pilgrimage of faith over the security of sight.

Sight is not faith, and hearing is not faith, neither is feeling faith; but believing when we can neither see, hear, nor feel *is* faith; and everywhere the Bible tells us our salvation is to be by faith. Therefore we must believe before we feel, and often against our feelings, if we would honor God by our faith.[15]

This brings us to the existential dimension of faith, that faith is a risk and venture. It is the readiness to enter confidently into the darkness of the future (Luther). The risk element in faith is conveyed in this rather free translation of Isaiah 50:10: "He who walks in darkness, to whom no light appears, let him trust in the Name of Yahweh, let him rely upon his God."[16] There are no rational guarantees in the life of faith. The Levitical priests carrying the ark over the Jordan river had to stand in the midst of the Jordan before the waters receded (Joshua 4). What Karl Barth says is very apropos concerning the nature of true faith: "Faith is not, therefore, a standing, but a being suspended and hanging without ground under our feet."[17] We are not only justified by faith alone, but we must also walk by faith alone. The man of faith clings to the promises of Christ in Scripture even though he may not have a direct awareness of the divine presence. He ventures forth without any outward security even though he may not understand the direction in which God is leading him. He ventures forth sometimes against all logic and reason out of fidelity to the inward call that comes to him from God. His believing is a joyous daring upon the unknown and untried goodness of God (Luther).[18]

Faith is not only a risk but also a struggle. It involves a daily battle against sin, death, and the devil (cf. 2 Tim. 4:7). Paul confessed, "I die daily" (1 Cor. 15:31 KJ), since he had to face ever new trials and tribulations. It is not enough to believe once: we must believe again and again. Our faith is renewed when we look evermore to Christ and throw ourselves on his mercy. Though our flesh and our heart may fail, we can press onward to victory knowing that the promises of God will never fail (Ps. 73:26).

Finally we need to remind ourselves that the object of faith is not a doctrinal formula but a living Person, Jesus Christ. As Kierkegaard phrased it, "The object of Faith is not the *teaching* but the *Teacher*." [19] Yet although faith is much more than doctrinal rectitude, it certainly entails adherence to doctrine. In our trust and commitment to Jesus Christ we must acknowledge him as the Savior from sin as well as the Lord of all creation. In following Christ we must also commit ourselves to the Gospel concerning Christ. We do not really know him until we understand his mission. We do not really believe in him unless we also believe what he tells us in the Scriptures. Yet our beliefs about him must not be confused with our personal fellowship and communion with him, which is deeper than belief though inseparable from it. This personal relationship with Christ definitely involves a belief in his deity and saving work, but it is possible to have the right belief without a living faith.

JUSTIFICATION BY FAITH

The theme of justification by faith alone *(sola fide)* can be found throughout the Bible, but it is especially evident in the writings of St. Paul. Paul drew a sharp contrast between the righteousness of works and the righteousness of faith (Rom. 3:21, 22). By the "works of the law," he declared, "shall no one be justified" (Gal. 2:16). If "justification were through the law, then Christ died to no purpose" (Gal. 2:21). The law was our custodian until Christ came, but "now that faith has come, we are no longer under a custodian; for in Christ Jesus you are all sons of God, through faith" (Gal. 3:24–26). For Paul "a man is justified by faith apart from works of law" (Rom. 3:28; cf. Eph. 2:8). The law cannot justify because no one can keep the law perfectly, since the infection of sin has spread throughout the human race. Therefore we can be saved only through God's grace and mercy which are apprehended and received by faith alone, not by works, lest any man should boast. We can do nothing to bring ourselves to faith, since apart from faith man is dead in sin. Indeed, it was precisely when "we were dead through our trespasses" that he "made us alive together with Christ. . . ." (Eph. 2:5; cf. Col. 2:13).

While Paul's main concern was the righteousness of faith (Rom. 3:22; 4:13) which is imputed to us and implanted within us, he also referred to the righteousness of outgoing love (Rom. 5:5; 14:15-17; Col. 1:4), which molds our character and instills hope (Rom. 5:5; 13:10; 15:13). Faith alone justifies and regenerates us, but faith working through love sanctifies us (Gal. 5:6). We are engrafted into the righteousness of Christ by faith, but we become righteous in personal life through works of love (Phil. 1:9-11).

For those who adhere to the full inspiration of Scripture, as we do, the Epistle of James presents some difficulty, since it is expressly stated that "a man is justified by works and not by faith alone" (James 2:24). How can this be reconciled with Paul's emphasis on faith apart from works? Luther did not attempt any reconciliation and relegated James to the level of Law, not Gospel. Wesley is better here for he points out that James has in mind a different kind of faith and a different kind of works from Paul. James is speaking of faith as intellectual assent, not faith as the commitment of the whole person to the living Christ (as in Paul). Moreover, he is referring not to the works of the law (which preoccupy Paul) but to the fruits of faith. Our justification is exhibited and carried forward by the practice of our faith, though its ground or basis is in the free mercy of God.

The biblical motif of *sola fide* was indubitably compromised in the early church and medieval periods. Irenaeus saw faith as leading to the observance of the commandments of Christ and therefore as sufficient to make man righteous before God. For Origen faith was only a preliminary though necessary step to salvation and must be supplemented by repentance. The emphasis in many of the fathers was on the obedience of faith rather than the gift of faith.

At the same time a commitment to salvation by free grace through faith in the righteousness of Christ is evident in some Catholic theologians, such as Ambrose, Augustine, Bernard of Clairvaux, and Thomas Aquinas. All these men insisted that justification is to be attributed not to the works of the law or to what man can accomplish on his own but to faith in the atoning sacrifice of Christ.

Ambrose, who had a marked influence on Augustine, foresaw many of the concerns of the Reformation. While open to the then emerging sacramentalism, he was above all a man of the Scriptures. In words that anticipate Reformed theology he declared:

I will not glory because I am righteous, but because I am redeemed. I will not glory because I am void of sin, but because my sins are forgiven. I will not glory because I am profitable or because any one is profitable to me, but because Christ is my Advocate with the Father, and his blood was shed for me.[20]

According to Ambrose "no one is justified by his deeds," but the one who is righteous "has received a gift," namely, "faith . . . which sets us free by the blood of Christ."[21] It is well to note that the Reformers frequently cited Ambrose with approbation because of his unmistakable witness to the free gift of salvation to be received by faith alone.[22] Faith, for Ambrose, is not simply assenting to the Gospel but opening one's heart and life to Jesus that he may enter as Savior and Lord.[23]

At the same time Ambrose contended that our justification is also accomplished through baptism, since it is in baptism that we are buried with Christ and rise with him to newness of life. Both baptism and the Eucharist mediate the forgiveness of sins and regeneration by the Holy Spirit. For grievous sins after baptism, such as apostasy, there is forgiveness only through the sacrament of penance, which involves grieving over sin, afflicting ourselves, and turning to God. Faith, of course, plays a significant role in all the sacraments, but it seems that through his stress on the sacramental mediation of grace Ambrose is not able to hold consistently to *sola fide*.

While it is generally known that Thomas Aquinas stressed salvation by grace, what is not so well known, at least by Protestants, is that he also spoke much of justification by faith alone. He saw "no hope of justification" in the precepts of the law "but in faith alone."[24] With Paul he held that "God saves man by faith without any preceding merits, *that no man may glory* in himself but refer all the glory to God."[25] "In vain," he said, "would anyone listen to the word of truth if he did not believe, and the believing itself is through Christ."[26]

At the same time Thomas was not content to rest the whole of justification only on faith, on faith simply by itself but instead joined faith to love so that our justification might be fulfilled. He spoke of a "faith formed by love" *(fides caritate formata)* and attributed the justifying power in faith to the love which "informs" it. Faith was seen as a virtue which makes one acceptable to God, provided, of course, that it is united with love. Charity or love was regarded not as an element in faith but as something added to faith: "What brings faith to its form, or makes it alive, does not belong to the essence of faith."[27]

The Council of Trent followed Thomas in this respect. For the Council faith is simply "the beginning of human salvation," not its essence or center. It was also affirmed: "For faith, unless hope and charity be added thereto, neither unites man perfectly with Christ, nor makes him a living member of his body" (Chapter VII). Faith justifies not because it appropriates the righteousness of Christ but because it works through charity.

Philip Watson astutely observes that this position irretrievably compromises the biblical doctrine of the justification of the godless:

The thought of faith formed by love as the ground of justification, rests on the assumption that God cannot receive man into fellowship with Himself unless man merits it by fulfilling His law. God's law is a law of love, and man must therefore possess the love it requires, if he is to be acceptable to the Lawgiver.[28]

For the Reformers faith is not a virtue that merits grace, but it is the action of grace itself in the soul of the sinner that justifies and redeems him. Luther passionately declared: "Now the article of justification, which is our sole defense, not only against all the force and craft of man, but also against the gates of hell, is this: that by faith only in Christ, and without works, we are pronounced righteous and saved."[29] Excluded by the Reformers from the work of man's justification were not only the works of the law but also the works of faith. For Calvin this means "not only works which are morally good, as they are commonly termed, and which are performed by the natural instinct, but also all those which even believers can possess."[30] Martin Bucer cited with approval Bernard of Clairvaux: "All our acts of righteousness, when examined in the light of truth, are found to be like the polluted rag of a menstruous woman."[31]

While seeing the truth that faith must give rise to works of love, the Reformers were adamant that such works do not justify but only attest a justification already accomplished. Calvin declared that "no other faith justifies 'but faith working through love.' . . . But it does not take its power to justify from that working of love. Indeed, it justifies in no other way but in that it leads us into fellowship with the righteousness of Christ."[32]

It is commonly thought that Luther emphasized faith to the detriment of love, but this is a gross misconception. The only faith that justifies, in his estimation, is a faith that bears fruit in love. By faith the Christian "is caught up beyond himself into God. By love he descends beneath himself into his neighbor."[33] For Luther,

Faith always justifies and makes alive; and yet it does not remain alone, that is, idle. Not that it does not remain alone on its own level and in its own function, for it always justifies alone. But it is incarnate and becomes man: that is, it neither is nor remains idle or without love.[34]

What is important to understand is that for the Reformers justification is not a divine process within the soul but an act of God by which He declares the sinner righteous, even though he inwardly remains a sinner. This act is extrinsic to man, but it does not remain so, since it has immediate concrete effects in the life of man through his faith. Man can apprehend and receive his justification only through the power of the Holy Spirit working in him. This means that justification and regeneration are correlative. One might even say that regeneration is the subjective pole of justification. Man is justified by the free grace of God, but this act becomes effectual in and through man's faith which is itself a gift of God. Melanchthon moved away from this position in maintaining that faith precedes the gift of the Holy Spirit to man, and he thereby separated justification and regeneration. For him justification was exclusively forensic and extrinsic, but this was not the case for Luther and Calvin.

The revolutionary character of the Reformation can be seen in the way Christians in that tradition generally interpret the parable of the rich young ruler who was barred from the kingdom (Luke 18:18–23; Matt. 19:16–22). He had done good works since his boyhood, but he refused to make the supreme sacrifice—selling all that he had and giving to the poor. This passage is traditionally interpreted in Roman Catholic circles as referring to the counsels of perfection, works that assure or expedite salvation. The rich man by embracing poverty could merit an increase in his justification and gain an eternal reward in heaven. The Reformers on the other hand rightly perceived that the virtue that Jesus was upholding was not the external act of voluntary poverty but unconditional faith. The rich young ruler lacked the one thing essential—faith. He hesitated to follow Jesus all the way. It was not so much that he was rich but that his trust was in his wealth; this is why he was unable to enter the kingdom.

The salient themes of the Reformation in the area of Christian salvation are nowhere better summarized than in the Heidelberg Catechism (1562), composed by the Reformed theologians Kaspar Olevianus and Zacharias Ursinus. The Catechism is very clear that the motivation in good works is not to gain salvation but to show our gratefulness for a salvation already accomplished in Jesus Christ. This answer is given to the question on why one must say that he is righteous by faith alone (question 61): "Not because I please God by virtue of the worthiness of my faith, but because the satisfaction, righteousness, and holiness of Christ alone are my righteousness before God, and because I can accept it and make it mine in no other way than by faith alone."[35]

In Evangelical Pietism and Puritanism the doctrine of justification by faith alone was vigorously reaffirmed. At the same time an emphasis was placed on the Christian life that is not found in the mainstream of the Reformation. It was said that Christian practice is the cardinal evidence and consequence of a genuine faith, and if such practice is not visible in the lives of believers then this proves that they are in fact not justified. Yet the Pietists were always quick to affirm that a godly life does not itself procure the remission of sins, for this is already a reality in the person's life through his faith. Philip Spener gladly acknowledged "that we must be saved only and alone through faith and that our works or godly life contribute neither much nor little to our salvation, for as a fruit of our faith our works are connected with the gratitude which we owe to God, who has already given us who believe the gift of righteousness and salvation."[36]

In the view of Jonathan Edwards: "Men are not saved on *account* of any work of theirs, and yet they are not saved *without* works."[37] Works of charity do not perfect faith in the sense of bringing a supposedly dead faith to life, but "they may 'perfect' faith in this way: for they may exhibit faith's own liveliness and thereby demonstrate the nature of faith."[38] Edwards diverged from the Reformation in his marked emphasis on the decision character of faith. Faith is not a mere instrument but the condition of the covenant of grace. It is not wholly passive but active, since it entails a decision of the will. He also went beyond the Reformation in seeing love as belonging to faith itself. For him, the faith that justifies already contains within it the impulse of love.[39] Edwards possibly lays himself open to the charge that he makes faith a meritorious work, but he is quite adamant that justification is unearned.

John Wesley also stood in continuity with the Reformation in the area of justification, although he too manifested a slightly different spirit primarily because of the changed religious situation. Writing in 1740 he described his doctrine as *"the old way,* of salvation by faith only"* as opposed to "the *new path,* of salvation by *faith and works."* [40] His inveterate Protestant orientation is very much apparent in these words:

Paul declareth nothing on the behalf of man concerning his justification but only a true and lively faith, which [itself] is the gift of God. And yet that faith doth not shut out repentance, hope, love and the fear of God, to be joined with faith in every man that is justified. But it shutteth them out from the office of justifying, so that although they be all present together in him that is justified, yet they justify not all together.[41]

Wesley was, of course, concerned that faith be inward and living and not merely outward or formal. The only faith that justifies is a faith characterized by the dedication and commitment of the inner man: "This is the true, [living] Christian faith, [which] is not in the mouth and outward profession only, but it liveth and stirreth inwardly in the heart."[42]

At the same time Wesley was disturbed to find that in much preaching faith was emphasized almost to the exclusion of good works. He consequently came to oppose what he termed *solifidianism,* a stress on faith alone which belied the need for sanctification and spiritual growth. Many evangelicals today would do well to heed his trenchant admonition:

If we *duly join* faith and works in all our preaching, we shall not fail of a blessing. But of all preaching, what is usually called gospel preaching is the most useless, if not the most mischievous; a dull, yea or lively, harangue on the sufferings of Christ or salvation by faith without strongly inculcating holiness. I see more and more that this naturally tends to drive holiness out of the world.[43]

In contemporary Catholicism efforts are being made to reassess the conflict with the Reformation and to reformulate the complex relationship between faith and good works. Karl Rahner contends that faith is an act inspired by grace and that it in no way merits justification.[44] At the same time he reaffirms the traditional view that faith precedes justification and that justification can be acquired by a cooperation with prevenient grace. In line with Catholic tradition he understands the righteousness of faith as a quality within us, not a righteousness credited to us by virtue of our faith in Jesus Christ (as in the Reformation). We contend that in faith we do not cooperate with God in procuring justification, but we gratefully receive the gift of justification, we surrender to his justifying grace but through the power of the Holy Spirit.

Hans Küng more closely approximates the Reformation position in maintaining that we are justified not by works, even works of faith, but only by faith itself. "Justification occurs," he says, "through faith *alone,* inasmuch as no kind of work, not even a work of love, justifies man, but simply faith, trust, abandoning oneself to God, giving oneself over to God's grace in response to God's act. . . ."[45] At the same time "faith, even 'dead faith,' has the seed of love in it. How else could it grasp God's mercy without a seed of love?"[46] He also is emphatic that faith must be seen as a human act as well as a divine gift:

Every human work, every human achievement, is excluded, but not every human *act*, which does not set itself up as the achievement of some work but rather as renunciation of achievement, which does not desire to force itself through by works, but rather trustfully to abandon itself. This fundamental deed of man, which is supremely active in its extreme passivity, is *faith.* "[47]

Louis Bouyer in his noted work *The Spirit and Forms of Protestantism* contends that such themes as the free gift of salvation and justification by faith alone are solidly Catholic as well as Protestant. He declares

that faith *alone* saves us means . . . that we, on our part, have nothing to add to it, nothing outside or independent of it. Any such addition would result, of necessity, in a denial of the essential. For if, believing in principle in the saving action of God, we were obliged to add something of our own initiative, what would be the result? We would fall back at once into the impossible situation from which grace had rescued us; we would have to accomplish our salvation in part, in the hope that God would do the rest. But our actual state of wretchedness comes from our incapacity for any effective initiative, even incomplete, towards salvation; in short, we have not only to be assisted to save ourselves, we need to be saved.[48]

On the Protestant side Karl Barth has pioneered in a rethinking of past positions on the question of justification. He insists that God not only turns to man in free grace (justification) but converts man to Himself (sanctification). The atonement consists not only in the humiliation of God but in the exaltation and sanctification of man. For Barth the declaring righteous is also making righteous. While justification must be distinguished from sanctification, it is inseparable from it. Justification has logical priority over sanctification but not chronological priority.[49] Neither movement of God's grace is superior or inferior to the other. Both aim for the glory of God and the salvation of man. Just as we are justified by faith so we are sanctified by love. Both love and faith play an integral role in the salvation of man; love is received in faith and invariably accompanies faith.[50] Just as we do not justify ourselves, so we do not sanctify ourselves. Rather our sanctification consists in our participation in the sanctification of Jesus Christ.[51] Where I differ from Barth is that I believe that we are called to cooperate in the process of our sanctification, while we simply submit and receive in the event of justification.

THE CERTAINTY OF FAITH

One of the perennial conflicts between Roman Catholic and Reformed theology concerns the subject of certainty in faith. While the
Reformers held that man can and must be certain of his salvation, the
Catholic position has been that one cannot be absolutely sure that he
is saved. The Council of Trent rejected the view that man could rise
above conjecture and attain certainty without a special revelation. In
the light of fresh research into the thought of Thomas Aquinas on this
question, there are grounds for maintaining that the Council here
reflected only one side of his position.[52]

Karl Rahner is willing to recognize certainty in faith, but in line
with his tradition he is unwilling to affirm that the certainty of faith
(certitudo fidei) implies the certainty of our salvation (certitudo salu-
tis). He contends that we must not suppose that "the believer's relationship with God is . . . contingent and open to doubt: this relationship
means an unshakable decision for God, regardless of how clearly he is
revealed, and for the truth of his testimony, a decision which acknowledges no other norm or judge."[53] At the same time he repudiates "a
belief in justification so firm that this belief is inconsistent with any
doubt of a man's ultimate salvation."[54]

In some Catholic theologians, certainty concerning our final salvation is based on works of love. According to the Dutch Catholic theologian Scheeben "we . . . have the certainty that we shall only attain the
final goal of predestination, heavenly bliss, if we merit it through good
works."[55]

Calvin was very emphatic that faith entails certitude concerning
our salvation. For him "faith is a firm and effectual confidence, and not
just a bare idea."[56] Indeed, "the knowledge of faith consists more in
certainty than in comprehension."[57]

For to have faith is not to waver, to vary, to be borne up and down, to hesitate,
to be held in suspense, to vacillate—finally, to despair! Rather, to have faith
is to strengthen the mind with constant assurance and perfect confidence, to
have a place to rest and plant your foot.[58]

Yet we would be doing an injustice to Calvin if we represented him
as upholding a view of the Christian life that is characterized only by
inward peace and certainty. He recognized the presence of doubt and
fear even in the most saintly Christian but insisted that they have their
source not in faith but in the old man, the man crucified in the decision
of faith. He declared: "When we inculcate, that faith ought to be cer-

tain and secure, we conceive not of a certainty attended with no doubt, or of a security interrupted by no anxiety; but we rather affirm, that believers have a perpetual conflict with their own diffidence, and are far from placing their consciences in a placid calm, never disturbed by any storms."[59]

Calvin maintained, moreover, that the Christian could be certain not only of his present salvation but of his perseverance in the faith to the very end. This is the doctrine of eternal security, and it was particularly objected to by the Catholic opponents of the Reformation. For Calvin the truly elect have been given the certain knowledge that they are not only saved by grace but will be kept by grace. This is not to deny that through stubbornness and presumption they may fall time and again, but they will never fall out of the sphere of grace.[60] Because God's grace is more powerful than their weakness, they will never be abandoned to the darkness.

Luther also understood faith as giving certitude and confidence to the Christian: "Faith is a living, daring confidence in God's grace, so sure and certain that a man could stake his life on it a thousand times."[61] Doubt is not an element within faith (as in Tillich) but a contradiction of faith. As he put it: "If we are in doubt about our being in a state of grace and about our being pleasing to God for the sake of Christ, we are denying that Christ has redeemed us and completely denying all His benefits."[62] The certainty of faith lies not in itself but in its object, the living Christ. Our faith is certain "because it carrieth us out of ourselves, that we should not lean to our own strength, our own conscience, our own feeling, our own person, and our own works, but to that which is without us, that is to say, the promise and truth of God which cannot deceive us."[63] Luther perceived that our works of love can deepen our certainty of salvation, but again such works take us out of ourselves into Christ and our neighbor, for we do such works to glorify God by upholding his Son and serving his people. Luther was emphatic that the born again Christian will feel in his heart the joy and certitude of his salvation (cf. 1 Pet. 1:8), but even when these inner consolations are absent he can still believe, since his faith has a sure and certain anchor in the promises of Christ in Scripture.

On the question of certainty of final salvation or eternal security, Luther's position was that our eternal security is with Christ in heaven. We have this eternal security by faith. It is ours so long as we believe and continue to believe. Unlike Calvin, Luther maintained that the Christian could fall from grace into condemnation, and that this was a distinct possibility throughout life.[64] The security that is now ours by faith will become ours by actual possession at the second coming of Christ.

In Protestant orthodoxy the certainty of faith came to be understood primarily as a rational certainty, one that has special reference to the trustworthiness of the biblical record. Faith itself came to be seen as intellectual assent, though the other elements were by no means denied. In place of the immediacy of the Spirit in our hearts witnessing that we are children of God (Rom. 8:16), the Spirit now witnesses to the authenticity of the Bible as a document of revelation. Johann Gerhard believed that the existence of God could be proved rationally. Yet this rational proof does not give us certainty. "Although the proof is correct," he declared, "we believe it because of revelation."[65] Francis Turretin contended that we can have certainty not a priori but only a posteriori by examining the effects of election in ourselves.[66]

It was customary in orthodoxy to define faith in terms of knowledge (notitia), assent (assensus), and trust (fiducia), but the latter was made contingent on the first two. Martin Chemnitz held that "after this knowledge and assent (which are in the mind), the heart or the will, under the Spirit's influence," feels the burden of sin and then asks for those blessings promised in the Gospel.[67] Ideally the three elements of faith should be viewed as three aspects of the same event, as was the case with a great many of those who stood in this tradition. For John Theodore Mueller notitia should be seen not simply as an historical knowledge but as a "true spiritual knowledge of Christ, which the Holy Ghost works through the Gospel". The term assensus should be conceived as "spiritual assent to the promises of the Gospel, which the Holy Ghost likewise works through the Gospel."[68] In this case both of these terms "include the fiducia cordis, or the sincere confidence of the heart in the grace of God offered in the Gospel."[69]

Whereas the Reformers saw the ground of certainty in Jesus Christ himself and the promises of the Gospel, certainty came more and more to be associated with rational corroboration (as in the rationalistic orthodoxy of the Age of Enlightenment) or with the Christian life and experience (as in Pietism). It is well to note that the Heidelberg Catechism, which found a hearing in the circles of both Orthodoxy and Pietism, maintains that "we are assured from the fruits of our faith" (question 86). This stands in apparent contradiction to Calvin who based the assurance of faith not on good works but on faith itself. According to Berkouwer, however, we misunderstand the Catechism if we think that it teaches that works are the ground of the assurance of salvation. Instead the Catechism affirms that they become the source of joy as we walk the Christian life.[70]

While Protestant Orthodoxy emphasized the content of faith, the belief one holds (fides quae creditur), Pietism emphasized the act of "believing," the belief with which one believes (fides qua creditur).[71] The point of reference consequently came to be the religious experience or internal disposition of the believer. The Christian life also loomed very significant as a source of certainty for the believer.

For Jonathan Edwards, an Evangelical who sought to stay clear of some of the pitfalls in his tradition, "Assurance is not to be obtained so much by self-examination, as by action."[72] He opposed the excessive searching of one's own experience, a morbid preoccupation with the status of one's soul. Assurance is gained chiefly as one perserveres in Christian practice. Faith itself is prior to genuine assurance, since it is possible to struggle with doubt and still be a person of faith. In contrast to the Reformers, Edwards maintained that true assurance is not an integral element of faith but its effect.

For John Wesley the assurance of faith is a special gift which ordinarily occurs at the time of the new birth. This assurance derives from both the witness of the Spirit and the fruits of the Spirit. Yet Wesley also spoke of an assurance of perfect sanctification, of being perfected in love by the purifying work of the Spirit. He sometimes referred to this as the "full assurance of faith." "As when we were justified, the Spirit bore witness with our spirit, that our sins were forgiven; so, when we were sanctified, he bore witness, that they were taken away."[73] Against Calvinism he maintained that the Christian can be assured of present salvation but not of final salvation. At the same time he allowed for the possibility that some Christians may be given the "assurance of hope" (cf. Heb. 6:11), the inner knowledge that they will be kept sound and secure until they meet Christ at death.

Soren Kierkegaard, who definitely belongs to the tradition of Evangelical Pietism, affirmed a subjective certitude of salvation but also an objective uncertainty. Faith is the passion of inwardness, not a knowledge of truths that are accessible to reason. Against the rationalism that dominated the Christian orthodoxy of his time he declared:

It is easy to see, though it scarcely needs to be pointed out, since it is involved in the fact that the Reason is set aside, that Faith is not a form of knowledge; for all knowledge is either a knowledge of the Eternal, excluding the temporal and historical as indifferent, or it is pure historical knowledge. No knowledge can have for its object the absurdity that the Eternal is the historical.[74]

For Kierkegaard the object of faith is the Absolute Paradox, God becoming man, the Eternal becoming historical, and this not only eludes but repels reason, since it cannot be mastered or comprehended. Faith must cling to the reality of this event against reason's inclination to explain away or resolve the paradox in a rational system. Kierkegaard's emphasis was definitely on faith as an act of believing, though he did not deny that faith has an objective basis in the action of God in Jesus Christ. Since faith can never possess its object, it must always cling to it fervently and allow itself to be sustained by its object. There is no rational certainty in faith, but there is an inward assurance which persists in spite of reason's attempts to fathom what is basically inscrutable and paradoxical. Kierkegaard perceived that a man of faith could use his reason to point others to faith and to demonstrate why reason of itself cannot comprehend the absolute in time. He was not an irrationalist, since for him the truth of faith makes sense once we believe. Once on the other side we see the meaningfulness and truth of the absurd so that it is no longer the absurd. Yet even for the Christian who as a sinner is inclined to place too much trust in his own rational powers, the truth of Christianity will remain somewhat paradoxical and offensive.

Emil Brunner, who was profoundly influenced by Kierkegaard as well as by the Reformers, contended that faith involves both the gracious God, the Eternal Thou, who is other than man, and the existing individual who is called into fellowship with God. Faith is a personal relationship that entails trust and obedience.[75] Its certainty is founded on the call of God but realized in the response of man. It is a certainty that must be constantly renewed as we walk the pathway that God has marked out for us. As he put it: "Faith is the process of continually *becoming* sure; as in faith we *may* continually renew our assurance, so also it is true that we *must* continually renew our certainty."[76]

In our own constructive statement we seek to learn from the great teachers of the past but especially from the inspired prophets and apostles of the Scriptures. In Hebrews 11:1 faith is defined as "the assurance of things hoped for, the conviction of things not seen." Faith is an assurance that concerns not only present salvation but final salvation, since the latter is the object of our hope. It is also a conviction that refers to a reality that transcends the senses of man and is, therefore, inaccessible to empirical verification. It is not a rational but an existential certainty. Its objective basis is the Word of God, but its subjective pole is the decision and surrender of the will of man. The Christian life is the field of certainty, the arena in which we constantly renew our assurance. The assurance of faith and hope is not something gained once for all but something that must be realized in the practice of Christian living (Heb. 6:11; Rev. 2:10). We are summoned to make our calling and election sure as we engage in the struggle of faith, for only in this way will we remain in the faith (2 Pet. 1:10; Heb. 10:23, 35, 36).

On the question of eternal security I am closer to Luther's than to Calvin's position. Christ is our eternal security, and we therefore have eternal security so long as we have faith in Christ. Our hope of remaining in Christ till the end is "sure" and "steadfast" (Heb. 6:19), but it is something that must be renewed daily. I do not discount what Karl Barth calls the absurd but undeniable reality of falling away from the ground and mainspring of our being, but this is not a cause for uncertainty, since we have the assured knowledge that as long as we look to Christ we shall never fall away. By calling upon him, by clinging to him as our only hope and salvation, we can be assured that we are secure for eternity. No worldly or spiritual force can pluck us out of the hand of Christ (John 10:28, 29), though we must allow for the impossible possibility that Christ himself may let us go if we go back upon our promise to serve Christ till the end (cf. Heb. 10:26–29; Rev. 3:11). Eternal security is a property not of the mind of the believer but of the relationship between the believer and Christ, and it exists only in this context.

The paradoxical relation between the promise of eternal glory and human responsibility is admirably brought out in the Living Bible translation of 1 Peter 1:4, 5:

And God has reserved for his children the priceless gift of eternal life; it is kept in heaven for you, pure and undefiled, beyond the reach of change and decay. And God, in his mighty power, will make sure that you get there safely to receive it, because you are trusting him. It will be yours in that coming last day for all to see.[77]

What is being said here is that we will arrive safely by the grace of God but not apart from our faith and trust in the God of grace. Or as the New English Bible phrases it, the "inheritance to which we are born is one that nothing can destroy or spoil or wither." It is "kept for you in heaven, and you, because you put your faith in God, are under the protection of his power until salvation comes. . . ." We can be assured of the protection of his grace because we have placed our faith and hope in the living God.

One of the signs of hope today in the Christian world is the apparently growing convergence in Catholic and traditionalist Protestant circles on the question of the certainty of salvation. Stephen Pfürtner holds that there is a remarkable correspondence between Aquinas' view of hope and Luther's view of faith.[78] Both contain the notes of certainty and confidence. In Aquinas' theology, says Pfürtner, "For the believer as such there remains neither uncertainty in regard to what he believes nor in regard to his own believing. And the case is similar with one who hopes, in so far as he hopes."[79] This, of course, is completely in accord with Luther's position.

The question that remains is whether the Christian can have absolute certainty of his salvation. Pfürtner points out that for both Luther and Aquinas true faith looks beyond itself to Jesus Christ and insofar as faith does this, it contains the note of absolute certainty. In his doctrine of faith Aquinas emphasized primarily the intellectual certainty of the objective truth of revelation, but in his doctrine of hope "the absolute certainty of our personal confidence of salvation emerges".[80] Pfürtner here very well expresses our own point of view:

Christian existence in the state of pilgrimage is and remains paradoxical: it remains balanced on that sharp point at which absolute certainty of God and his mercy meets persistent uncertainty about ourselves and our own state. No rational insight into God's grace-giving action, no psychological experience of his comfort, no judgment of conscience based on good conduct or a right use of the sacraments, none of these can give us absolute certainty of our own state of grace. Our certainty of confidence, based on faith, comes to us only because and in so far as we look to God and to his work. If at this point we doubt his grace and his forgiveness of sin, then we have neither faith nor hope in him.[81]

Similarly Juan Alfaro holds that faith entails an "absolute certainty" which excludes doubt, though not the psychological possibility of doubt or denial.[82] He recognizes that the certainty of faith is entirely different from philosophical or scientific certainty, since it is not based on that which is rationally obvious: "The believer does not accept divine revelation, because he sees the truth of the mystery, or knows from rational evidence that God has spoken, but because under the guarantee of the external signs of divine revelation and the impulse of grace within him, he freely decides to rely on the word of God, who of himself is absolutely worthy of credence."[83]

Most Catholic theologians while acknowledging the certainty of faith agree with Karl Rahner that this does not predicate a certainty of ultimate salvation. Rahner maintains that the Christian can have a *practical* certainty" of salvation but must commit his "eternal destiny to the sovereign discretion of the gracious God."[84]

While contending against Rahner that we can have *assurance* of the eternal glory that God has promised, I oppose any claim to *rational* or *evidential certainty* of eternal salvation.[85] We still must walk by faith and not by sight (2 Cor. 5:7). The "once saved, always saved" syndrome of latter-day Calvinism cannot be maintained in the light of the scriptural warnings against presumption in faith (1 Cor. 10:12; Heb. 10:35). At the same time there is an element of truth in this notion, namely, that we can and must hope with exceeding joy that we will be kept by grace, since God does not deceive (cf. Rom. 5:2; 15:13). He remains true to his promise that whoever calls upon the name of Christ will be saved (Acts 2:21; Rom. 10:13). Karl Rahner points to Paul's words in Philippians that we must work out our salvation "with fear and trembling" (2:12) as proof that there can be no final certainty of salvation. With Berkouwer we retort that this must not be understood as the anxious fear of losing salvation but the fear and trembling that spring from faith itself, the awe and reverence that come upon man as he is confronted by the numinous, the divine majesty.[86] The Christian is called to work out his salvation without any doubt as to the outcome, since he knows that the gifts and the call of God are irrevocable (Rom. 11:29). We also have the assurance that our Lord is able to keep us from falling and to present us without blemish before the presence of his glory (Jude verse 24). The one who abides in Christ will never fail; yet this is not an occasion for presumption but a call to action (cf. Rev. 3:11). In Christ there is complete certainty, outside of Christ nothing but uncertainty.

MODERN MISCONCEPTIONS

One of the pitfalls on the modern scene is intellectualism whereby faith is defined primarily in terms of intellectual assent, and the object of faith is seen less as a Person than as a creedal formula. Those who define revelation as exclusively propositional nearly always depict faith as predominantly a rational act. The search for evidences and rationalistic proofs of God and the validity of his revelation figure prominently in this kind of orientation. Likewise the fascination with extraordinary gifts and experiences attests a yearning for rational or experiential certainty in addition to faith. Modern fundamentalism is particularly vulnerable to this temptation, but certain strands in the old Catholicism are also open to question in this regard. The elements of risk and venture are entirely missing in such an approach. It seems that faith needs to be buttressed by the authority of sight. Some seek to ground faith in historical proof, but such proof can only ensure a high degree of probability. Faith, however, must be grounded in certainty.[87]

How much more biblical is this excerpt from an old hymn quoted by Karl Barth: "For where He is most truly thine/ Is hidden from thy seeing."[88] Brother Lawrence also reflects the biblical position when he says: "He sometimes hides Himself from us: but faith alone, which will not fail us in time of need, ought to be our support, and the foundation of our confidence. . . ."[89]

At the other extreme are those who contend that faith has no cognitive content, that it is basically a suprarational or nonrational act. We frequently come across this misunderstanding in the circles of mysticism and existentialism. For William Law faith is a magnetic desire for the perfection that is in Christ. In Tillich's theology "absolute faith" transcends the divine-human encounter and therefore has "no special content."[90] It is the condition of being grasped by the power of Being-itself. Thomas O'Meara proffers this definition: "Faith is simply a word for my openness to presence."[91] According to Leslie Dewart Christianity has a mission but not a message. Christian faith, he says, "excludes *belief* in the truth of belief."[92] Faith is nothing other than "the existential response of the self to the openness of the transcendence disclosed by conscious experience."[93]

Henry Nelson Wieman, American process theologian, also reflects the new mood which disassociates faith from cognition: "Faith is not esentially belief at all. Religious faith is basically an act—the act of giving one's self into the keeping of what commands faith, to be transformed by it, and to serve it above all."[94] He defines faith as giving oneself totally to the creative event. Theology consequently cannot be ruled or governed by faith, since Christianity is a way of life and not intellectual assent to a rational message. Theology must not impose traditional formulations upon the ever-new process of creative transformation. Therefore in order to understand our faith and the world about us we do not appeal to any rational criterion in faith itself but to the empirical method. God is depicted as the source of human good, the creator and preserver of values, but not as the One who has revealed his will and purpose to the world.

Against the standpoint of existentialism, mysticism, and process theology we maintain that faith is indeed a rational as well as a suprarational act. The object of faith is not only a living Person, Jesus Christ, but the message concerning him, which is disclosed in the Scriptures. Faith entails not only risk and venture but also knowledge—knowledge of the mystery of the plan of salvation. It is a knowledge that transcends the senses, to be sure, but it is still knowledge. For a correct understanding of faith we must appeal not to the truth-claims of secular thought but to the truth-claims of faith itself. Faith can only be understood in the light of its object—the Word of God revealed in the Bible.

In opposition to a resurgent Pelagianism we must reaffirm with Augustine and the Reformers that faith is an undeserved gift of God. It is commonly assumed in some revivalist circles that salvation is only an offer from God and that it is up to man in and of himself to lay hold of this salvation.[95] In the new liberalism faith is regarded as the supreme exercise of man's freedom. Among many of the latter day mystics faith is simply a venture into the future having its basis in man's own imagination and volition. Gerald Heard writes: "We can, if we choose consciously to continue our evolution . . . go forward, refuse to decline and enter on the Eternal life now."[96] When faith becomes a decision or act of man's will independent of grace, then we are confronted with the heresy of faith-moralism. Faith indeed is a decision of the will, but this is a will liberated by God's free grace. Faith is also a venture and pilgrimage, but it is one made possible and inevitable by the action of grace upon man and within him.

Finally we must warn against the current, popular view that salvation is possible without explicit faith in Jesus Christ. Of all the misconceptions listed this is by far the most widespread and pernicious, for it undermines the New Testament message that there is salvation only in a living communion with Jesus Christ (Acts 4:12). Heinrich Ott alludes to a hidden faith on the part of non-Christians.[97] For him God's redeeming grace is universal and not confined to the Christ revelation. In Schubert Ogden's view faith is a universal and inescapable anthropological fact. It is part of the human condition, and therefore everyone already partakes of salvation or at least is on the way to salvation. In Tillich's theology those who do not consciously believe are in the latent church and therefore still within the realm of grace. Karl Barth emphasizes the need for conscious faith in Jesus Christ, but only in order to enjoy the benefits of salvation. Salvation itself includes all people, and therefore we may regard the whole human race as belonging to the kingdom of Christ and the body of Christ.[98]

In the new Catholicism also, salvation without faith has become a guiding motif for many theologians. In the thinking of Hans Küng the non-Christian religions typify the ordinary way to salvation while Christianity signifies the extraordinary way of salvation.[99] Karl

Rahner equates self-acceptance with implicit faith in Christ and there-fore deems it quite possible that one can be justified without a conscious commitment to the Jesus Christ of history. The Second Vatican Council has affirmed: "Those also can attain to everlasting salvation who through no fault of their own do not know the gospel of Christ or His Church, yet sincerely seek God and, moved by grace, strive by their deeds to do His will as it is known to them through the dictates of conscience."[100] Daniel Callahan sees love rather than faith as the con-dition for salvation and justification:

Faith in the person of Christ does not save us. . . . Some do not have the gift of Christ, at least not consciously. But they do have the gift of their own potentialities for love. Insofar as they are able to realize these potentialities will they be fulfilled—will they become one with themselves and with others.[101]

It is very clear that in the New Testament, on the contrary, *pistis* means conscious faith and commitment to Jesus Christ as the only Savior of the world. Paul held that "if you confess with your lips that Jesus is Lord and believe in your heart that God raised him from the dead, you will be saved. For man believes with his heart and so is justified, and he confesses with his lips and so is saved" (Rom. 10:9, 10). Our Lord himself declared to the Pharisees, "I told you that you would die in your sins, for you will die in your sins unless you believe that I am he" (John 8:24). The world is portrayed not as the kingdom of Christ but as the domain of the prince of darkness, and only those who believe are regarded as being in the realm of salvation. In Paul's words: "But the Scripture declares that the whole world is a prisoner of sin, so that what was promised, being given through faith in Jesus Christ, might be given to those who believe" (Gal. 3:22 NIV). The church of Jesus Christ is a beachhead of light on enemy occupied territory.

As has been indicated true faith entails assurance of our salvation. It is impossible to believe without having joy and confidence that we are indeed saved (1 Pet. 1:8). We here concur with John Wesley: "That no man can be justified and not know it appears farther from the very nature of things—for faith after repentance is ease after pain, rest after toil, light after darkness. . . ."[102] To speak of implicit or latent faith as itself being sufficient for salvation or as meriting eternal life has abso-lutely no scriptural warrant and is indeed a grave error.

We recognize the heresy that many of the new theologians are trying to guard against, namely, that those who have never had the opportunity of hearing the message of salvation are nonetheless con-demned to hell. It is more proper to hold that such persons are spiritu-

246 Essentials of Evangelical Theology

ally lost and headed for perdition unless they come to a saving knowledge of Jesus Christ. We believe as did Jonathan Edwards, P. T. Forsyth, and many others that God in his mercy will see to it that no person is bereft of the opportunity to come to Jesus Christ, and we would add with Forsyth even if this be not in this life. Yet we must not fall into the delusion that persons who are not yet in conscious fellowship with Christ are already saved or that their salvation is already assured. There are many persons, of course, who are truly seeking for salvation on the basis of grace given in the Word or sacraments but who have not yet made an open confession of faith. They have an acute awareness of their guilt and of their need for God but not yet a true knowledge of their sin and of God's mercy. Such persons are better understood as pre-Christians rather than Christians or infidels. The disciples of Jesus before Pentecost illustrate this particular category very clearly. On the other hand those who have no contact whatsoever with the redemptive grace of God, which is given only in the Word and sacraments, are still in darkness and need to hear the message of salvation. To contend that they already believe even though implicitly is a dangerous delusion, dangerous to them and to the church. Those who truly hear the Gospel and harden their hearts against it and those who hear and fall away are most certainly on the road to hell and should be special objects of our missionary concern. Yet in our missionary endeavor we can proceed with a holy optimism knowing that sovereign grace can restore even the most hardened backslider. Does not Paul declare that some might be grafted back into the body of Christ (Rom. 11:23, 24)?

Even in the circles of confessional orthodoxy the idea of salvation without conscious faith is very much present. In traditionalist Reformed circles it is alleged that birth in the covenant community assures one of salvation even apart from conscious faith, since, of course, infants and little children cannot have such faith. In Catholic and Lutheran circles it is commonly assumed that baptism itself regenerates one and that one is therefore saved even without faith in Christ. Luther himself who held to baptismal regeneration nevertheless maintained that baptism is only a beginning and that salvation is forfeited apart from a vital, living faith in Christ. At one place he declared that the sacraments of grace far from being beneficial harm all unless " 'they draw near in full assurance of faith.' "[103] Luther was here combatting the doctrine of *ex opere operato,* that the sacraments work simply by being performed. Augustine also pointed to the need for faith if the sacrament is to be fully efficacious: the Eucharist "justifies not because it is performed, but because it is believed."[104]

Soren Kierkegaard, who remained true to his Lutheran heritage, nevertheless perceived the dangers in an overemphasis on baptism to the detriment of personal faith. The practice of infant baptism in particular is viewed as an enemy of New Testament faith. "One accentuates the sacrament of baptism," he declared, "with such exorbitant orthodoxy that one actually becomes heterodox on the dogma of regeneration, forgetting the objection raised by Nicodemus and the reply to it, because with hyperorthodoxy one decrees that a little child has actually become a Christian by being baptized."[105]

An emphasis on personal faith, as Louis Bouyer has rightly recognized, is inimical to a purely collective religion and to a religion reduced to externals.[106] One cannot be religious by proxy (Dean Inge), and this great evangelical truth must indeed be incorporated in any ecumenical church that seeks to be truly ecumenical and truly biblical. The church of the New Testament was a gathered church, not a folk church, a church that one enters by profession of faith and not a church where membership is automatically guaranteed by birth or by baptism. The New Testament ideal of a believers' church is one we sorely need to recover in our day.[107]

NOTES

1. Thomas Aquinas, *Commentary on Saint Paul's Epistle to the Ephesians*, p. 96.

2. John Calvin, *Institutes of the Christian Religion*, ed. John Allen (1936 ed.), III, 2, 7, p. 604.

3. *Ibid.*, III, II, 14, p. 613.

4. Bernard of Clairvaux, *Sermo* 76: 6 *super Cantica Canticorum* III, 6. *S. Bernardi Opera*, vol. 2, ed. J. Leclercq et al. (Rome: Editiones Cistercienses, 1958), p. 258.

5. *Wesley's Standard Sermons*, vol. I (London: Epworth Press, 1935), p. 125.

6. P. T. Forsyth, *The Soul of Prayer*, 5th imp. (London: Independent Press, 1966), p. 68.

7. D. A. Schlatter, *Das Christliche Dogma* (Stuttgart: Verlag der Vereinsbuchhandlung, 1911), pp. 119 f.; *Die Theologie des Neuen Testaments* Zweiter Teil. (Stuttgart: Verlag der Vereinsbuchhandlung, 1910), pp. 335, 336; *Der Glaube im Neuen Testament* (Stuttgart: Verlag der Vereinsbuchhandlung, 1905), pp. 123, 546.

8. Karl Barth, *Church Dogmatics* III, 3, p. 247.

9. Calvin, *Institutes of the Christian Religion* III, 20, 12, ed. McNeill, p. 864.

10. *Luther's Works*, vol. 36, p. 248.

248 Essentials of Evangelical Theology

11. Quoted in H. R. Mackintosh, *Types of Modern Theology*, p. 98.

12. Martin Luther, W. A. 57, 144, 10. Cited in Gordon Rupp, *The Righteous-ness of God* (London: Hodder & Stoughton, 1963), p. 212.

13. Martin Luther, W.A., 27, 223.

14. Martin Luther, *Treatise on Good Works* in *Works of Martin Luther* (Philadelphia: A. J. Holman, 1915), vol. 1, p. 192.

15. Hannah Whitall Smith, *The Christian's Secret of a Happy Life* (West-wood, N.J.: Fleming H. Revell 1952), p. 63.

16. This is Thomas Merton's paraphrase of Isa. 50:10 in his *Contemplative Prayer* (Garden City, N.Y.: Doubleday, 1971), p. 17.

17. Karl Barth, *Church Dogmatics* II, 1, p. 159.

18. Martin Luther, "Sermon on July 25, 1522," W.A., 10, III, 239.

19. Soren Kierkegaard, *Philosophical Fragments,* 2d ed. trans. David Swenson (Princeton: Princeton University Press, 1962), p. 77.

20. Ambrose, *De Iacob et vita beata* I, vi, 21. Quoted in Arthur B. Crabtree, *The Restored Relationship,* p. 99.

21. *Saint Ambrose: Letters,* trans. Sister Mary Melchio Beyenka (New York: Fathers of the Church, 1954), p. 468.

22. Note that the citation in the Augsburg Confession of Ambrose's defense of the "forgiveness of sins, not through works but through faith alone, without merit" (Part I, Article VI) is actually derived from a contemporary of Ambrose, pseudo-Ambrose or Ambrosiaster in his *The First Epistle to the Corinthians* 1:4. It nonetheless definitely reflects Ambrose's own position.

23. Note that Ambrose sometimes viewed faith as itself a meritorious work and thereby fell short of the Reformation conception: "We are not justified by works but by faith, because the weakness of the flesh is a hindrance to works but the brightness of faith puts the error that is in man's deeds in the shadow and merits for him the forgiveness of his sins." *Saint Ambrose: Seven Exegetical Works,* p. 151.

24. Quoted in Hans Küng, *Justification,* p. 250.

25. Thomas Aquinas, *Commentary on Saint Paul's Epistle to the Ephesians,* p. 96.

26. *Ibid.,* p. 65.

27. Thomas Aquinas, *Nature and Grace, Selections from the Summa Theologica,* trans. A. M. Fairweather. *Library of Christian Classics,* vol. XI (Philadelphia: Westminster Press, 1954), p. 270.

28. Philip S. Watson, *Let God be God!* (London: Epworth Press, 1947), p. 53. For Watson's discussion of this concept in Thomas Aquinas see p. 52 f.

29. Martin Luther, *A Commentary on St. Paul's Epistle to the Galatians,* ed. Philip Watson, p. 218.

30. John Calvin, *The Epistles of Paul the Apostle to the Romans and to the Thessalonians,* ed. Thomas Torrance and David Torrance, p. 71.

31. Bernard of Clairvaux, *Sermons on the Dedication of a Church* 5:3 in *Patrologia Latina* 183, p. 531.

32. John Calvin, *Institutes of the Christian Religion* III, XI, 20, ed. McNeill, p. 750.

33. Martin Luther, *A Treatise on Christian Liberty,* rev. ed. trans. W. A. Lambert (Philadelphia: Fortress Press, 1970), p. 34.

34. *Luther's Works,* vol. 26, p. 272.

35. *The Heidelberg Catechism with Commentary,* eds. Allen Miller and M. Eugene Osterhaven (Philadelphia: United Church Press, 1963), p. 108.

36. Philip Spener, *Pia Desideria,* trans. & ed. Theodore G. Tappert (Philadelphia: Fortress Press, 1964), p. 63.

37. Ralph Turnbull, ed., *Devotions of Jonathan Edwards* (Grand Rapids: Baker, 1959), p. 58.

38. Conrad Cherry, *The Theology of Jonathan Edwards,* p. 135.

39. According to Conrad Cherry, "Edwards includes the human act of love in saving faith in two ways: either as the working love directed primarily to the neighbor, which is at least potentially included in every act of faith; or as the propensity of heart directed to God, involved in the very essence of faith itself." *Ibid.,* p. 71.

40. In Philip Watson, *Let God be God!,* p. 4.

41. Albert C. Outler, ed., *John Wesley* (New York: Oxford University Press, 1964), p. 125.

42. *Ibid.,* p. 130.

43. Quoted in W. L. Doughty, *John Wesley Preacher* (London: Epworth Press, 1955), p. 173.

44. "Even this faith which leads to justification in no way merits this justification, even though it is a gift of God's free grace." Karl Rahner, *Theological Investigations* IV., trans. Kevin Smyth (Baltimore: Helicon Press, 1966), p. 207.

45. Hans Küng, *Justification,* p. 252. For a cogent Reformed critique of Küng's position see Rudolf J. Ehrlich, *Rome—Opponent or Partner?* (Philadelphia: Westminster Press, 1965), pp. 101–205. Ehrlich contends with a certain degree of validity that Küng misunderstands both Barth's position and that of the Council of Trent.

46. Hans Küng, *Justification,* p. 256.

47. Hans Küng, "Justification and Sanctification According to the New Testament" in Daniel J. Callahan, Heiko A. Oberman, and Daniel J. O'Hanlon, *Christianity Divided* (New York: Sheed & Ward, 1961) [pp. 309–335], p. 322.

48. Louis Bouyer, *The Spirit and Forms of Protestantism,* p. 12. Bouyer holds that even in Luther's view faith implies love in that it issues forth into love, though, as we have seen, Luther would not attribute the justifying power of faith to love.

49. Karl Barth, *Church Dogmatics* IV, 2, p. 507.

50. Barth writes that "faith and love, reception and surrender are two indivisible but distinguishable moments of the one vital movement and act which constitutes Christian existence." *Ibid.,* p. 731.

51. *Ibid.,* p. 517.

52. See Stephen Pfürtner, *Luther and Aquinas on Salvation,* introd. by Jaroslav Pelikan (New York: Sheed & Ward, 1964). Pfürtner raises the interesting question whether a Catholic critique of the Council of Trent is possible (p. 46 f.). According to Pelikan in his Introduction not all Catholic and Lutheran scholars would concur with Pfürtner's thesis.

53. Karl Rahner, *Theological Dictionary,* p. 169.

54. *Ibid.,* p. 70.

55. In Berkouwer, *The Conflict with Rome,* p. 142.

56. John Calvin, *The Epistles of Paul the Apostle to the Romans and to the Thessalonians,* ed. David Torrance and Thomas Torrance. 10:10, p. 228.

57. John Calvin, *Institutes of the Christian Religion,* 6th ed., ed. John Allen, 1902), III, 2, 14, p. 614.

58. *Institutes of the Christian Religion,* ed. McNeill, III, 13, 3, p. 766.

59. *Institutes of the Christian Religion* 6th ed., ed. Allen, III, 2, 17, p. 616.

60. That Calvin's own position must be differentiated from the presumption of many of his followers is made clear in this remark about David: "He confesses that prosperity had so stupefied and benumbed his senses that he disregarded the grace of God on which he should have depended, relied on himself instead, and imagined that he could not fall. If this happened to such a great prophet, who of us should not be fearful and cautious?" John Calvin, *Golden Booklet of the True Christian Life,* 4th print. A modern translation from French and Latin by Henry J. Van Andel (Grand Rapids: Baker Book House, 1975), p. 48.

61. Martin Luther, *Preface to the Epistle to the Romans* trans. C. M. Jacobs. In *Works of Martin Luther* Vol. VI (Phil.: A. J. Holman Co., 1932) [pp. 447–462], p. 452.

62. *Luther's Works,* vol. 26, p. 380.

63. Martin Luther, *A Commentary on St. Paul's Epistle to the Galatians,* trans. & ed. Philip Watson p. 372.

64. In contrast to Luther Barth maintained that falling away from grace is not a possibility within the new man but an "ontological impossibility," which nevertheless happens. Because it is not presupposed in either the original or regenerate nature of man, it is thereby all the more inexcusable.

65. Quoted in Paul Tillich, *A History of Christian Theology,* ed. Carl E. Braaten (New York: Harper & Row, 1968), p. 279. Cf. Heinrich Schmid, ed., *The Doctrinal Theology of the Evangelical Lutheran Church,* p. 32 f.

66. John W. Beardslee, ed., *Reformed Dogmatics* (New York: Oxford University Press, 1965), p. 393.

67. Heinrich Schmid, *op. cit.,* p. 413.

68. John Theodore Mueller, *Christian Dogmatics* (St. Louis: Concordia, 1955), p. 326.

69. *Ibid.*

70. G. C. Berkouwer, *The Conflict with Rome,* p. 143 f.

71. Cf. Charles Spurgeon: "It will not save me to know that Christ is a Savior; but it will save me to *trust* Him to be *my* Savior." *The Treasury of Charles Spurgeon* (Westwood, N.J.: Fleming H. Revell, 1955), p. 160.

72. From his *Religious Affections.* In *The Works of Jonathan Edwards,* ed. Edward Hickman (Edinburgh: Banner of Truth Trust, 1974), vol. 1, p. 263.

73. In Harold Lindstrom, *Wesley and Sanctification* (London: Epworth Press, n.d.), p. 155.

74. Soren Kierkegaard, *Philosophical Fragments,* p. 76.

75. Emil Brunner, *The Divine-Human Encounter,* trans. Amandus W. Loos (Philadelphia: Westminster Press, 1943), p. 66 f.

76. Emil Brunner, *Revelation and Reason,* trans. Olive Wyon (Philadelphia: Westminster Press, 1946), p. 188.

77. From this passage we can conclude that the perseverance of the saints

is to be attributed to both divine election and the struggle of faith. Like the doctrine of eternal security, the doctrine of the perseverance of the saints must always be seen in the context of the relationship of faith.

78. Stephen Pfürtner, *Luther and Aquinas on Salvation*.

79. *Ibid.*, p. 134.

80. *Ibid.*, p. 93.

81. *Ibid.*, p. 113.

82. Karl Rahner, ed., *Encyclopaedia of Theology*, pp. 507, 508.

83. *Ibid.*

84. Karl Rahner, *Theological Dictionary*, p. 70.

85. My position on this question is not very far from Rahner's, even though there remains a certain tension because of our differing traditions.

86. It is interesting to note that James Moffatt translates Phil. 2:12 "with reverence and trembling." See J. Hugh Michael, *The Epistle of Paul to the Philippians* (New York: Harper & Row, 1927), pp. 98, 102, 103. When we compare Eph. 6:5 and 2 Cor. 7:15 where the phrase is also used, we see that this interpretation makes sense.

87. See Donald G. Bloesch, *The Ground of Certainty* (Grand Rapids: Eerdmans, 1971).

88. Karl Barth, *Church Dogmatics* II, 2, p. 337.

89. Brother Lawrence, *The Practice of the Presence of God* (Old Tappan, N.J.: Fleming H. Revell, 1958), p. 58.

90. Paul Tillich, *The Courage to Be* (New Haven, Ct.: Yale University Press, 1958), pp. 176, 177.

91. Thomas O'Meara, *Loose in the World*, p. 13.

92. Leslie Dewart, *The Future of Belief* (New York: Herder & Herder Co., 1966), p. 70.

93. *Ibid.*, p. 64.

94. Henry Nelson Wieman, *The Source of Human Good* (Chicago: University of Chicago Press, 1946), p. 46.

95. Such gospel songs popular in fundamentalist and revivalist circles as "I Am Determined, I've Made Up My Mind" and "I Have Decided to Follow Jesus" often betray a Pelagian or synergistic orientation. Yet it is possible to sing these songs in the context of Reformed theology as well, since God's free grace liberates the will for decision and surrender to Christ, and apart from such a decision man is not yet fully or truly in the body of Christ (cf. Rev. 22:17 KJ). In our theology faith is not a decision made possible by enabling or preventive grace (as in popular Arminianism) but a decision made inevitable by transforming grace. It is nevertheless a bona fide human decision; with Augustine, Edwards and Barth we maintain that faith and every act that proceeds from it are the only bona fide decisions, since true freedom is freedom for obedience.

96. Gerald Heard, *The Creed of Christ* (New York: Harper & Row, 1940), p. 160.

97. Heinrich Ott, *God* (Richmond, Va.: John Knox Press, 1974), pp. 38, 69, 116.

98. At the same time Barth is emphatic that though all people are in the body and kingdom of Christ by the pronouncement of God (de jure), they are

not necessarily in Christ de facto in that they have not all appropriated the fruits of his saving work by his Spirit.

99. Hans Küng, *Freedom Today* Trans. Cecily Hastings (N.Y.: Sheed & Ward, 1965), p. 141.

100. *Dogmatic Constitution on the Church* II, 16 in *The Documents of Vatican II,* ed. Walter M. Abbott., trans. Joseph Gallagher (New York: America Press, 1966), p. 35.

101. In *The Sign* 48:6 (Jan. 1969), p. 16.

102. Albert Outler, ed., *John Wesley,* p. 137.

103. *Luther's Works,* vol. 29, p. 193.

104. Cited in *Ibid.,* p. 172.

105. Soren Kierkegaard, *Concluding Unscientific Postscript,* p. 527.

106. Louis Bouyer, *The Spirit and Forms of Protestantism,* p. 97 f.

107. The New Testament ideal of a believers' church was partly recovered by the Anabaptists and Pietists. For relevant books see Donald F. Durnbaugh, *The Believers' Church* (New York: Macmillan, 1968); and F. Ernest Stoeffler, ed., *Continental Pietism and Early American Christianity* (Grand Rapids: Eerdmans, 1976).

SCRIPTURE INDEX

NAME INDEX

SUBJECT INDEX

adoption 179
agnosticism 1, 19, 36
Anabaptists 11, 100, 115, 194, 252
analogy 75, 85
angels 108, 118, 124, 138, 158
Anglo-Catholicism 21, 133
Anglo-Israelism 62
anthropology 89 f., 96, 106
anxiety 100, 101, 105, 112, 236
apokatastasis 168
Apollinarianism 134, 135
apologetics ix, 14, 18, 76, 101, 199
apologists 98, 101, 131, 188, 200
Arianism 35, 134
Arminianism x, 4, 77, 164, 167, 177, 199, 207, 251
asceticism 115
assurance of salvation 235 ff., 245, 246
Athanasian Creed 128
atheism 1
Augsburg Confession 22, 248

Bahaism 62
baptism 91, 135, 166, 169, 189, 190, 207, 221, 229, 246, 247
Bible, the Holy
   its authority 4, 51 ff., 209, 237
   its inerrancy 3, 20, 64 ff., 82 f., 237
   its inspiration xi, 12, 55 f., 104, 228, 239
Brethren of the Common Life 216
Buddhism 170, 213

Calvinism x, 4, 22, 29, 48, 77, 113, 133, 164, 167, 178, 238, 242
Camps Farthest Out 5
Campus Crusade for Christ 5
Chalcedonian Definition 127, 132
cheap grace ix, 172, 207, 214
Christadelphians 20, 83, 156
Christian and Missionary Alliance 204
Christian Science 62
Christomonism 18, 44, 140, 141, 147
church
   its authority 57 f., 63
   its infallibility 58, 59
   unity of 60
Church of the Living Word 62
common grace 91, 103, 187

communion of saints 18
conversion 2, 7, 20, 99, 101, 115, 185, 189, 193, 197, 202, 204, 213, 225
Council of Nicaea 35, 127
Council of Trent 57, 80, 99, 193, 194, 229, 235, 249
counsels of perfection 231
Counter-Reformation 190
creation 25 f., 36, 38, 42, 46, 47, 106, 118, 154, 227
culture-religion 46

damnation ix, 40, 103, 220, 236, 246
Darwinism 16
death 98, 117, 126, 152, 153, 155, 156, 161, 171 f., 178, 180, 238
deism 31, 37
demonic powers 25, 47, 106, 108, 109, 110, 117, 149, 152, 154, 155, 158, 203, 245
dialectical theology 45, 60, 123
Disciplined Order of Christ 5
dispensationalism 20, 181
docetism 52, 79, 134 f., 137, 140, 142, 145
dogmatics 18
Donatism 81
doubt 97, 235, 236
dualism 37, 47, 158

ebionitism 52, 79, 134 f., 137, 140
election 11, 29, 45, 141, 154, 165, 168, 173, 178, 204, 215, 220, 221, 237, 240, 251
empiricism 67, 83, 243
Enlightenment 14, 17, 23, 54, 102, 109, 114, 200, 237
eschatology 14, 20
estrangement 78, 93, 149
eternal life 170, 190, 240, 245
eternal security 236 f., 251
Evangelical and Reformed church xi
evangelical revivalism 11, 165, 199, 214, 244, 251
evangelism 12, 14, 32
evil 24, 26, 34, 47, 88 ff., 109, 110, 130, 151, 189
evolution 16, 50, 106, 112, 135, 145, 180, 212, 244
existentialism 5, 23, 56, 71, 121, 243